RUNNING IN THE ZONE:

A HANDBOOK FOR SEASONED ATHLETES

EDITORS

STEVE KING AND DAN CUMMING

Foreword

Rob Reid

Note for Librarians: A cataloguing record for this book is available from Library and Archives Canada at www.collectionscanada.ca/amicus/index-e.html
ISBN 1-4120-6857-6

Printed in Victoria, BC, Canada. Printed on paper with minimum 30% recycled fibre. Trafford's print shop runs on "green energy" from solar, wind and other environmentally-friendly power sources.

TRAFFORD
PUBLISHING™
Offices in Canada, USA, Ireland and UK
This book was published *on-demand* in cooperation with Trafford Publishing. On-demand publishing is a unique process and service of making a book available for retail sale to the public taking advantage of on-demand manufacturing and Internet marketing. On-demand publishing includes promotions, retail sales, manufacturing, order fulfilment, accounting and collecting royalties on behalf of the author.

Book sales for North America and international:
Trafford Publishing, 6E–2333 Government St.,
Victoria, BC v8t 4p4 CANADA
phone 250 383 6864 (toll-free 1 888 232 4444)
fax 250 383 6804; email to orders@trafford.com
Book sales in Europe:
Trafford Publishing (uk) Limited, 9 Park End Street, 2nd Floor
Oxford, UK ox1 1hh UNITED KINGDOM
phone 44 (0)1865 722 113 (local rate 0845 230 9601)
facsimile 44 (0)1865 722 868; info.uk@trafford.com
Order online at:
trafford.com/05-1768

10 9 8 7 6 5 4 3 2

ACKNOWLEDGMENT

We wish to thank all our contributors, extraordinary people who have worked with us to share secrets, insights, methods, motivations and more than a few personal thoughts. It has been a pleasure working with each and every one of them.

We want to recognize Rob Reid for providing the Foreword and for the special and invaluable role he has played in making *Running in the Zone* a reality.

A special thanks is due to Danielle Krysa, cover designer and daughter of Dan, for her professional assistance and for her grace and good humour in putting up with Steve and her Dad asking for "one more" revision and just another "small" change.

As co-editors, we each have to recognize the other for the unique contributions brought to this project. Without Steve's contacts and ability to assemble such a marvellous, interesting and talented group of contributors, *Running in the Zone* could never have been what it is. But, had Dan not had the idea and vision of the project in the first place, backed up by his editorial skills and ability to work with a diverse group of people, *Running in the Zone* still would not have happened. We want to salute and thank each other and to 'tell the world' that we recognize neither of us could have done this alone and especially not without our generous and talented contributors.

Thanks to Marathon & Beyond for the rights to reprint "*The Ancient Marathoner*" by Joe Henderson and "*Trying Harder*" by Richard Benyo.

Thanks to Meyer and Meyer Sports re material reproduced in "*Aging Slower than Your Competition*" by Earl Fee. The material in this contribution is mainly from *How to be a Champion from 9 to 90* and the *Complete Guide to Running*, both by Earl Fee.

Thanks to Harper Collins Publishing and Bernd Heinrich for permission to reprint "*The Race*".

Finally, we both wish to acknowledge all the people who have influenced and supported us in our athletic, professional and personal lives and contributed to us having become who we are today, including being co-editors of *Running in the Zone*.

RUNNING IN THE ZONE:
A HANDBOOK FOR SEASONED ATHLETES

ZONES AND CONTENT

PHOTO CREDITS (Contributor Biographies)

Roger Robinson	Robert Cross Image Services, Victoria University of Wellington
Wally Hild	courtesy of Joints in Motion Team
Neville Flanagan	Kent Wong, Copyright 2004
Moe Beaulieu	Bryan Smith Photography
Bob Dolphin	Smiles Photography (Victoria, BC)
Rob Reid	René Haché
Evan Fagan	Ed Walsh
Lorne Smith	VeriSmile Photography
Paula Fudge	Robert Fudge
Herb Phillips	Teresa Nightingale
Steve King	Mike Van Ert
Diane Palmason	Rick Rickman

FOREWORD

Rob Reid

This book, *Running in the Zone*, is the result of a collaboration between Steve King and Dan Cumming. According to his wife Jean, the announcing guru Steve King recites marathon and triathlon performances in his sleep. Steve has competed in every known distance worthy of calling a race from sprint to ultra and in conditions from freezing rain to desert heat. He has also been the motivational spirit behind this project. He has gathered the runners you have in the pages before you into a new zone. Sitting down and writing on the many topics in this enlightening book was a marathon in itself for many of the contributors. Co-editor, Dan Cumming, has taken the novice writers in the group and articulated their experience to benefit the reader. Dan can do this so well because of his experience as a writer, marathon runner and race organizer. The two of them are a potent combination for those of us who have participated in this book. We thank Steve for convincing some of us that we really could write about this thing we love to do and Dan for his patience and diligence in bringing out the best of our latent or long forgotten writing skills.

The phases or zones we experience in our lives change like the seasons. At first everything is new and fresh. We absorb abundantly the nutrients offered to us for growth and development. We then train to maximize our potential. Eventually, we settle into a maintenance zone where we continue to utilize our talents but strive for and define success in a different manner. This is less performance defined and more based on the knowledge we impart to others both directly through teaching or coaching and indirectly through the examples we set. What the sport of running means to us, our training methods, the Zen-like state it creates, its social and societal benefits, and the heroes we know and admire that motivate all of us, enables every zone in every season to remain enriched and to teach us lessons for a healthier and fuller life.

The array of contributors includes writing professionals Rich Benyo, Joe Henderson, Roger Robinson, Bernd Heinrich, Don Kardong and Bart Yasso. The twenty additional runner-writers are all seasoned experts in the sport and range from enthusiastic and dedicated mid-pack runners to Olympic medalists such as Lynn (Williams) Kanuka and World Record holders like Paula Fudge, not to mention many age-class record holders at both national and world level. They enlighten us with both information and motivational pieces. No matter what zone you may be in currently, these pages will take you to new heights of experience. You will learn from the technical greats such as Zatopek, and be inspired by age group heroes like Jack Foster. As an added feature, Doug Alward, Terry Fox's closest friend, shares powerful events from "The Marathon of Hope", revealing how it continues to inspire him on each and every run. Energy, attitude, will power, goal setting and having fun are all evident in our sport as well as camaraderie and community. Each of these elements is reflected in the following pages.

The benefits and developing values sport creates in our being are long lasting and make us "seasoned runners" of quality and substance. It is this that allows us to "go the distance" the way we do. By sharing lessons learned through our experiences in this wonderful sport, we leave behind a legacy for those coming up the road or trail, and create an environment where the wind blows strongly at our backs.

INTRODUCTION

Running, especially long distance running, was once the province of relatively young fleet-footed men. It was largely structured on a competitive model, meaning that the lower echelons were mostly meant to identify and develop potential performers. And, once a runner passed some "best before" date, the running career generally ended. Naturally, the longer distances, starting at one time with 800 meters, were too long to be *safe for women*. It was only in 1972 that the 1500 meters for women was included as part of the Olympics, and again we find ourselves speaking of young strong women, not to mention 'reckless' and a little 'foolhardy'. The Olympic Marathon for Women began only in 1984. That is not to say that women weren't running longer distances prior to those dates, and in fairness to the Olympics, they have a practical and necessary policy of requiring a defined level of practice and number of countries actively participating in the sport prior to its being accepted into the Games. Getting back to long distance running in general, the first Boston Marathon had 15 competitors and as recently as 1970, the first New York Marathon had just 55 finishers.

How times have changed!

Running began to turn a corner some 30 years ago, when "fun runs" started to appear. Jogging was a part of the story and the acknowledged guru in North America was Jim Fixx. Health and longevity were linked to jogging and the cardiovascular exercise it represented. The naysayers still abounded and when Mr. Fixx expired at a rather young age of a heart attack, they quickly pointed to the folly of his opinions on the benefits of jogging. Naturally, most of them seemed to have missed the fact that Jim Fixx had outlived his father and a brother by some six years, perhaps **due** to his exercise program. Still, a movement had begun and it was not to be turned back.

Various forms of running began to become popular and road racing was right up there. People began to realize that while things change in the human body over time, there was no magical point at which a person must simply stop. Well, actually, this is not strictly true. There is a point where one must stop. It is called death. Up to that point most people have options.

People who got into "jogging" for exercise began to enjoy the many benefits of running, including the camaraderie of the running community of which they were a part. We could go on and on about how the running phenomenon really began and who the most important proponents were, exactly when it started and when it turned various corners. It really doesn't matter. One thing that can be said is that almost all the contributors to *Running in the Zone* were there when it happened. Just look around today. You will see people enjoying one form of running or another, almost everywhere you look.

Not only will you see people running, you will see lots of women and you will see lots with grey, and in the case of some men, no hair. Many are still "jogging", but many more are in some kind of organized program of running, with a goal in mind. In Vancouver, Canada where editor Dan Cumming lives, the Vancouver Sun Run (10K) celebrated its 20th Anniversary in 2004 and each year for the last few has flirted with exceeding 50,000 participants.

All over North America and the world, for that matter, marathons are being run in which thousands of competitors take part. New York (35,000 plus) and London (46,500) stand out among the largest marathons. The Boston Marathon has existed for well over 100 years now, but began with just 15 elite runners. In its centennial running in 1996, Boston recorded 38,708 entrants and 35,868 finishers. Indeed, how times have changed.

And, speaking of times and older runners we see that among the elite, age is not so daunting. The fastest times recorded at Boston are 2:07:15 for men and 2:20:43 for women. However, the top masters (40+) men's time is just 2:08:46 (Andres Espinosa, Berlin, 2003) and the fastest women's masters time is 2:26:51 (Priscilla Welch, London, 1987). Just to complete the picture, the fastest ever marathon at time of writing, was recorded in Berlin in 2003 by Paul Tergat with a 2:04:55 clocking, followed ONE second later by his Kenyan countryman, Sammy Korir. But what of the "weaker" sex, the one that until 1984 wasn't allowed to have a marathon event in the Olympic Games? Well, also in 2003, in London, one Paula Radcliffe of Great Britain crossed the finish line at 2:15:25. To put this performance in perspective, Paula Radcliffe would have won every men's Olympic marathon up to 1960, when she would have been second to Ethiopian Abebe Bikila who ran 2:15:16. Her time would have placed her second in 1964 and would have won again in 1968!

Outside the spotlight of World and Olympic competition we still see amazing performances from our best women and men. Simply as an example, most people might find it interesting to know that the fastest marathon time for a 70 year-old is held by Canadian, Ed Whitlock, at a speedy 2:54:48*, and just by the way, Ed also holds a 10K record of 38:04:13. In actual fact, Ed was 73 when he posted his record marathon time in Toronto, Canada. [* Note: chip time was 2:54:45 and has been accepted as the official time for age class records.]

Now don't forget. This book is not just about elite running. All of these records are simply to put into context the fact that age is not so big a detractor as one might think. Few of us are setting world records. But that isn't the point. Young or old, running is something you can do and keep doing. If you do it properly and with respect, you can keep doing it for a very, very long time. And, as some of our contributors aptly demonstrate, you can keep doing it well, if that is your chosen approach.

We used marathon records and facts to discuss distance running. Naturally, there are other distances with 5K and 10K events being the most popular. That said, ultra-running has been developing and people involved in these events now cover distances that make the marathon look like a short training run! A few of these hardy folks have agreed to grace our pages with their thoughts and suggestions. Where will it all end?

This book is primarily about one component of the running population – the "older" runner. When we set out to bring this book together, we as editors somewhat arbitrarily looked at the "older" runner as being 50-plus years of age. However, as we worked on the concept and with our colleagues and contacts in the running community, we realized that the older runner is someone who self-identifies in that category. This book is for all those people, regardless of chronological age.

Naturally, to some observers, a runner who is 50 years of age or older **is** an older runner. Of course, if you have been an elite runner competing at or near world standards, then you MIGHT be an older runner at 40. But, what does that really mean? Forty isn't old, and what some 40 year-olds can do by way of running is nothing short of amazing. As a matter of fact, as you read through this book, you will see that what some people can do at 50 and 60 is stunning. A few of our contributors didn't even start running seriously until they hit their 40's and recorded improved performances well into their 50's. Nonetheless, everything is relative and age or perhaps more appropriately, "aging", does bring challenges.

Running in the Zone tries to address as many as possible of the issues and opportunities facing the older runner. And, yes, there are many very real opportunities. We asked a wide range of men and women with long-term histories in running to participate. We looked for people with broad-based experiences. Each was asked to address a particular area and to do so in his or her own words and from a personal perspective. As editors, we only tried to help our contributors get their message across, and did our very best to let each tell his or her story in their own way. One contributor who knows a lot about running but claims not to know so much about writing, had this to say about the process when all was said and done:

"I actually enjoyed reading it (!) and thought...hey, did I write that? (!) It really is me, and reflects exactly how I feel and think, and hope the end result is that some of what I say will help people stay motivated, realize they can be in charge of their own lives, and that exercise will make such a difference in the quality of their lives."

We considered the advisability of making this a "how to" book for older runners and doubtless some of the articles may indeed be of that nature. However, there are many good books on running, including those for the absolute beginner. And have no doubt, there are beginners even among our older runners. Not only that, as the so-called Baby Boomers swell the ranks of the older runners and as people look for the answers to health and wellness challenges, we expect that there may be a good many more beginners from the ranks of the, shall we say, *"**seasoned**"* population.   However, another "how to" guide on running, even if we did concentrate on the issues of older runners, would simply be repeating so much that is already out there.   As much as possible, where it is a matter of technical information, we have tried to refer to a range of books or information sources that are widely available.   In a few instances, we have reproduced certain information, with permission.

The focus of *Running in the Zone*, is inspiration and the conveyance of new ideas for older runners.   If you can't be inspired by some of the stories in these pages, maybe you should consider another pastime.   Running takes on a different aspect for participants as they age and with these changes can come some very positive and enjoyable experiences, regardless of the relative abilities of the individual.   Being older often means greater time, flexibility and opportunity for running and running-related activities such as coaching, mentoring and volunteering.   At younger ages, career and family can throw real challenges at runners.   Time is at a premium for training and even competition.   With advancing age and changes in careers and family dynamics, the older runner may see many options opening that just weren't there earlier.

Research continues to demonstrate the resilience of the human body.   Some studies have even shown that octogenarians living in nursing homes were able to regain amazing amounts of mobility and flexibility through physical exercise. Others have shown how even modest exercise programs (walking and jogging) performed on a regular basis will restore lost strength and lung capacity.   No wonder, once people become involved in running, they tend to stay with it after reaching some basic threshold of fitness and comfort.   Of course, we are not going to say that getting to the threshold is all that easy.   It is not.   Part of this book is intended to help newcomers or re-starters to make it over the "hump" that will get them to a stable, healthy running program that can be maintained for the long term.   That content is both practical/technical and inspirational. Before you can meet a challenge you have to want to meet it: you must be motivated.

We have tried to include some tools and guidelines, which can be used for achieving specific goals and putting those achievements into personal context. Some of the most important contributions attest to the mental approach to running as age marches forward.   For many, the biggest deterrent to continuing is the mental rather than physical side of running.   A number of our contributors have addressed the matter of how to mentally approach running.   If not being able to run a three-hour marathon anymore is failure for someone, then he or she might as well stop running, because sooner or later that just isn't going to be possible.   Just to be clear, there are a good many people running for whom a three-hour marathon was never a possibility!   The point is, everything is relative and requires perspective.   Change of performance due to age is just one of those things.

Make no mistake, the pieces in this book include practical information for the serious runner that will inspire, but also help with fundamental technical transitions as well. The idea is to run happily and to keep healthy for as long as possible. The advice you will find here can help you do that. It will be up to the reader to find what he or she most needs. Because of the range of writers we have been fortunate to attract, we believe **Running in the Zone** will have a dynamic place in the life of the older runner. What is of interest today may be replaced by other content a year or two from now. What you are not ready for today will become important tomorrow. We sincerely hope you will agree and will use **Running in the Zone** in that way.

As editors, it has been our privilege and pleasure to work with the amazing people who authored the individual chapters of **Running in the Zone**. We should make it very clear that these people are amazing as much for their personalities and outlooks as they are for any physical performance they may be able to claim and make no mistake, some of them are able to claim awe-inspiring performances.

The book includes sections that will assist the performance of even elite older runners to continue at that level. It includes sections that will help average runners adjust training programs to remain injury-free and to meet new goals. Some chapters suggest entirely new viewpoints or goals for runners to use in planning their running programs. We have included some stories which are just plain inspirational in nature. Nothing is as satisfying as meeting or exceeding a personal challenge, particularly one that may have seemed unattainable. We expect readers to find and take what they need at any given moment and come back for more as time goes on. *Running in the Zone* was not written as a "cover to cover" read, though we expect that some will do just that. All sections have been kept short and to the given point. Where a topic is more complex, we have asked more than one author to participate.

As creators of the concept for *Running in the Zone* and editors, we set out to develop a book that would encourage, instruct and inspire older runners of all interests and levels of accomplishment. To our delight, we also reaped all of the same benefits for ourselves! We will be eternally grateful to our fellow runners and writers.

In a quiet moment during the writing of *Running in the Zone*, Steve was moved to create a poem, which has since become a lyric put to rock music by Bill Head (a runner himself) and "The HeadBand". Listen for it, and when you hear it you too may find yourself:

RUNNING IN THE ZONE

It keeps me running
Till the twilight of the day
It keeps me running in all weathers
Come what may

I'm fleet of foot
I'm heavy and I'm slow
But I'll never stop
Because I'm -
Running in the zone

The time moves on
and my pace is steady
I'll finish this off
When I'm good and ready

I'm having a blast
Over country and the road
For peace of mind it's the only mode
Because I'm -
Running in the zone

I'll run alone
Or in a pack
I'll take on the hills
Or hit the track

I love to race
To be at my best
To make the pace
And to complete the test

Because I'm -
running in the zone

Never alone
Away from the phone
My body's just on loan
Yes ET's going home

(Steve King 2005)

THE PREPARATION ZONE

"Running taught me valuable lessons. In cross-country competition, training counted more than intrinsic ability, and I could compensate for a lack of natural aptitude with diligence and discipline. I applied this in everything I did."
[Nelson Mandela]

Roger Robinson

Roger Robinson is known internationally as a leading writer and speaker on running. Senior writer for *Running Times* and author of *Heroes and Sparrows* and *Running in Literature*, he has also been a successful runner, coach, TV commentator, and stadium announcer.

An advocate of the "balanced life," he has always lived by the philosophy of this book, sustaining a top level running career for over forty years, and competing as an elite until nearly 60. He still runs an hour daily, at 66, despite one knee that announced its retirement eight years ago. He represented his native England and then his adopted New Zealand in the World Cross-Country (a unique double), but his biggest impact internationally came when he turned 40. He won several world masters championships, was top-ranked master in American road racing in 1980, and moved to the marathon with spectacular success, winning at New York, Vancouver, Canberra, Auckland, and others, with a best of 2:18:14. At 44, he set a masters record at Boston (2:20:15). At 50 (1989), he again compiled an unbeaten series of over twenty top American races, setting over-50 records that included the New York City Marathon (2:28:01).

Running has always been fitted into his full schedule as a distinguished professor, academic administrator, and writer. (His Boston record came in a five-day Easter return excursion from his post as Faculty Dean in New Zealand.) Outside running, he has published such major literary-scholarly books as the *Oxford Companion to New Zealand Literature, Katherine Mansfield: In From the Margin* and *Robert Louis Stevenson: His Best Pacific Writings.* He also had a leading role in the revision of New Zealand's schools English curriculum in the 1990s. He recently took part-time retirement from Victoria University of Wellington, where he had served as Head of School, Dean, and Academic Assistant Vice-Chancellor, and is now Emeritus Professor. He lives in Wellington and New York with his wife, women's running pioneer Kathrine Switzer. They are currently finishing a joint book on the marathon.

The Seasoned Runner As Hero, In History And Literature

Roger Robinson

"Though I look old, yet am I strong and lusty." - Shakespeare, As You Like It

In the very first race in literature, the old guy wins. He's Odysseus (aka Ulysses), pushing forty at the time, and he beats the best of the united Greek army gathered outside Troy.

The race comes late in Homer's long poem *The Iliad*, written down about 720 BC, the earliest great story in Western culture. It's one of the events in the "funeral games" (which is how the track meets of ancient Greece began) for Patroclus, killed in battle. His friend Achilles puts up good prizes - a silver bowl, an ox and some cash - for the first three, in a race that seems to be about 400 meters. The top entries are the warrior Ajax, "famous for his speed," Antilochus, "the fastest among all the younger men," and the "cunning Odysseus". Ajax charges into the lead with Odysseus following so close that "Ajax could feel his breath on the back of his neck". But Odysseus cannot get past, and with the finish near, he does what many an older runner has done in that position - he prays. "Give it me, Goddess, help me, move these legs!"

Athene not only "infused new power and lightness into his pumping hands and feet," but she makes Ajax skid and crash on a piece of greasy offal. Seasoned runners don't waste an opportunity like that. "Odysseus had the silver bowl triumphantly above his head before Ajax staggered up," the poet says. Young Antilochus makes a nice speech about how Odysseus "belongs to an earlier generation, but man, he's still fast". For the history and literature of older runners, it's a good beginning.

Cunning as ever, Odysseus dodges the race in Homer's *The Odyssey*, the later poem that tells of his long journey home. He wins the discus, but excuses himself from any running because he is out of shape from his sea travels. He tactfully omits to mention that he has just loitered away several years on a temptation island with the beautiful Calypso.

*

Older runners are rare in earlier literature, and in the historical records of running, as you would expect when few people of any kind lived much past 40. There were some "freak races" during the 18th century gambling craze. Montague Shearman's seminal history of track and field records one such race between an elderly overweight man and a young runner carrying a jockey on his back (pick your odds for that!). Fanny Burney, in her novel *Evelina* (1778), attacks the exploitative side of the betting craze, in a scene, quite likely derived from real life, when some arrogant young gents set up a race between two old women, both "more than eighty years of age". Feeble and frightened, the old ladies "hobble, stumble, and fall," enraging those who have put money on the result. Some of today's 80-plus masters women could have outrun the gamblers.

Another good seasoned runner, a woman this time, turns up in an 18th century poem about women's "smock races". These were customarily held at village sports, and take their name from the prize, traditionally a smock (chemise or underskirt, usually of glazed "holland" cotton or linen). A small group of poems were written about these races, almost unknown (and very hard to find) today but a useful source for the history of women's running. They are entertaining and often wickedly funny. Most of the attention is on attractive young competitors, who can be described in close-up detail in their gauzy and revealing running attire, which quite often falls off during the race. A more seasoned competitor, Tabitha the "veteran," enters the smock race in a poem called *Hobbinol*, by William Somerville (1740). She doesn't win, but she makes an exciting race of it with her courageous challenge to the speedy and sexy little Gandaretta, with her "heaving breast" and "taper thighs". "Tabitha the tall, known far and near/For matchless speed" goes out, the poet says, like a shooting star, and looks to be heading for an upset win. But she has pushed too hard, and runs into what we would call oxygen debt:

> Sudden she stops, nor longer can endure
> The painful course, but drooping sinks away,
> And like that falling meteor, there she lies
> A jelly cold on earth.

(Some of us have felt like that after a marathon.)

*

The older runner who is over the top and liable to collapse is a common disparaging stereotype, in fact and fiction. By contrast, I found one who is very much in charge. He is also the most horrific runner anywhere in literature. He is a Polynesian cannibal tribal priest who runs for three days in a narrative ballad by Robert Louis Stevenson, called "The Feast of Famine" (1890). The story and details are based on rituals that had only recently died out when Stevenson cruised observantly around the South Pacific islands. The poem describes with disturbing vividness how the frenzied priest prepares for a coming feast by running non-stop for three days round and round the village, dressed grotesquely in the hair of those slain for previous meals. When he stops running on feast day, he will name which villagers he has chosen to be on that night's menu:

> All day long in the land, by cliff and thicket and den,
> He ran his lunatic rounds, and howled for the flesh of men...
> Three were the days of his running, when valleys were heavy with musk,

Then the wreck of the red-eyed priest came gasping home in the dusk

It would add to spectator interest at marathons, I guess, if the race winner picked three from the crowd to get barbecued for the post-race party. Stevenson provided another account of the running ritual in his travel book *In the South Seas*, wisely explaining about the lack of protein in the diet that partly caused cannibalism in some of the islands.

*

Searching through both imaginative literature and old historical sports books for attitudes towards "seasoned" people who continue to exercise, I found an underlying inconsistency, the extremes of approval and disapproval. On the negative side there are the ageist stereotypes, images that suggest it is merely ridiculous for older people even to try to run. There is a very dismissive passage about what we would call masters track races in a French book about sports, *Wonders of Bodily Strength and Skill* by Guillaume Depping (1871), which says almost indignantly how embarrassing it is to watch frail and elderly runners who still try to compete, especially in front of spectators.

But in another chapter, where he writes about the "running footmen," the servants who used to be the couriers of the European aristocracy, Depping is full of praise for the senior footman of the King of Saxony, striding out in front of the King's coach at Dresden, "an old man, 70 years of age, six feet high, and nimble as a stag". So sometimes it can be admirable to run. Some writers recognized that it can also be beneficial. "Athletic sports" as a means to good health and longevity are strongly advocated in an important early book, *The Code of Health and Longevity* by Sir John Sinclair (Edinburgh, 1806-07). Another French book (*Customs and Costumes of Provence*) writes lyrically about races for older runners, and "how good it is to see runners who look like a beautiful day in winter...who have kept the fire of youth under the creases of age...Young people can say, if we would like to reach such a fine old age, let us live as they have lived".

"A sunny day in winter" is a nice way of describing the seasoned runner. I've heard worse.

So alongside the ageist stereotypes runs this contrary and fairly well sustained belief that continued exercise is a way of enriching life as you attain old age. You still meet both attitudes today. The satiric poet Ogden Nash lamented the onset of middle age by punning "when I jog I joggle." On the positive side are George Sheehan and a myriad other writers, including everyone in this book; or to go further back, the Scottish novelist Smollett, at the end of his novel *Humphry Clinker* (1771). The bad-tempered and chronically constipated old squire Matthew Bramble has learned in the course of the story that sitting around feeling sorry for himself only made things worse. Travel, adventure and vigorous exercise have cured him:

> I have put myself on the superannuated list too soon, and absurdly sought for health in the retreats of laziness...We should sometimes increase the motion of machine, to unclog the wheels of life.

Since I turned 40, that has been one of my favourite quotations.

*

Other cultures where running is a necessity have no doubts on the issue. Running is so essential to the survival and belief systems of many Native American and Canadian First Nations that no one is excluded. The Navajo held races for all age groups, including girls and an "old man's race". Hopi and Tarahumara men habitually keep running well into their sixties. Peter Nabokov (in *Indian Running*) recounts the story of how the Cheyenne chief Little Wolf, aged well over 50, outran a young Sioux challenger in a race of about four miles. Like the cunning Odysseus, Little Wolf sat in behind for most of the distance and came through near the finish.

When Walt Whitman wrote poems about his long walks as a source of freedom and independence ("The east and the west are mine, and the north and the south are mine"), he was expressing something very close to the Navajo running chant "The mountain, I become part of it...The wilderness, the dew drops, the pollen, I become part of it." Walking or running makes us part of the living cosmic unity, and that is not something restricted to the young.

Another real-life model for achieving this kind of fulfillment by staying in shape was the late Victorian scholar and man of letters, Sir Leslie Stephen. A top miler as a student at Cambridge, and mainly responsible for starting the annual Oxford-Cambridge athletics meet, Stephen in later life kept himself in the exercise zone, becoming a prodigious mountaineer and long-distance walker, covering thirty mile walks every Sunday with a group that called themselves the "Boa Constrictors" (possibly because of the resultant appetite). At the same time he produced a body of important essays and editions.

If you know Stephen only through his daughter Virginia Woolf's limited version of him in *To the Lighthouse*, check on a more balanced portrait of him, as the vigorous fast walker Vernon Whitford in George Meredith's novel *The Egoist* (1879). The lively heroine Clara says, "I chafe at restraint: hedges and palings everywhere," so chooses the energetic Vernon over the idle egoist who gives the book its title. Being in the fitness zone equated even then with moral and spiritual health. The wisest Victorians believed, as Charles Kingsley put it:

No man would deny that a thoroughly healthy state of body is the normal and most essential condition of athletic excellence. And just the same thing may be said of spiritual and intellectual health.

*

The more formal annals of the sport of running, even in the early days, show a few whose careers as top competitors extended beyond the usual limits - like the Cheyenne Little Wolf. Mainly, as you would expect, these were in the longer events. One of the best was the 18th century Yorkshire "pedestrian" (professional walker/runner) Foster Powell, whose performance range went from one mile to many hundred miles, and whose active career extended from his early twenties to nearly 60. At 44, Powell could run two miles in 10:30, at 57 a mile in 5:23, and at the same age he walked/jogged from London to York, and back, 400 miles/640 k, in less than six days.

Another versatile runner/walker who went on well beyond 40 was Captain Robert Barclay Allardyce, whose training methods provide most of the substance of the first "how-to" book on running, Walter Thom's *Pedestrianism* (1813). Barclay's system started with "physic" (purging with emetics and laxatives), and included a lot of vigorous walking, intense bursts of fast running, a meaty diet, and plenty of sleep; nowhere does the book say that the regime of a committed pedestrian is only for the young.

Later in the 19th century, the fashion for six-day "go-as-you-please" races, some of them drawing contestants from both sides of the Atlantic, naturally attracted a few seasoned competitors. The American Edward Payson Weston, the most popular celebrity of the series, had one of his best victories at age 40, in London, when he covered a record 550 miles/880 km.

Perhaps the greatest seasoned runner of them all before the establishment of masters racing in the modern era was the British-born South African Arthur Newton, who brings us into the 20th century. (Not to be confused with the American Arthur Newton who ran the 1900 and 1904 Olympic marathons.) Newton took up running at 39, almost immediately won the 54.6-mile Comrades ultra-marathon, won again by a huge margin the next year, and soon after lowered the world record for 50 miles by 20 minutes (5:53:05), and for 100 miles by 22 minutes (14:22). In thirteen remarkable years, 1922-1935, Newton shuttled between events in Britain, South Africa, and North America, turned professional, ran an average of twenty miles a day, totalling over 100,000 miles, twice entered the trans-America Bunion Derby, and broke every world record longer than the regular marathon. Two of his best record runs, for 24 hours and 100 miles, came at ages 48 and 51. His book, *Running in Three Continents* (1940) is a classic, though his how-to books are less convincing. By becoming a runner at nearly 40, he transformed his own life, from an obscure South African farmer into an international celebrity, and made a lasting contribution to the sport. The urbane Arthur Newton led the way for all seasoned runners into the zone.

*

A scattering of older runners was a familiar feature of the mid-20ᵗʰ century running scene, especially in the marathon, road running, and inter-club cross-country. The first stirrings of the modern masters movement, as it is fair to call it, came in the 1950s, with the foundation of a special over-40 road and cross-country club called Veterans AC. Other Commonwealth countries like New Zealand soon followed. In the 1960s, New Zealand's great coach, Arthur Lydiard, whose runners had stunned the world at the 1960 and 1964 Olympics, began, with the missionary energy that characterized the man, to apply his training principles to older people, including those convalescing from heart attack, totally contrary to what was then standard medical practice. Lydiard's *Run for Your Life* (with Garth Gilmour, 1967) was the first book to promote running to groups other than elites or school athletes, as something beneficial even to those with little competitive ability.

The wave swept the world. University of Oregon coach Bill Bowerman made a famous visit to New Zealand, was outrun by some of Lydiard's plump heart-attack-recovery joggers, and returned home to publish *Jogging*. Pioneering masters in the 1970s founded IGAL (a German title for an international road running association of "older long-distance runners"), and WAVA - the World Association of Veteran Athletes (now called World Masters Athletics). Both introduced world championships, the first WAVA at Toronto in 1975. Also in the mid-1970s, Jacques Serruys in Belgium created the Veterans 25k road race in Brugge, a race that for many years was an unofficial championship attracting top over-40 runners from around the world. *National Masters News* started publication in USA, taking information to a much bigger circulation than its British precursor *Veteris*. In USA, the Fifty-Plus Fitness Association was founded in 1979 and hosts significant annual conferences on ageing and performance, with a "fitness weekend" of sports events. National age-group championships were established in many countries, and age-group awards introduced in America's rapidly growing road events. When prize money was legitimized in the early 1980s, the masters, as they were now known (because American English has another meaning for "veterans") got a small but tempting slice of that cake. And their bit of the running boom boomed even louder than most. The increasing world population of over-40s and over-50s were ready to enter the zone.

Stars emerged. Jack Foster of New Zealand brought fire to the movement in 1974 when he won the silver medal in the Commonwealth Games marathon in Christchurch, inspiring all older runners with his 2:11:19. A few years later a reformed smoker called Priscilla Welch did the same for over-40 women, winning the New York Marathon and running 2:26:51 at age 42. A Dutchman, Piet van Alphen, and two clerical Americans, Baptist minister Rev. Norman Green, and Dominican teaching nun Sister Marion Irvine, were soon setting equally extraordinary new marks in the over-50 grades. New Zealand sheep farmer Derek Turnbull simply kept running as he got older at the same speeds he had done as a young club runner: 2:12 for the 880 at age 20, 2:12 for the 800 at age 58 (and still sub-2:30 at over-70). At 60, Turnbull ran a marathon in 2:38, and at 65 in 2:42. Now Ed Whitlock runs 2:54:48 hours at 73. Ruth Anderson, Ed Benham,

Clive Davies, Toshiko d'Elia, Alan Gilmour, Payton Jordan, Johnny Kelley, Evy Palm, Diane Palmason, Ruth Rothfarb, Joyce Smith, and many more contributed to this historic rewriting of humanity's understanding of what is possible at later ages.

There have been many such heroes. There are also tens of thousands, even millions, of runners who now continue well beyond the age when society used to think it more appropriate to concentrate on growing cabbages or playing cards. We are looking (as I wrote in *Heroes and Sparrows* twenty years ago) at a worldwide social movement whose contribution to community health, improved lifestyle, and changing values is one of the best developments of the modern era.

Has this major change in social attitude to ageing fitness made any mark on our culture's imagination? Yes, to judge from the many popular movies and TV series in which older characters (sometimes very old) are central, such as *Cocoon, On Golden Pond* or *The Golden Girls*. Jack Nicholson and Sean Connery can now play seasoned characters who are romantically active. I have seen Shakespeare's Beatrice and Benedick played as 50-plus-year-olds, and the romantic sparkle was increased by the maturity of their witty sparring. Even in a Broadway musical like *Mamma Mia!* the narrative turns out at the end to be essentially about the older generation making changes in their lives, not the less interesting 20-somethings who start the show. Dynamic things can happen in relationships, careers, or lifestyles after 40, our culture now accepts. No longer do we think, with one Jane Austen heroine, that 27 is an age at which a woman "can never hope to feel or inspire affection again". No longer is the senile and ranting King Lear the only stereotype. These days he'd take up the marathon.

And runners? Yes, they are there, in literature at least, though not yet in the movies, or in big numbers. Bernard Malamud's major late novel *Dubin's Lives* (1979) focused the hero's mid-life crisis in the tension between the fulfilling simplicity of his daily run through the upstate New York countryside and the complications of his unfulfilling love life. The running scenes are much better than the sex scenes in my opinion. I think a few hard half marathons would have solved Dubin's problems - especially if he won an age-group award.

Some established poets who are also runners have written well about running, from the perspective of the older, slower runner, including Marge Piercy, William Stafford, Marvin Bell and Brian Turner.

One recent book takes the other side. Brooks Stanwood's running-gothic horror story, *The Glow* (1979), has to be set against all the endorsements of running as beneficial for the body and spirit. Its older runners are the villains. It's a creepy tale about an eagerly vigorous group of senior joggers in New York who turn out to be macabre vampires, who rejuvenate themselves every few months with the blood of the young runners they have befriended, and then murdered. The novel reflects disturbingly on modern society's obsession with prolonging youth. That old discomfort, lingering from 200 years ago, the feeling that it is somehow inappropriate to try to be a runner at an advanced age, has not entirely disappeared.

*

To end on the positive note, however. The figure of the wise and toughened older runner (always male, so far) has appeared in several of the best running novels in the last 25 years. It's a welcome change from the familiar running-fiction formula, borrowed from school stories, of "rejected-young-hero-defies-authority-and-earns-fame-by-winning-dramatic-race-in-the-last-chapter". Now (to take them in order of publication) we have the refreshingly astute Doc Cole, the 54-year-old ex-Olympic marathoner who is one of the stars of Tom McNab's powerfully entertaining *Flanagan's Run* (1982); and the wiry, canny, unwashed, hard-training Scotsman Watson Doyle, still good at 53 for a sub-2:30 marathon, in Paul Christman's fine fantasy of the first London Marathon, *The Purple Runner* (1983); and the delightfully flamboyant actor-runner-entrepreneur Douglas Cameron/Professor Moriarty, well past youth in McNab's vivid running Western, *The Fast Men* (1986).

In non-fiction, Bernd Heinrich's remarkable *Why We Run* (2001) is both an enthralling scientist's meditation on running, and a dramatic inside-the-mind account of a seasoned runner winning the USA 100 km championship. Heinrich was 41 when he won that race, but the book was written nearly twenty years later, from the zone of a highly intelligent thinker with a lifetime of experience and vigorous knowledge.

These are heroes for any seasoned runner to enjoy. More should follow soon. We now have many interesting older heroes who are currently active in running, as anyone knows who has enjoyed a conversation with Bill Rodgers, Joan Benoit Samuelson, Ed Whitlock, Helen Klein, or John Keston. No doubt fiction, and our culture more widely, will soon recapture their vitality, giving us new characters to join Odysseus and Tabitha and Matthew Bramble - seasoned heroes of the imagination, who remind us that it is always better, at any age, to increase the motion of the machine, and unclog the wheels of life.

- The literary references in this essay are more fully discussed and quoted in Roger Robinson's *Running in Literature: a Guide for Scholars, Readers, Runners, Joggers, and Dreamers* (Breakaway Books, 2003, $22; available signed from **rogerrobinson61@hotmail.com**).

- Translations in this essay are by Roger Robinson, ©.

Select Reference Sources:

Richard Benyo, *Running Past Fifty* (Human Kinetics, 1998)

Richard Benyo and Joe Henderson, *Running Encyclopedia* (Human Kinetics, 2002)
Guillaume Depping, *Wonders of Bodily Strength and Skill* (Paris, 1871)
Tom McNab, Peter Lovesey, Andrew Huxtable, *An Athletics Compendium* (British Library, 2001)
Peter Nabokov, *Indian Running* (Ancient City Press, 1981)
Roger Robinson, *Heroes and Sparrows. A Celebration of Running* (Southwestern, 1986)
Roger Robinson, *Robert Louis Stevenson: His Best Pacific Writings* (Exisle, 2003)
Edward S. Sears, *Running Through the Ages* (McFarland, 2001)
Montague Shearman, *Athletics and Football* (Badminton Library, 1887)
Kathrine Switzer, *Running and Walking for Women Over 40* (Harper Collins, 1998)
Noel Tamini, *La Saga des Pédestrians* (Edior, 1997)
Walter Thom, *Pedestrianism* (Brown & Frost, 1813)
Bruce & Sue Tulloh, *Running over Forty* (Tulloh Books, 2001)

THE INSPIRATION ZONE

"When people wish me 'good luck' before a race, I say luck has nothing to do with it – it is all of the hard work and effort I have put into my training that will pay off – so simply say, 'Have a good race'. The only people I say 'good luck' to are those who are going to Las Vegas!"
[Dick Hartnett, masters runner and coach extraordinaire]

Doug Alward

Doug has every right to join the other contributors to *Running in the Zone*, as an active and dedicated runner in his own right. But, Doug Alward has another unique reason for participating and that reason transcends age or any personal running accomplishment. Doug was the teenage friend of Canada's Terry Fox and was there with Terry through early school days, the bout with cancer that cost him his leg, his recovery and steely determination to achieve a superhuman goal. Doug was there through the run that branded Terry Fox's image on our minds and finally at the point of his untimely death.

Doug Alward drove the support van for Terry Fox and tells the story of determination and inspiration represented by the Marathon of Hope. That inconceivable objective to run across Canada and raise money for cancer research began 25 years ago on a cold beach in Newfoundland. As most people know, the cancer that took Terry's leg, also took his life before he could complete his run. It could not defeat his dream and the continuing, even growing movement to achieve Terry's dream is active around the world in over 50 countries. Doug was there and the story is moving as he recounts it.

Today Doug is 46 years old, just on the edge of the "older runner" category perhaps, and an avid participant who is accomplished at his chosen distances. As an example, in 2002 Doug won the Peach City Half Marathon (Penticton, BC) with a time of 1:15:46 and in 2005 set an age-class record of 2:45:46 at the Peach City Marathon, coming second overall by just six seconds. Still, Doug has chosen not to talk about his own accomplishments, challenges, theories or trials, but to share his knowledge of Terry Fox instead. As the years pile on and perhaps the physical abuse the more enthusiastic of us heap on our willing bodies, the injuries, small and not so small, the aches, pains and arthritic joints test us and slow us. Doug Alward uses his long ago friendship and continuing memory of Terry Fox to go beyond those physical challenges to keep striving to meet his personal potential in running and in life.

All contributors to *Running in the Zone* have received a modest compensation for their participation. Doug Alward has donated his honorarium to the Terry Fox Foundation in support of cancer research, and to respect the policy that no-one should profit personally from the Terry Fox story or image. Anyone wishing to contribute financially or to participate in a Terry Fox Run can learn more by going to **www.terryfoxrun.org**.

Inspiration And Determination
A First Hand Account Of The Terry Fox Story

Doug Alward

"Anything is possible if you try.....
Dreams are made when people try."

Terry Fox, 1980

The Marathon of Hope to raise funds for cancer research began on a cold and foggy day in St. John's, Newfoundland (April 12, 1980). Snow covered the roadside as winter still gripped the landscape.

Terry Fox dipped his artificial foot into the icy Atlantic Ocean, then turned landward to begin one of the most historic and inspiring runs ever. It was a run that would take him over 3,339 miles (5,373 km) across Canada through snow, wind, rain, and stifling heat before the cancer would strike again, killing his body but not his indomitable and enduring spirit.

It was a run that sceptics said was impossible. How could a boy who had lost one leg to bone cancer run a 42.2 km or 26.2 mile marathon EVERY day across hilly and mountainous highways, all the way across the second largest country in the world? Such a feat was considered impossible for most two-legged people. How could a one-legged person even think about it? Only one one-legged person, a man named Dick Traum, had ever tried a marathon on the primitive artificial legs available in 1980. Terry was going to try to RUN a marathon EVERY DAY for several months. It was a run that would carry Terry Fox into the hearts of a nation and inspire millions of people across Canada and around the world, then and for decades to come.

As Terry's friend and driver on the "Marathon of Hope for Cancer Research" and as Terry's best friend from the age of 13, I learned much about his character and dreams. By sharing what I was so blessed to be a part of, I hope to inspire you to reach out for your dreams, regardless of your present age, condition or situation.

One step at a time! One telephone pole at a time! One Marathon Run on one leg, one day at a time! Over 5,300 km across Canada through 100 km/hr wind, rainstorms, snow, -20°C late winter weather and searing 35°C summer heat; enduring freight trucks and inattentive drivers barrelling along the Trans-Canada Highway at him; living in a small camperized van with the world's worst cook (me) feeding him canned beans and peanut butter and jam sandwiches, Terry Fox ran a marathon a day for over 130 days taking only a couple of days off. Those "off" days were spent doing publicity events, television and newspaper interviews and meeting politicians and Prime Ministers. For Terry, the daily fundraising speeches and interviews were often more exhausting than the run. Miraculously, Terry Fox did it. He proved it IS possible to do the impossible.

When Terry first mentioned to me his idea of running a marathon a day, EVERY day, for 200+ days in a row across Canada to raise money for cancer research, I never doubted he could accomplish such an unbelievable feat. Terry was always a possibility thinker. Terry believed in reaching for dreams with the abilities he had, not dwelling on what he didn't have or what he might have done. I believed Terry could do it. Terry believed he could do it. The rest would just be detail and hard work.

To understand how Terry and I could believe such a feat was possible, you have to know something of Terry's background. When I first met Terry we were the only two Grade 8's on the school cross-country running team. The school's huge football coach, who was our Physical Education instructor, semi-threatened us into joining the team even though running was not something Terry particularly enjoyed. In the first race of the year Terry came a distant dead last.

Untrained and new to competitive running, Terry was glad just to finish that first race, but he wouldn't quit. With the encouragement and direction of outstanding teacher and running coach Mr. Fred Tinck (five of the athletes he coached went on to make the Olympic Games in various sports), Terry worked hard every day through cross-country and track seasons. By the time Terry was 15 he could run a mile in under five minutes. In other words, were it not for events yet to come, Terry was at the threshold of becoming an elite runner. But, as we know, Terry was destined to be not just an elite athlete, but an elite human being.

Similar to his efforts on the track, Terry improved dramatically as a basketball player. By way of a daily plan of training, believing in himself and just plain working his butt off, Terry went from being the shortest, least skilled Grade 8 player (possibly in all of Canada), to making the basketball team at Simon Fraser University five years later. Academically, Terry went from being a 55% student in Grade 8 to holding an 88% average in Grade 12. Believing he could accomplish each of these goals, then planning and working towards them was the key to Terry achieving his dreams.

When Terry was 18 years old he felt a pain in his knee, a pain that got progressively worse over the next three months. Terry was stubborn. To him, pain was not to be a barrier to achieving his goals. He would not go to a doctor until he could no longer walk. Finally, after the doctors had done a battery of tests, Terry's right leg was amputated a foot above his knee. Such a drastic measure was needed to try to prevent the spread of bone cancer that had started in his knee.

After surgery, several months of sickening chemotherapy treatments followed to try to kill any cancer cells that may have spread to other areas of Terry's body. He lost his hair and vomited almost daily.

Terry did not dwell on his amputated leg and illness. He decided to get off his butt and show people what he could do. He said,

> *"I'm a dreamer, I like challenges. I don't give up. I go all out...Nobody is ever going to call me a quitter."*

Terry focused on carrying a full course load of tough science and math courses at university. At the invitation of world wheelchair traveller "Man in Motion" Rick Hansen, he began playing wheelchair basketball. The British Columbia wheelchair team with Rick and Terry playing key roles, won the Canadian Championship three times.

After two years of treatment Terry vowed to do something to help all the kids he had seen suffering and often dying in the cancer clinic. He came up with the dream of running across Canada on one leg, doing a marathon a day to raise funds for cancer research. How could he accomplish such a feat on one good leg and a primitive artificial leg that was held on by air suction and a strap? The normal running gait was impossible so Terry invented a motion where he hopped with his real leg and swung the artificial leg through. Some people called it a triple jump and others appropriately called it the "Fox Trot". One person said his running looked like that of a three-legged horse. To Terry all that mattered was that he was RUNNING. Problem number one had been solved by thoughtful experimentation.

The next problem to tackle was running a marathon a day. Terry had to come up with a training plan. He consulted everyone he knew who might be able to help him. Running and weight training coaches as well as nutrition experts helped Terry develop a plan. The first day Terry "RAN" just a single lap around the local dirt track and collapsed with an exhausted real leg and a bleeding stump, the result of the chafing of his stump in the bucket of the artificial leg. Terry went home with only one thing in his mind: a plan to do better the next day. The next day he ran two laps. After one week he was running a mile. By five months he was up to twenty laps a day. Terry said:

> *"I had some blisters man. It was like running on coals. I had some sores on my stump where the artificial leg was. They just rubbed raw and there is no protection. Sometimes the sores would bleed right through my valve in the bucket and the blood would run down my knee and my leg. I developed bone bruises. My toes and heel were totally blistered raw and I lost three toenails. I had shinsplints for two months...You have to get over a pain threshold. There were times where it really hurt, but I kept going."*

Then, with my crazy encouragement, Terry decided to pre-register for a 28 km race in Prince George, BC on the Labour Day Weekend of 1979. He still had two more months to increase his mileage and train his body. Slowly and systematically Terry increased his mileage to 18 km a day. Also, three times a week intensive two-hour sessions of strength and conditioning exercises followed the daily running sessions. These exercises worked particularly hard on back, abdominal, and lower leg muscles. Finally, race day in Prince George arrived and Terry ran the entire 28 km without walking a single step.

Terry had now made up his mind. He would begin planning his run to cross the country at a marathon a day pace. The run would begin in April of 1980, just seven months later. He prepared a letter to get sponsors to help him in his dream. Terry wrote:

> *"The night before my amputation I read an article on an amputee who completed the New York City Marathon. It was then I decided to meet this new challenge head on and not only overcome my disability, but conquer it in such a way that I could never look back and say it disabled me. But I soon realized that would only be half my quest, for as I went through the sixteen months of the physically and emotionally draining ordeal of chemotherapy I was rudely awakened by the feelings that coursed through the cancer clinic. There were faces with the brave smiles and the ones who had given up smiling. There were the feelings of hopeful denial and the feelings of despair. My quest would not be a selfish one. I could not leave knowing these faces and feelings would still exist, even though I would be set free from mine. Somewhere the hurting must stop and I am determined to take myself to the limit for this cause.... I am not saying this will initiate any kind of cure for cancer, but I believe in miracles. I have to."*

> *Terry Fox (September 1979)*

From September 1979 to Christmas Eve Terry ran 101 days in a row increasing his mileage from 10 miles (16 km) per day to 20 miles (32 km) per day by Christmas Eve. His mother ordered him to take Christmas Day off. Even when his wheelchair basketball team toured Washington and Oregon in early December Terry kept the streak of 20 mile days going by rising by 5:00 a.m. and running his miles.

Terry's dream gave him amazing drive. He wanted to help kids dying of cancer. This dream kept Terry going through injury, lack of sleep and the pressures of university exams and term papers.

In his speeches Terry would often say that the pain he felt was nowhere near as bad as that of the pain the kids were feeling on the cancer wards. Some kids had tumours growing out the side of their head. Others had tumours throughout their body. Some would be there one week and dead the next. This suffering motivated Terry into action: one step at a time, one telephone pole at a time, one mile at a time. Now the dream was within reach. Running a marathon a day on one leg, across the second largest country in the world was just one step away.

On April 12, 1980 in St John's Newfoundland Terry dipped his leg into the Atlantic Ocean. He filled a bottle with Atlantic Ocean water and tucked it away in the small camperized van we would share over the next several months. CBC television was there to capture the historic moment although much prodding was needed to convince CBC to have a film crew out to film such an impossible feat. A news reporter recorded the following quote from Terry:

> *"If it's only up to me and my mind I've got a lot of positive attitude. But you never know what might happen....I wanted to try the impossible..."*

The first day fog limited visibility to fifty meters. The second day it snowed. The third day was sunny but with sub-zero temperatures that Terry said "Froze my balls off." Seventy kilometre per hour freezing winds in his face made the running extremely difficult. On and on I watched Terry struggle. Day after day he accomplished the marathon goal. Day after day and step after step he captured the hearts of the kids and adults he spoke to at schools, receptions, and by doing countless interviews on radio and television. After three weeks he had run across the province of Newfoundland, a distance of 933 kilometres. By six weeks he had conquered Nova Scotia, Prince Edward Island and New Brunswick. By seven weeks Terry had lost ten pounds, mostly due to my sub-par cooking. By eleven weeks Terry was through Quebec and at the Ontario border. Terry would say:

> *"I broke the run down. Get that mile down, get to that sign, that corner and around that bend."*

If I could describe Terry in one word it would be RELENTLESS.

Terry had accomplished what doctors, other amputees and sceptics had said was impossible. Terry Fox had proved them wrong. Now news editors hurried to record the story of the miracle boy who was capturing the imagination of people from coast to coast.

His story was simple. He had lost his leg from cancer. He had seen kids dying of cancer. He was determined to do something about it. He was asking people to donate to cancer research. A one dollar donation from each person was his goal.

His day would begin shortly after 4:00 a.m. Before 5:00 a.m. he had to be at the spot on the Trans-Canada Highway that he had stopped the day before. In the pitch-black darkness Terry would step onto the highway under every conceivable weather condition. There were no excuses for taking a day off. Pain, blisters, and exhaustion were no excuse. A broken foot "MIGHT" be. Walking was NEVER allowed. He had to RUN every step.

Entering the province of Ontario in mid-July, temperatures soared upwards of 35°C. In major population centers thousands lined the streets to see and be inspired by Terry as he struggled onwards. Terry added several hundreds of kilometres to the run by heading south to Toronto, Mississauga, Hamilton, and London, Ontario. Terry wanted to go to large population centers to inspire as many people as possible to give for cancer research.

Terry relentlessly fought onward through the hot summer finally nearing Thunder Bay, Ontario. At mile 3,339 (5,373 km) the cancer struck again. The bone cancer cells that had spread from his knee had grown into tumours larger than baseballs in his lungs, causing one lung to collapse so that he could hardly breathe. The Marathon of Hope had ended on Labour Day Sunday, exactly one year to the minute after Terry had run his only race, on one leg, in Prince George.

The run was over, but the dream of raising funds for cancer research was not. Telethons and fundraising ventures spread like wildfire across Canada as Terry received treatment for the cancer that was now surely and steadily killing his physical body.Terry died just before 5:00 a.m. on June 28, 1981. Ironically, one year before at 5:00 a.m. on June 28, 1980 Terry ran across the Quebec/Ontario Provincial border. Ontario was the province where the fundraising skyrocketed. It seemed as if Terry was asking us to continue his dream.

I was sad to physically lose my best friend, but relieved he was free of the horrible suffering cancer had caused. Spiritually, Terry's attitudes and values continue to inspire me. Several times I have thought of giving up running as my aging body breaks down. Three years ago my doctor did a bone scan on my swollen feet and discovered the beginnings of arthritis. Muscle pulls, tendon problems and even a broken upper arm that sidelined me from any running for two months have slowed me down. Due to a modified training program, improved diet, the support of other runners, and Terry's attitude to take "ONE STEP AT A TIME', I have achieved some of my best ever running performances.

Do you have a dream? Think of Terry's perseverance against unbelievable handicaps: bone bruises, shinsplints and severe blister-like cysts on his stump that often bled into the artificial leg. Whether they be trivial or major, physical or mental, let Terry's perseverance and spirit inspire you through your tough times and personal challenges.

Today, Terry Fox Runs are held in over 50 countries and have raised more than $360 million for cancer research. Terry is still running, still taking one step at a time, one mile at a time. As Terry said:

> *"You only live once and if you want to get something done you have to do it while you have the chance."*

Terry tried and his dream to find a cure for cancer lives on.

Wally Hild

In 1994, oncologist Dr. Jack Chritchley told Wally Hild that he had less than a year to survive because of advanced Hodgkin's disease. That grim diagnosis and subsequent eight months of harsh and aggressive chemotherapy changed Wally's life – forever.

Because of his faith, family and friends, he began his metamorphosis with the first of his two Ironman Canada Triathlon finishes in 1996. He's also finished numerous short course triathlons, short distance races and half and full marathons. He says that training for triathlons and marathons is like 'eating the elephant'. It's impossible to do in a single sitting but by breaking down all of his challenges and endeavors, he's been able to achieve his dreams and goals, one bit and bite at a time.

There is another spectacular twist to this family's history. Caroline, Wally's wife of 33 years, suffered a massive stroke at age 49 from a congenital blood disorder she was not aware of. Because she received the clot-busting drug, TPA within three hours, she not only survived, but completed the Honolulu Marathon in December 2002 with Wally at her side. She, like Wally, agrees that it's not important what happens to you in life, but how you respond. She says we can be victims or victors – it's our choice.

Wally has authored two books, "From Hodgkin's to Ironman", released in 1999 and "Through The Valley Of The Shadow", to be released later this year. His story can also be read in "The 6th Bowl Of Chicken Soup For The Soul". Wally and Caroline have two children, daughter Jodi (26) and son Chris (28).

After a 32-year career in radio and TV, he's now studying to earn his real estate license. Wally continues to re-invent himself, having formed a rock band at the age of 58. Until November 2004, he'd never played an instrument and is now the drummer and lead vocalist in the band, "Phoenix". He says, "I've risen from the ashes and am now following my passion to create music. I've found out that the only person stopping me from achieving my dreams and goals is me – and I'm getting the hell out of my way".

Will Power Can Make Things Happen

Wally Hild

In February of 1994, I was told I was dying of Hodgkin's disease, a lymphatic cancer. Oncologist Dr. Jack Chritchley explained the four stages of the disease and said I was at 3-B, almost at the final stage, which would be terminal without treatment. Many of my internal organs were compromised by cancer, including my spleen and lymph nodes. I'd lost over 20 pounds, my weight dropping from 162 to 140. I had two baseball-sized tumours in my chest, one behind each lung. It hurt to breathe. Dr. Chritchley told me, without treatment, I had less than one year to live.

After a month of invasive tests and procedures, he sentenced me to eight months of harsh and very 'aggressive' chemotherapy. Aggressive means you throw up a lot and lose all of your hair. As well, Dr. Christchley told me there were no guarantees that the treatment would be successful. I had to put all my trust in my faith, my family and friends as well as in him, to help get me through the difficult and black days that were in front of me.

In retrospect, it is interesting, even fateful, to notice how different parts of a life fit together like two jigsaw pieces. It was during my chemo protocol that my wife Caroline and I ended up watching our very first Ironman Canada triathlon, which is held in Penticton each August. We had moved to the Okanagan from southern Alberta the previous autumn. The valley is Canada's version of Napa Valley in California where many different kinds of fruits and grapes grow abundantly.

Six months into my chemotherapy I could barely walk for more than 10 minutes without having to stop and rest. I was totally bald and because sunshine is dangerous to chemo patients, and with the daytime temperatures rising as high as 40° Celsius, staying covered was a formidable task for me. In my tattered straw hat, long-sleeved cotton shirt and loose fitting jeans, I looked like someone who had his seasons confused.

As I stood there on the beach in Penticton at 7:00 a.m. I could not believe what I was seeing as almost two thousand triathletes from countries around the globe hit the water for the 2.4 mile swim. It was like a divine inspiration that came over me, but my eyes teared up as I turned to Caroline, and in a choking voice, said, "I'm going to do this someday." I so desperately wanted to live and I felt that wrapping an anchor chain around something like Ironman might help. By blurting out that seemingly irrational statement, I'd given myself authority to take my healing into my own hands.

Through my faith, the support and encouragement of my family and friends and the expertise of Dr. Chritchley and the team of cancer professionals, I survived

21

the treatments, which can be as harsh as the cancer itself. I thought of Friedrich Neitzsche's observation: "that which does not kill me, makes me stronger".

In September of 1995 I decided to train for the 1996 Ironman Canada Triathlon. Caroline and I met with Dave Bullock, a director of the race and a previous two-time finisher. For three hours we interrogated him about what it takes to finish such an arduous event. I came away from the meeting with a new enthusiasm for taking on the challenge. I met with Dr. Chritchley a few days later to undergo a rigorous cardio-pulmonary function stress examination to determine if the chemotherapy had caused any irreparable damage to my internal organs, especially my heart and lungs. It was not a routine test, but because I had met with him for his input into my desire to do the race, he ordered the evaluation. I asked him if I was crazy to attempt it. With the usual twinkle in his eye, he said, "You've come through an Ironman-type medical procedure. Go for it." He told me the examination showed no damage from the chemotherapy and I was thrilled when he gave me "thumbs up" after the test.

On August 25, 1996, just after 11:30 p.m., I crossed the finish line to achieve the greatest goal of my life. I'd blown out my right knee during the bike portion and had to walk the marathon leg of the triathlon. I was on the course for 16 hours, 34 minutes and 17 seconds. With tears of joy, I collapsed into the arms of my wife Caroline, daughter Jodi and son Chris as I passed beyond the tape. We'd all experienced something that would profoundly change the way we looked at life.

I knew from that day that I would be physically active for the rest of my life. Buoyed by the Ironman finish, I kept a modicum of fitness by occasionally running 10K races and became more interested in training for a marathon. I'd read books by Joe Henderson and Jeff Galloway, which helped in my decision to train for the 26.2 mile odyssey.

But as they say, the best laid plans of... well you know the rest of the story. I started the Okanagan Marathon in Kelowna in October 1999 but after 14 miles, I had to drop out of the race. Eight months earlier, while playing in a no-contact old-timers hockey tournament where there was to be no body-checking, a Neanderthal on the other team who obviously hadn't read the rules (or couldn't read) nailed me with an NHL-style hip check. He sent me flying through the air. I crash-landed on my right knee, damaging the meniscus. It was the same one injured during Ironman.

The incident forced me to evaluate the sports love of my life. I'd been playing hockey before Wayne Gretzky was born, but the orthopaedic surgeon who examined my knee and performed the arthroscopic repair told me bluntly, "Hockey and marathon training have nothing in common. You'll have to choose which one you want to do. It's one or the other - unless you like lying here with me poking holes in your knee."

Late that fall I made the tough decision to prepare for the 2000 Peach City

Marathon the following May. It was difficult and I regretfully hung up my skates for a season. I apologized to them each time I passed them in the basement room where I stored all my athletic equipment. I lovingly fondled my hockey stick whenever my wife wasn't looking. But, my decision had been made. I garnered as much information from books and friends who were much better runners than I and began my winter training. The second item I bought after a new pair of runners was a heart rate monitor. I was to run at no faster than 130 beats per minute, which was 70 percent of my maximum heart rate.

With my mind overflowing with information and inspiration, a watch on my left wrist and heart monitor receiver on my right, I set out on my 24-week regimen. I'd never used a monitor before and was shocked at how slowly I had to run to stay in my target zone. I can walk faster than this I thought to myself. But I persisted and was on my way to running five days a week with a swimming session thrown in for good measure. My goal: finish in 4:45.

Penticton is known for mild winters, but below freezing temperatures and some snow are assured even though the season is not nearly as severe or lengthy as that experienced in most Canadian provinces and northern US States. As it got colder through December and January, one of Dr. Chritchley's prophesies came true. He'd told me that because chemotherapy is accumulative and does not dissipate as a prescribed medicine might over time, I had suffered permanent side-effects from the drugs in my fingertips and toes. I could no longer tolerate the cold as I once was able to when I was growing up in the prairies of Alberta where the mercury could plummet to -40 degrees. The nerve endings and capillaries in all 20 digits were in danger of freezing quickly. It was dangerous for me to be in cold weather without adequate apparel.

I asked Dr. Chritchley if he could give me a prescription to live in Hawaii or southern California, which to my surprise he said he could do. However, a follow-up phone call to the American Consulate in Vancouver soon dashed any hopes of a move to where palm trees blow and the only ice you find is in the freezer.

On some of the colder days, I had to wear two pair of gloves and heavy wool socks in my runners. When it was just too miserable, I ran indoors at the city's community center, which I disliked. Running on a treadmill is clinical and I sweated profusely. Without the wind, I was drenched within twenty minutes.

In early January, I woke up one morning with flu-like symptoms. I coughed and dragged my butt for a few days but continued to run in spite of my discomfort. I increased my intake of vitamins and echinacea to help boost my immune system and carried on. The rest of January passed relatively smoothly and before I knew it, February was nearing a close. In spite of the inclement weather, I was able to run mostly outdoors. The valley where I live is situated north-south so I often ran face-first into wet snow. My cough lingered and my lungs were sore as I sucked in the cold air. In the shower, I cried out in pain as my frozen fingers and toes thawed under the stinging hot water, which felt like millions of tiny needles were being rifled into my digits. On such days, I thought back to my cancer battle and remembered how I vowed to never quit believing I could win it. So it was with my marathon training. I promised to let nothing stand in my way and just grimaced as another toe thawed out.

As winter gave way to spring, I was able to discard some of the layers of clothing making me finally look more like a runner than a displaced Eskimo high on the fumes of old, unwashed hockey jerseys. Once the temperatures hit into the 20's, I finally stripped down to shorts and just a single T-shirt.

Slowly I began to see the positive results of training with the heart rate monitor. After three months, I was going nearly a quarter-mile farther in a 50 minute run at the same pulse rate. It was still too slow for me, but I pressed on. Although four business trips to Vancouver and Victoria put me several long runs behind schedule, I was able to stick to most of my running program. I took my gear with me on each trip and was able to at least do the shorter 8 to 12 mile runs called for by my program.

By the time the cherry, apricot and apple blossoms had burst into full bloom in early May, I had shaken off the cold and was feeling great. My runs between the orchards and vineyards were exhilarating as I drank in the fragrance from the white and pink petals lining the road. Bathed in glorious sunshine, I ran along the east side of the mountain, a thousand feet above the city, the valley spread out below me.

Three weeks before the marathon, I received an interesting proposal from the sales manager at the radio station where I worked. "Do you think you could do an on-location broadcast while you're running? Peach City Runners would like you to do a play-by-play as you're doing the race. It's never been done on radio before. We'll give you a hands-free cell phone with a special microphone and earpiece."

"It's a cool idea", I said, not really thinking about the ramifications and I agreed to do it. My stomach began to tighten because there was no turning back from the decision I'd made. I had to shake the thought out of my head that I may have bitten off more than I could chew. The days quickly passed and before I knew it, it was Sunday May 21st - race day. On the Friday before, I'd awakened with a sore throat and by Saturday morning it had morphed into a head cold.

On Sunday morning my nose was running faster than I could at the best of times. My head was swimming and the floor seemed to undulate under my shaky legs. I knew, however, I could not drop out at the last moment. I sucked back another glass of orange juice, ate a bowl of porridge, popped a couple of echinacea capsules and just after 6 a.m., headed out with my wife Caroline.

It was slightly overcast and 15°C (59°F). Caroline kissed me goodbye and at 7 o'clock, the gun went off, signalling the start of the race. I was near the end of the pack and it was a good thing. With my dripping nose and gritted teeth, my goal was to get from aid station to aid station, situated two miles apart. Caroline had agreed to bring the cell phone to me by car just before 8:30 when the radio broadcast was to begin. The remote broadcast was to end at noon, and I was hoping to be at the finish line by then. I was to do four cut-ins per hour. When the phone rang, I stopped running and walked while I reported on the race.

As the miles slowly melted away under my red and white runners, the phone progressively got heavier. My breathing became more laboured as I spoke. But, I kept up my excitement about Peach City Runners to give them the best I could under the circumstances. Of the thousand or so remote broadcasts I'd done over a 32-year career in radio and TV, I'd never before done one where I was panting and breathing hard - until that date. About mile 18, I began to struggle and happened upon a runner who appeared hurt. His name was Ed, and he lived in Vancouver. We shook hands and agreed to help each other finish the race, especially when it came to the hilly portion of this particular marathon. By 11:00 a.m. The sun was directly over us and the famous Okanagan heat began to take its toll. I increased my intake of Gatorade and water. My thighs and shins were burning as we walked and jogged north, toward the finish where the Voice of Ironman, Steve King, was welcoming the tired and spent finishers.

At 11:30, Ed and I were still three miles away from the tape and I knew I would not make the noon finish. I did my last radio cut-in at 11:50 with the beach in sight. On the air, I thanked Steve Brown, the owner of Peach City Runners for the opportunity to do the remote but signed off with, "please don't ask me to do this again."

Ed and I hobbled through our collective pain and crossed the finish line together with a time of 5:17. Caroline held me up as I received my Finishers Medal and jacket. I hugged Ed and thanked him for his support and motivation.

As I lay on the foam table, getting my sun-burned and aching legs massaged, I squeezed Caroline's hand and smiled weakly at her. I had achieved another goal; conquered another challenge. There would likely be another marathon sometime in the future, but I knew that afternoon, I could enjoy what I had accomplished. I was so very grateful that I was alive to enjoy the aches and pains of stepping outside my comfort zone.

My life has never been the same since my cancer experience. I've taken on challenges that in the past, might have seemed insurmountable. There are no mountains in my life anymore. I now have the desire, confidence and fortitude to achieve anything that I want. My wife will attest to that. When I come home excited with the idea of something I want to do, she now simply rolls her eyes upward, and with a knowing smile, says, "OK, go for it".

The only thing stopping me from achieving my goals is me. And believe me, I'm getting out of my way!

Joe Henderson

Joe Henderson is one of running's senior writers. His magazine career began in 1967 at *Track & Field News*. From there he served in various capacities at Runner's World through 2004. Recently his columns have appeared in *Marathon & Beyond* magazine and on his website (**www.joehenderson.com**). Joe is the author or co-author of some 27 books on running and is widely recognized for his written contributions.

Born in 1943, Henderson began running 14 years later. He won several state high school titles in Iowa, then competed in track and cross-country at Drake University. From there he graduated to longer distances, racing as far as 70 miles.

He is a three-time winner of the Road Runner Club of America's Journalistic Excellence Award and is a member of the RRCA Hall of Fame. He lives, with his wife Barbara Shaw, in Eugene, Oregon. There he teaches university running classes and coaches a marathon team.

The Ancient Marathoner
[Reprinted with Permission from Marathon & Beyond]

Joe Henderson

We met in person only once, and then for less than an hour in 1976. Yet I count Jack Foster as one of the greatest friends I've ever had. Like all the great ones, he has never stopped giving.

Measured by the most said in the least words, one of the best books ever written about running was really just booklet length -- Foster's Tale of the Ancient Marathoner. Its first words, and far from its best, aren't his but mine that introduce him to readers.

"If a friendship can be measured by the number of letters two people exchange," I wrote in the Foreword, "then I can count Jack Foster among my best friends. On my desk here now is an inch-thick folder of lightweight blue aerogrammes postmarked 'Rotorua, New Zealand.' I feel I know Foster about as well as I know any runner,"

At the time we hadn't yet met. We tried at the Munich Olympics, before the marathon he ran there at age 40.

I wormed my way into Olympic Village, found the New Zealand compound and knocked on the door that I'd learned was his. No one answered.

Oh well, I thought at the time, I'll try again later in the Games. But a few days later everything changed for that Olympics and for all to follow. No intruder sneaked into the Village again.

Our writing back and forth continued, peaking during his writing of that wonderful little booklet (which I edited for publication in 1974). He handwrote it in tiny script across almost 100 pages of aerogrammes.

By then the sport knew him as the world masters marathon record-holder. His mark of 2:11:19, set at age 41 while silver-medaling at the 1974 Commonwealth Games, would stand until 1990.

We finally did meet, briefly, at the Boston Marathon in 1976. The meeting was awkward, as we tried to reconcile the person imagined from written words with the one now standing before us, speaking.

Though his measurements (about 5-feet-8 and weighing in the 130s) were known to me, I was surprised by how small he looked. We expect people who've done big things to be bigger than life.

Jack and I didn't say much that night, at least not to each other. We stood together at a question-and-answer clinic, where he wowed the crowd with his simple wisdom.

He did the same for me as he now gave voice to what he'd told me by letter over the years. Though we never talked again, I would never stop repeating his words.

Other runners feel that way too. Jack's booklet was a treasure when published 30 years ago and is much more so now. Originally priced at $1.50, a copy sold recently on E-Bay for more than $100. I wouldn't part with my one tattered copy for 100 times more.

WHERE HE CAME FROM

Running humbled Jack at first, which might be why he retained humility about his later successes in the sport. He remembered where he came from, and that by not running he would soon return there.

His first sport was bicycling. After taking long, hard rides with friends in his native England, Jack "drifted into racing" on the bike. This continued through most of his 20s, until he settled into family and working life in New Zealand.

Biking only to work and back, and playing some soccer, he imagined himself to be fairly fit at almost 33. "Surely a half-hour run would be no trouble," he said of his first try.

After going what seemed to be several miles, Jack arrived back where he'd left his wife Belle. "What's wrong, have you forgotten something?" she asked. "You've only been gone for seven minutes."

"Impossible," Jack recalled in his booklet. "I was sure I'd run at least six or seven miles. I was soaked in perspiration and felt tired.

"Now I was worried. If I felt like this at 33, how would I be when I was 40?"

We now know that by 40 he was an Olympian, with his best marathon time still to come. But he couldn't have known that when he began running only every second day, and I was working to maintain that 20-minute jog even on alternate days.

"I kept at it. I liked the feeling after the run, feeling the glow which comes after exercise. Sometimes the glow was a whole fire, in fact a real burnt-out feeling!"

Running led to racing. "I noticed I was still very competitive," he wrote. "A hangover from my cycling days perhaps, or maybe my nature.

"My competitiveness might better be described as a desire to excel, for I have no 'killer instinct' at all, no real will to 'win at all costs.' Getting my times down was the motivation to do more and more running."

Better times led to more training, to better times and... You now know where the repeated cycles led.

Other runners have climbed this high, but none was a later starter. Jack Foster wasn't like the young superstars who seemed to drop in from another planet, bringing with them apparent immunity to the limitations imposed on us mere mortals. He was more like one of us, one who made very good.

He ran while raising four children and working fulltime. He knew the feeling of starting to run as an adult, and of recovering from hard runs slower than the kids of the sport did.

He wrote for us. We lacked his late-blooming running talent. (His son Jackson, himself a competitive bicyclist, called Jack "a white Kenyan -- an oxygen-processing unit on legs".) But he spoke a language that any older, part-time runner could understand.

WHAT HE TAUGHT

The highest form of flattery for a writer isn't imitation. It's repetition -- quoting the writer's words as better than any you could make up, or better yet adopting his or her recommended practices as your own.

He left me with three lasting lessons for enjoying a long and happy running life. I've repeated them often in writing and speaking, and practiced all three myself.

1. The one-day-per-mile rule. Jack could race as hard and fast as runners little more than half his age. He just couldn't race that way as often as those that much younger. Watch time doesn't necessarily slow with age, he said, but recovery time usually does.

He outlined his recovery needs in the Ancient Marathoner booklet: "The after-effects [of a hard race] vary, with me anyway. Sometimes I feel fully recovered in two or three days. Other times I have a drained feeling for as long as three weeks.

"My method is roughly to have a day off racing for every mile I raced. If I've run a hard 26-mile road race, then I don't race hard again for at least 26 days. I'll go for daily runs okay but no really hard effort."

One easy day per racing mile. That's the Jack Foster Rule -- my term, not his.

2. Not training. "A reporter once asked about the training I did," wrote Jack. "I told him I didn't train.

"The word 'training' conjures up in my mind grinding out 200- and 400-meter intervals. I refuse to do this."

Nor did he run "the 150 miles a week that some of the top marathoners are doing. I rarely did more than half that. I believe it is possible to achieve results in a less soul-destroying way."

He concluded, "I don't train; never have. I don't think of running as 'training.' I just go out and run each day, and let the racing take care of itself.

"It has to be a pleasure to go for a run, looked forward to while I'm at work. Otherwise no dice. This fact, that I'm not prepared to let running be anything but one of the pleasures of my life, is the reason I fail by just so much."

3. Timeless racing. Jack added to the paragraph above that "failing" didn't bother him. Nor did "the prospect of running 2:30 or even 2:50 marathons in the future."

This would have been almost unthinkably slow to him at the time he penned this line, but "slow" is a relative term. Jack's times would slip to levels that were slow only to him -- a 2:20 marathon at 50, and to six-minute miles for 10K's in his 60s.

He claimed not to let the old times haunt him. "The dropoff in racing performances with age manifests itself only on timekeepers' watches," he wrote. "The running action, the breathing and other experiences of racing all feel the same. Only the watch shows otherwise."

Jack chose to define a good race by the effort, not by the numbers of a watch. He said, "All the other experiences of racing that attracted me initially are the same as they have always been, and they still appeal to me."

AFTER THE FAME

A fourth tip, one I often quote and always follow, almost went unrecalled here. It deals with wearing the least shoe we can tolerate, not the most we can carry (or afford).

Jack Foster wrote, "I was introduced to running over farmlands, where the underfoot conditions were soft and yielding, developing good foot strength and flexibility. I ran first in light tennis shoes because there were no suitable training flats in those days." Jack believed that those shoes forced him to learn proper running style. "We ran in those flimsy, light shoes and developed a 'feel' for the ground," he said. "We learned to land properly or got sore legs, since we couldn't rely on the shoes to absorb any shock.

"We got into a light-footed gait that moved us over hill and dale very effectively. I'm certain this [style] helped me stay injury free."

Even after he set world records and ran in the Olympic Marathon as a master, and shoe companies begged him to wear their latest high-tech training models, he remained a minimalist. He ran daily "in shoes most people consider too light even for racing."

This preference would clash with the onrushing trends in running shoemaking, toward bulkier and better-cushioned or more-supportive models. The clash would affect him personally, but not for long.

Jack's successes led to a job with Nike. The company moved him to Oregon, where he knew right away that he didn't fit in.

He didn't like having to wear the latest high-tech shoes. He didn't like running on suburban streets instead of his beloved sheeplands. Most of all didn't like acting the role of hired celebrity, Jack Foster World Record-Holder, Mr. Masters 2:11.

Jack had lived too long as a normal adult to believe he was as famous as others made him out to be. He had written years earlier: "People tend to think success in some field or other changes a person. In some cases this is true, but more often it is the other person's attitude toward the successful one that changes. Before success, no one knows him. After success, everyone wants to.

"Our sense of values is quite lopsided. Music stars, film stars and to a lesser degree sports stars all get media coverage, public acclaim and, for professionals, remuneration out of proportion to what they contribute to society."

Our brief stays with Nike (mine with its short-lived magazine, Running) almost overlapped. Just before I arrived in Oregon, he left, fleeing in joy and relief back to New Zealand. Our letters after that were few.

One came in the mid-1990s, when I asked for his contribution to my book Road Racers and Their Training. Then 63, he spoke apologetically of his running.

"I feel like a fraud completing your questionnaire," he wrote. "But I do run some, so I'll answer it."

He told of choosing what he liked best from his past program and discarding all else. His favorite: a run as long as 1-1/2 hours over hilly countryside, taken two or three times a week. He wasn't training for anything, just running.

Jack told of "indulging in a fun race now and then, but at about half-throttle while finding someone to chat with." He didn't pay much attention to the watch time, so neither will I. I'd rather recall his words than his numbers.

The last lines of his booklet read, "Perhaps what I've achieved as a runner may have inspired other 35-year-plus men to get up and have a go. I'd like to think so."

I know so.

FRIEND TO THE END

Bicycling was Jack Foster's first sport, and his last. He was struck and killed by a car in early June 2004 while riding near his home in Rotorua, New Zealand -- the same place he'd started to run almost 40 years earlier. He was 72.

He wasn't the first friend I've lost to a bike accident. It's a riskier sport than running.

But Jack wouldn't have wanted anyone to speak ill now of his favorite sport, any more than Jim Fixx would have wanted to tarnish running by dying of a heart attack on the run. Anyway, I'm not a runner-biker, so it's better to let one of them speak here.

Steve Goldberg, a law professor at Northwestern University, writes, "I was shocked and saddened by the news of Jack Foster's death. I never met Jack, but we were the same age, and his successes were both an inspiration and a challenge. They also served to keep my own successes in perspective."

He recalls telling a friend in 1974 how proud he was of running a 2:31 marathon at age 41. The friend responded as only a good one can, "Congratulations. You're only 20 minutes off your age-group record."

Goldberg says, "The fact of Jack's death while bicycling was also sobering since, with a decreasing amount of cartilage, I have increased the amount of time I spend on a bike. Riding with the traffic, not against as I do when running, has always created a sense of vulnerability, and that is increased by this news.

"I have no intention of stopping, however. What will be, will be."

Jack Foster went quickly, doing what he loved. That's not all bad.

It's worst for his family, of course, and bad for his friends near and distant. The day after hearing about his accident, I quoted advice from Jack in my talk at Dick Beardsley's Marathon Training Camp in Minnesota.

This wasn't a memorial tribute. I'd already planned to borrow words from Jack, as I nearly always did in talks and books, and will keep doing. Friends keep giving long after they're gone.

Richard Benyo

Richard Benyo is the editor of *Marathon & Beyond*, a bimonthly magazine devoted to the marathon and to ultrarunning. He is also the author of 17 books, the latest of which are **Running Past 50** (Human Kinetics, 1999) and **The Running Encyclopedia** with Joe Henderson (Human Kinetics, 2001). He was a newspaper editor (1968-72), editor of *Stock Car Racing* Magazine (1972-77), editor of *Runner's World* Magazine (1977-84), and running and fitness columnist for the San Francisco *Chronicle* (1985-90) and has contributed to numerous general circulation magazines. He is the veteran of 37 marathons and in 1989 along with running partner Tom Crawford, became the first maniacs to run from Badwater in Death Valley (lowest point in the Western Hemisphere and hottest place on Earth) to the peak of Mt. Whitney (at 14,494 feet highest point in the contiguous U.S.) and back, a distance of 300 miles, in midsummer. Rich  attempted the same feat in 1991 and again in 1992; his therapy has begun to take hold and he feels no urge to make another run on the course, although he has been known to detour hundreds of miles out of his intended route to visit Death Valley. In 2004 Rich and his partner Tom were inducted into the Badwater Hall of Fame. Rich is the race director of the Napa Valley Marathon and is also the 1999 winner of the RRCA journalist of the year award. (The RRCA apparently is unaware of his running abberations.) In early 2005 Running USA inducted Rich into its Hall of Champions. For more than a decade, Rich has portrayed Mark Twain at a mid-summer Koyote Howling Ritual in the middle of the wilderness with roughly 100 guys who spend the weekend drinking beer, smoking cigars, and howling at the moon. Rich and his wife Rhonda currently live in Sonoma County, California; in their spare time, they are attempting to learn to sail on the San Francisco Bay.

Trying Harder
(Reprinted from Marathon & Beyond)

Richard Benyo

The death of Emil Zatopek last November continues to exert a profound effect. A few nights ago I once again watched Volume VII (the use of Roman numerals on a series symbolized by a Greek discus thrower doesn't even seem incongruous) of Bud Greenspan's nine-part documentary *The Olympiad: Greatest Moments,* which was released in time for the 1996 Olympic Games by the then fledgling Dream Works.

Volume VII contains two documentaries: "The Soviets" and "East Europeans."

The "East Europeans" documentary is shorter than "The Soviets," as befitting a conglomeration of countries that were subservient to Moscow and that served as protection to its western boundaries against the evil Western Powers during the Cold War. "East Europeans" features athletes such as the Romanian gymnast Nadia Comaneci and Hungary's three-time gold medal boxer Laslo Papp.

It also contains a segment on Emil and Dana (pronounced Donna) Zatopek

Whenever I feel lackluster or that I'm not performing up to par, I fire up the VCR and watch Emil and Dana come walking toward the camera in their little garden in Prague, where they were filmed many years ago.

They walk toward the camera very much aware that they are walking toward a camera and not spending a quiet afternoon in the peace of their garden. They are already middle-aged. Emil is bald, and Dana has very bad teeth and is aware of it; she speaks with an effort to keep her mouth closed. Their clothes are the antipathy of fashionable, more befitting a 1950s lower-middle-class couple in the American Midwest. Yet they are noble and filled with life. Even on the fading film stock, there is a glow to them.

The film is a little confusing in that it was obviously filmed by a Czech film crew because Emil is speaking in Czech, yet the film has been overdubbed so that he is speaking to this audience in English, one of a half-dozen languages he mastered.

Emil speaks of the joy and purity of sport, and then the documentary veers off to take us through the highlights of his Olympic career: a gold in the 10,000 meters in the 1948 London Games and a silver in the 5,000 meters with his heroic sprint down the final straight in a vain attempt to catch the Belgian Reiff; then the 10,000-meter and 5,000-meter gold medal performances at the 1952 Helsinki Games, followed by the gold in the marathon. The documentary does not go to Melbourne in 1956, where he placed sixth in the marathon, following a hernia operation. Nor does it deal with his forced labor at a uranium mine after the Soviets invaded Czechoslovakia in 1968.

The tape devotes a little time to Dana's gold medal in the javelin in the 1952 Games, and she later comments on Emil's generosity in giving one of his gold medals to Ron Clarke of Australia (who never won Olympic gold, despite his holding virtually every world record from 5,000 meters to 20 miles); she claims that she has hidden his other gold medals because if it were up to Emil, he'd give them all away. Ron Clarke is then interviewed concerning the gift of gold, which Emil handed to him before he boarded his plane, Clarke never guessing what the little package contained.

The whole segment is less than 10 minutes - about the amount of time it took Emil to cover a couple of miles in his one-hour track run world record. There are marvelous little snatches:

- Emil embracing Alain Mimoun, following yet another second place for the little Algerian behind Emil at an Olympic final.
- Emil smiling in appreciation and weariness instead of his typical grimacing as he crosses the finish line at the 1952 Olympic Marathon, as though to say, "Man, am I glad that's done. .."
- Emil chattering a mile-a-minute to the press after he sits down following the marathon gold.

In each instance Emil is filled with life, which he exudes like a lamp burning in a cave.

Emil Zatopek was a man who had a little talent in running, which he polished by what today we would consider extremely hard work. His track workouts (sixty 400-meter repeats with a 200-meter jog between) were staggering. So were the results: for several years no other runner could touch him in the 5,000 and 10,000 meters - he went undefeated.

Burdened with a limited education, he read widely and taught himself six languages. He could talk on politics and physiology with equal ease and clarity.

Literally stripped of his fame by the Soviet invaders, he determined to do the best job he could digging for uranium many meters underground.

He emerged into the daylight smiling and speaking of the nobility of man.

They don't make men like Emil anymore.

People today are generally taught to wallow in the wake of little injustices done to them, to look for excuses to under-perform, to assign blame for failures and for failure to try. The radio psychologist Dr. Joy Brown, frustrated by the timbre of a series of callers looking to blame everyone else but themselves for their poor choices in life, put it simply: "We've become a nation of cry-babies and busybodies."

We want to be recognized for merely existing, a by-product of the mania for bestowing self-esteem like pollen on a spring wind.

And this cultural mind-set has infected running.

We demand recognition for doing something we should be doing for its own sake, because it is natural and good. We demand recognition even if we train haphazardly and race half-heartedly. We strive not to be the best we can be but merely to be. That's enough. We'll get by doing as little as we can and then demand some recognition for it.

And in the process we cheat ourselves. We never move far enough ahead in our training to hit that overdrive gear in our running, where the reality of a hard asphalt surface beneath our feet is negated, and we are floating, running strong and free like the human animal whose divine design infuses all of us. A result of our under-striving is that we never earn admission to that special place in our running where the joy of effortless movement resides,

We elevate our egos at the expense of our spirits. We orbit rather than dive to the calm eye of the center, and therefore we drift and scan the horizon for someone to rescue us so that we can then damn them for not rescuing us the way we wanted to be rescued.

We lower our goals while we raise our heads to be patted.

We lust for cheap brass medals, while Emil Zatopek joyfully gives away his gold.

We look at Emil, and we are humbled.

We look at Emil, and we are inspired.

Emil occasionally lost a race, but he never failed.

Isn't it time that we, long-distance runners, become children of Emil?

Laurelee Welder

When Steve King asked me to write a chapter for *Running in the Zone*, I was both honoured and astonished. Although I had a hard time starting, once I got a few notes down and began thinking about what running has meant to me over the years, the words just started to flow. Before I knew it, I was recalling special moments from each of my five decades of running, and the experience has brought back many memories, both good and bad!

I am the eldest of three siblings. My parents, Bob and Doris Nelson, are both active, and have always been big supporters of our athletic endeavours. They were each strong athletes in their day, and continue to be active in their 70's.

My younger sister, Cindy Rhodes (Davy) is a well-known runner not only in the Okanagan, but at a National level as well. She is best known for her motivational contributions to fitness and running, and holds the record for most wins in the Victoria Marathon (6 times overall winner for women). She has twice been to the Nationals representing B.C.

My brother, Garth Nelson, is also an excellent runner, although he has not tested his skills as much as Cindy and I have. He prefers the discipline of the Marshal Arts.

I have four very talented children (of course a mother can say that!) My eldest daughter, Jennifer, who was 24 at time of writing, has been involved in the sport of soccer since she was six. She continues to play in a Women's league every summer in Kelowna, while attending the University of BC. She has just completed her Bachelor of Science, along with her younger sister Melanie, another talented soccer player. In fact, all three daughters, including Ashley, the youngest, have played on the same women's team many times, along with their cousin Chelsea Davy, who is Cindy's daughter. Ashley has been to the Nationals twice for soccer, coached by her father, Doug Welder. My son, T.J. (Thomas John), is nearly 16 as I write this, and has athletic talents as well. He especially loves basketball.

Even though my children do not share my passion for running (yet!) I believe someday they will. Perhaps they too will come to realize how much the challenge of running contributes to their game, and their outlook on life. And then, there are always the grandchildren......!

Running: Reflections and Revelations

Laurelee Welder

OK! I confess! I'm addicted to running. Always have been, always will be. It's the one thing that has remained a constant in my life. It has taught me many of my life lessons, and molded my character. It has lifted my spirits when I have been down. It has taught me how to dig deep for that extra bit of energy to finish a race or meet a challenge. It has made me stronger, and has kept me honest. Sometimes I swell with pride, feeling that I have mastered the sport, but more often than not I am humbled by it. It is my calm when there is chaos; my comfort when there is stress; and my joy when there is sorrow. Let me tell you how running has influenced my life and why I intend to keep it part of my life as I enter the ranks of the "older runner".

From my early years when I participated in elementary school track and field, to running long distance in high school, I have always enjoyed running. The competition was exciting. I loved to compete, and I loved to win. I also loved the peace and tranquility I felt running the trails. In those days my family lived in Alberta. There were few wooded areas near home, so when our class headed out on field trips to the Provincial parks around Cochrane, a few of us would take to the trails and just run. Somehow it always ended up as a race. We would feel exhilarated and strong, taking turns at the lead, trying to outdo each other. I think we all just felt free. We had no worries.

After graduation, I went on to UBC where I gave up running for a while to become a serious student and discover stress. As I found out later, it was not the best time to put my running on hold,. Taking a break from studies to go for a run would have been the best thing for me at the time. Instead, I over-worked, under-slept, gained weight, failed exams, and wondered what the magic formula for success was. I should have figured out that it was something that had been with me all along. Still, somehow I knew I would always come back to running as a grounding point in my life.

After four years at UBC, a degree, and a marriage, I moved to Victoria with my husband, started a job, and started running again. My running was now for a different reason - I was trying to lose the weight I had gained as an inactive student. I found my passion again and along with it, my self-esteem. Being overweight and a couch potato can definitely bring you down! I soon discovered that running a short three km loop was not enough to seriously shed any pounds. I started riding my bike to work and took up sailing. Life was good.

When we moved to Kelowna to start a family, I continued to run recreationally, but soon settled into a familiar cycle of – pregnancy-baby-cooking-cleaning-no-time-to run-pregnancy.... Fortunately, my sister, Cindy, and her husband, Brent, moved to Kelowna to start up a fitness club, just in time to save me from the horrible 'barefoot and pregnant' syndrome. Cindy could tell that I was stuck in the mode, and losing my running-identity, and convinced me that I needed to get out of the house and start running again. This was just the motivation I needed, and not only did I get back into running, but also began a 10-year career teaching aerobics. This was fun! We carted babies with us to class, had babysitting available for those noon-hour runs, and proved that aerobics was the perfect preparation for any sport, including running! Not only did I get in shape, but we had some laughs, met Moms with the same stories, and made lots of friends along the way. We even converted many of them to running, once they found out how much fun it was to run and chat at the same time. So running took on a whole new meaning to me during this stage of my life - the late 20's, early 30's. It was a time of socializing and having a break from motherhood for an hour or so. It was a stress-release, which always allowed me to return to my family relaxed and rejuvenated. And my kids started to notice at a very young age that it certainly made me a happier mom!

One of the benefits of aerobics that my sister and her husband would endlessly promote was that it would get you in shape for any sport - whether it was skiing, swimming, cycling or running. To prove this to herself, and other members of her fitness club, she decided to tackle a road race. The first event she entered - the Kelowna half-marathon - to her own surprise, she won! This was the start of many years of competitive running for both of us. I was so inspired by her race result, and the easy transition between exercise classes and running, that I followed her example and began training with her in preparation for future race events. We were soon joined by other members of her club, who were also keen to test their level of fitness in another way. Cindy and I began participating in some of the local races, and eventually travelled to some of the other races up and down the Okanagan Valley. . . These road trips would later become the conversation topic of many family gatherings.

The racing bug had me in its grip again. Throughout the 80's and 90's, interspersed among pregnancies/children/school/sports/etc., I enjoyed competing in the BC Interior Road Racing series as well as many of the team relays in and around Kelowna. I soon learned relay running was a different kind of competition. Not only were we racing against our own personal times, but we had to meet the expectations of our team members. There were overall and individual estimated times to meet or beat. We were expected to 'give it our all', and our team-mates gave new meaning to the word 'support'. This was not a solitary race, but one that involved all team members every step of the way. It was as if each runner raced alongside the actual runner for the relay leg shouting words of encouragement, and urging him/her to 'do it for the team!'. It made you dig down deep for that last bit of strength to drive you to the transfer point. After all, your team was watching and cheering you on with every stride. You couldn't let them down!

Some of my favourite 'bonding' experiences resulted from participating in the Jasper/Banff relays with a team called the Prairie Lightning, originating out of

Saskatchewan. My sister and I also ran together on teams in the Okanagan Express Relay, and the Kamloops Relay, and neither of us will ever forget the many years of racing in the Haney-to-Harrison Relay. While we ran for fun, I can't deny our team's hopes of winning and even breaking records at these relays. Being part of the competition made the relays challenging and fun, while the award parties afterwards made the events truly memorable for years to come!

The racing bug not only had me now, it was taking over. I was training more, and getting better results.   I soon started placing in my age category. This, of course, spurred me to run faster, train harder, to see just how fast I could get. My 'last fastest' time was never supposed to be my best ever result, you know?

You always think you can get faster, but there comes a time when you have to admit to yourself that you won't get any faster than 'that Personal Best you did way back when'.... That's when you have to have the inner strength and wisdom to be satisfied with what you did then as your 'best ever', and what you do now as the best you can be.

During these years, I have to say that my running friends helped me through some pretty serious life challenges. Running seemed to give me the time for 'soul-searching' and in some way even helped me to accept my shortcomings, all the while making me mentally stronger. Running with friends allows me to vent and be vented to; to give and get advice; and to cry and laugh at ourselves and each other. We have all helped each other through good times and bad.

It was about this time that I started toying with the idea of longer races - like the half and full marathons. I was in my late 30's when I began training at longer distances, and prepared for my first Kelowna half-marathon. About 2/3 of the way into the race I remember thinking how awful I felt. I had started way too fast, and my pacing was all off. At about 18 km I was spent - out of energy - with no reserve. It was all I could do to drag myself to the finish. This was just a 'Half' and I wondered how anyone could ever run twice this distance for a full marathon!? It seemed unfathomable! And yet, a challenge. Could I ever do one? Slowly I began a plan to increase my distance from 21 km to 42. Thankfully, there were others to train with, which made it a little easier. The promise of cooler summer mornings and running mates to chat with made the miles and days go by quickly. The goal was a fall marathon the following year.

Finally the day arrived when I ran the entire distance for the Victoria marathon, and realized the draw, the lure of the 26 miles. I ran my first marathon in 1991 and had what I thought was an amazing first time of 3 hours 14 minutes. The following year I ran 3 hours 9 minutes. This was exciting! My first 2 marathons were decent times, and of course I wondered how much faster I might get with further training. It was 1993 and I was running more than ever in preparation for my third Victoria marathon. However, I was soon to find out that this race requires more than just 'putting in the miles'.

I now understood the marathon was an entirely different race with a whole new mindset. It was a race calling not only for physical endurance, but mental strength. This was a race that demanded respect, a race that could change from mile to mile and often did. You could be having the best race of your life for 20 miles, and suddenly find yourself struggling to hang on for the last 6. Even the strongest runner might fail to finish. Then, there is that 'wall' - the imaginary barrier that you try to run through, but often discover you can't. It plays games with your mind; telling your body to stop. You want to stop, but your brain tells your legs to keep moving. All those months of training, - there is no way you are not going to get to the finish. You deny your body's pain and your mind's demands ... instead you push through it, until you can't remember what happens next. From what people tell me, I began to wander off course and become disoriented. One of my best friends, Helen, was behind me and saw me struggling to stay upright. I was determined to keep going, even though I could barely put one foot in front of the other. I staggered a few hundred yards before I collapsed.... And it was all over. The race, never completed, ended one kilometre short of the finish. That was the one I never finished, but it was the only one.

I ended up in the hospital for several hours after I collapsed. The doctors informed me that I had experienced a Grand Mal seizure, but they were not sure why. The doctor who looked after me had also finished the marathon just minutes before, and was on call. He explained that having a seizure such as the one I had, was similar to putting your body through a full marathon; so in essence, I had almost run two that day! After many tests and follow up examinations, the consensus was that the seizure may have been brought on by an electrolyte imbalance which occurred during the race. Perhaps I had taken in too much or not enough sports drink and water. It was hard to say. The one thing I know for sure, is that I did not listen to my body when it was telling me I was in trouble. It is one thing to be mentally strong enough to 'run through the wall' but you also have to pay attention to the other signs. I have been in many races where I have run so hard I have almost collapsed at the finish line. That is called 'giving it your all', and it can be taken as a sign of mental as well as physical strength. However, as I had discovered, sometimes there is a fine line between running strong and running stupid.

It was difficult to start running again after that. I was second-guessing myself all the time. I doubted whether I would ever be strong enough, brave enough, to get out on the road again. This last race had taken a lot out of me, and I was afraid the same thing might happen again. How would I know I could finish the next time? Slowly I began to run again. In spite of the disappointment I realized I needed to get back to what I loved. This is what made me happy. As I came to understand myself and what had happened, I gained a new appreciation for being healthy and being able to run.

Running in my forties was still mainly competitive, and kept me happy. It gave me strength to deal with a difficult incident in our lives. Near the end of my forties, we almost lost our third child in a tragic car accident. I focused my energy and time on her recovery, but knew there would be a point when I would eventually run again. She was in her prime athletically, and I knew she was stronger than most kids her age. Still, she had sustained a serious head injury, and had been in a coma for days. Although I never doubted she would recover, I wondered if there might have been a higher force watching over her that night. This is when I came to believe in guardian angels. I spent many solitary runs reflecting on this very image and on how lucky we were to still have her with us.

And now, running in my fifties, I ask myself what motivates me to keep going, to get up and get out on the road three or four times a week. The answer is in the question! That's exactly what it does for me, it 'keeps me going' and I believe it 'keeps me young'. Whether it does or not, it's what I believe, so that's all that matters. Maybe I think that if I can keep running, I will never get old! When I run, I still feel like I did when I was 20 or 30, even thought my times show that age is catching up with me. I need more rest days. Recovery is a little slower. (Thank goodness for hot tubs and massages!) I want to keep active and happy, and running is the only thing I can do anytime, anywhere, with as much or as little effort as I choose. I can run easy or hard, it's up to me. I believe we run for a different reason as we get older. Now I am just happy to be out there on the road, on the trails, in the fresh air and feeling alive! Happy. Content.

Recently Cindy and I were running and each of us was whining about how slow we felt, how hard the run was and all the little aches and pains. We observed how it took us longer to warm up - 20 or 30 minutes, as opposed to 10-15 only a few years ago. But, as the run progressed we settled into an easy pace and began talking about more interesting things - non-running related. We got onto talking about our kids, work and friends. We began to realize how thankful we were for the many things that allowed us to enjoy this day. We reflected on how we came to this point in our lives; me at 50, she following close behind at 48, and how we were lucky to still be running. We talked about familiar places and routes; joked about how we would still be running them in years to come. We imagined how we'd look 10, even 20 years from now when we would still be running together. Would we have walkers? That brought back the memory of the relay when we dressed up as little old ladies and ran with grey hair, skirts and canes. What a sight that was on the streets of Kelowna! We were a team of grannies, shuffling along the relay route, loudly cheering each other on with scratchy voices and enthusiastic 'whoops', oblivious to the confused looks of bystanders. Was this a premonition of our running future? We hoped so. How lucky we would be to be doing exactly what we loved, just a little slower, and with a few more rest stops!

So what have I learned along the way? What has running taught me about life?

First, attitude is everything. Be positive about life, your family, your friends, your work and your play. It shows up in everything you do.

Second, wear good shoes. If you find a brand/model that works for you, don't change. I have gone through running injuries from, plantar's fasciitis (the worst!) to IT Band, and hamstring pulls. Once I found the best shoes for my body type and running style, I stuck with them. The right shoe won't prevent injuries but will definitely keep them to a minimum.

Third, have good running buddies: they keep you motivated, honest, committed, and loyal to the sport. You do the same for them. Running is one of the most unselfish sports in that you freely give your support and tips to other runners, and they give it back. Most of the runners I know are humble, non-egotistical, complimentary, and encouraging. Some people may argue that runners are selfish with respect to the time they take away from family and friends. I would disagree. In my opinion, based on my own experience, I believe running makes us better mothers/fathers/sisters/brothers/friends because we are generally happier and more content. You know the old bumper sticker that reads "when Mother's happy, everyone's happy!"; I love that one. And my kids do too!

The mental strength you gain from being a runner can take you through all sorts of adversities, and help you survive - especially as a 50-year old. I know it has done for me. I believe that, as you age, you find a certain purpose to life. You may find that your goals change as you get older, along with your focus. You reach a certain age where you try to be 'the best that you can be'.

I recently asked my eldest daughter, Jennifer, who is 23, to describe in her own words her impressions of what my running has meant to me. She had quite a bit to say! She understands that running is one of the easiest forms of exercise to do, yet is the hardest to maintain. She says it takes self-control and persistence. Jennifer also believes that running is a way for you to release the stress in your life. It takes you away from the world around and back to nature. It also helps clear your mind and lets you think things through without the influence of other problems at hand. She says it's not for everyone, but she notices that when I'm not running, I'm not happy. So, to her, running keeps me happy.

When I asked my sister what running has done for me, she says that running has made me stronger. She thinks I have tremendous mental strength and can 'run through the pain'. She says that it is my strength that stands out, but in many ways, she has been my strength - the motivating force telling me to 'get out there and run' whenever I am down - all the time knowing that I will feel better, stronger, after a run. While most people go through troubled times and difficult situations, not everyone can deal with their problems in a positive way. Sometimes it takes another person with an understanding of what drives you forward to keep you on track. Sometimes I think we know each other too well!

If you asked me what running does for me, it is what keeps me happy. When I run, I think about the good things in my life, as well as the bad, and I am thankful for both. The good because I realize I have been lucky in life. I have a wonderful family, I am proud of what has been my life so far. I am happy to be a mother, and look forward to the next stage in my life, which hopefully includes grandchildren. I am humbled by the challenges and tragedies in my life, and take nothing for granted. They have made me appreciate life even more. Running allows you to reflect on the stages of your life - there is only you and the road ahead, and the steady rhythm of your feet on the ground, and if you are lucky, someone beside you to share those revelations. Maybe even your guardian angel....

Neville Flanagan

Neville was born November 20, 1940 in Brisbane, Australia. After completing an electrical apprenticeship in 1962, he worked for a year on the Australian Gold Coast before traveling to New Zealand where he met his wife to be, a Canadian girl named Bonnie. They were married in Vancouver, Canada in 1964 and shortly after set out for travels around North America, to Europe and the Middle East, ending up back in Australia. Neville and Bonnie had their first son, Grayden in Australia in 1968, but soon returned to Canada where their second son, Darren, was born.

Because running generally doesn't pay the bills, Neville worked in Vancouver as an electrical draftsman with H.A. Simons, eventually moving north to a pulp mill under construction where he oversaw half of the electrical installation. They moved to Quesnel, BC in 1972 where they stayed until August 1975 when they moved to Kamloops. There, Neville attended Cariboo College and studied Recreation. The next move was to Eugene, Oregon where he obtained his Recreation and Parks Degree staying on to complete a Masters In Education.

Never ones to let moss grow, the Flanagans moved back to Kamloops where Neville had a position with Cariboo College teaching Recreation Management, continuing until 1991 when they opened two Subway Restaurants. By 1996 the Flanagans owned six Subway Restaurants and still do today. Although it may seem hard to know how he could do so, Neville ran in many races during that time, not only running but achieving some significant accomplishments.

From 1982 to 1995 Neville was a Nike sponsored athlete, having set a BC Masters Marathon record (2:30:20) in 1982, placing first in the 1983 BC Masters Marathon Championships (2:34:00) and posting seconds in the 1982 Canadian National 20K Championships (69:12, noting that the first place finisher also posted 69:12), in the 1983 Canadian Masters Marathon Championships (2:31:00) and in the 1983 Canadian Masters 20K Championships (70:04).

From 1982 through 1985 Neville was the top Masters Runner in the BC Interior Road Race Series. He also served the sport of running as Chairman of the BC Athletics Road Running Division, for a period of five years in the early 1980's.

To Run Or Jog: Is There Really A Difference?

Neville Flanagan

As I held my dying mother in my arms, I vowed I would do everything in my power to live past 45. Even at 16, I knew that meant I would not only have to eat right, but I would also have to be fit so I wouldn't have a lethal stroke and die in an ambulance on a Gold Coast highway. It was in that fateful year, when we had enough money to go on a family vacation, that we went to St. Leonard's Guest House at Coolangatta on the Gold Coast, south of Brisbane, Australia. We were about to have dinner one night and my Dad said, 'Go get your Mum'.

I went upstairs where I found her convulsing on her bed. I ran down and got Dad. A doctor and an ambulance were called. The doctor and the ambulance driver went upstairs with my Dad. The staircase was so narrow they had to put her into a blanket to carry her down. I've never forgotten my mother rolling around in the blanket as four men, who happened to be nearby, were told by the doctor to hold a corner each as they took her down the two narrow flights. I believed everything would be OK as I got into the ambulance. The doctor showed me how to hold my Mum's wrist to feel her faint and irregular pulse and how to scoop the vomit that was continually coming out of her mouth.

Dad and Jean, my 13-year-old sister, followed in our old Vauxhall along the coastal highway through the rolling hills back to Brisbane. About halfway through the three-hour trip, I couldn't find my mother's pulse at all. The ambulance driver pulled over and came back to check her. He turned to me and said that he was sorry, but my Mother had passed away. I didn't really believe him. I couldn't. She had been OK just a few hours ago. How could this happen so quickly? "She had a stroke," was all he said. Time stopped. It was very dark, but off in the distance I could see a farm house with its lights on and people walking around as if nothing had happened. It was so surreal.

My Dad and sister had pulled up by then. I ran to Dad and told him that Mum had died. We were all in a state of shock. The driver told us he had to take my Mum to the South Brisbane hospital and that we were to follow him. The drive took for ever. My Dad didn't know what to do with us, so he phoned my Mum's sister who lived on the other side of Brisbane. He told us to walk up to the Dutton Park tram terminus about a mile up the road and wait for her there. We sat on the curb and waited. By this time it was about 1 a.m. and no one around. We never felt so all alone. To this day I still don't know why we had to wait there and not at the hospital, but Dad wasn't thinking properly.

My Mum was too young to die and that fear of dying has been with me ever since. I didn't want to be fat. I wanted to be fit. Eventually running became my way of making sure I achieved both those goals. I was afraid I wouldn't live to be

45. When I did turn 45, that moment was as fresh as the snow I ran on that morning in my 10-mile run. Through the years I could still feel my mother in my arms, taste the panic and the fear, see the house that no longer exists on the now non-existent road. I made it to 45, but fear still kept me running, so I wouldn't feel death breathing on my shoulder. By the time I reached 50 that fear had gone, along with the miles I had run. Fear is not with me any longer as I have proven to my self over and over again that staying fit and healthy allows me to enjoy life with my wife, our two sons, daughter-in-law, and to watch our two grandchildren grow.

My Mum died in 1956 and in January 1957 I started an electrical apprenticeship. Although I didn't start running until years later on a ship from Southampton to Sydney, I didn't get fat: I swam and surfed. In those days my first love was my nine-foot 10-inch fiberglass surf board. On Friday nights, my mates and I would make the three-hour drive to the Gold Coast in just two and a half hours. The wind direction would determine which beach we would surf. As soon as it was light enough to see the waves and whether any sharks were lurking about, we hit the water and surfed till sunset. At night, we went to the local fish and chip shop, and, just like runners talking about training, compared the knobs on our knees and on the top part of our feet. Knobs formed from sliding over the surf board as we shifted the weight forward and paddled like crazy to make sure we had enough speed to catch the crest of the wave. We camped on the beach, waited for sunrise and did it all over again. Then, we drove back to Brisbane, telling stories about each wave we caught and whether we had hung ten. I did that almost every weekend during my five-year apprenticeship.

Between surfing weekends, and when it wasn't good surf, I also played Aussie Rules (Australian National Football) and Rugby League. When I became an electrical journeyman it was time to travel the world. I went over to New Zealand. It was there I met Bonnie from Canada, who was also traveling the world. After a short courtship we left New Zealand for Vancouver, where we married in May of 1964.

When I came to Canada for the first time in 1964, I worked out at the Men's Y in downtown Vancouver, which was near the consulting engineering company where I worked as an electrical draftsman. A year after we were married, we decided to travel North America, bought a 1965 Volkswagen sedan, a two-man tent and drove down the west coast of the US. I bought a surf board in Santa Cruz, California and surfed all the famous beaches I had only read about in magazines, including Rincon and Huntington Pier. We continued on down the west coast of Mexico surfing all the way.

Surfing is definitely a great way to keep fit. After waxing your board properly and checking the way the surf is rolling, you usually have to go through about 10 or so breakers to get out beyond the break. You kneel and paddle out and when a coming wave breaks you flip the board over and yourself and let the wave roll over you. Then you quickly flip back upright, kneel, paddle and go at the next wave, which is often almost behind the first one, flip over under the board, repeating over and over until you make it beyond the breaking waves. Then you sit and wait for your wave to come. When it does, you kneel and paddle quickly to pick up with the speed of the surging water, stand and ride the wave. After you finish with the wave or it decides it is finished with you, you then have to paddle back out and start all over again. That type of workout did keep me fit. Fit not fat.

We ended up in Montreal for a year. I put the board away and decided that the only way to keep fit through the harsh winter was to go to the Montreal Downtown YMCA. I did light weights and joined a fitness class, ran around a large gym, and stretched. From Montreal we traveled to England, Europe and the Middle East. After eight months of traveling those countries we boarded a ship back to Australia. This is where I met a friend who introduced me to running. Several days into running around the deck I felt that I had found the one thing I could really enjoy that would help me keep my weight down and stay fit. Running for quite a while made me realize how you sense your whole body, including how terrible you could feel in your throat and your chest and how your legs could feel the next morning. At first I couldn't really grasp how I could be fit in the way I was and yet feel so crappy after only running two or three miles. After all, I was still young and strong; obviously I was really wrong.

For those seriously starting into running for various reasons, such as obesity, doctors orders, or thoughts of regaining their youthfulness because they "did track" in high school, there are a few words of useful advice I can give. One has to realize that after leaving high school most people get into time consuming working positions, or meet the love of their life, get married and have children. It seems in a wink of an eye they are 35 or older - just a wink of an eye before their thoughts turn to self and physical conditioning. So here you have a dormant body, healthy but not fit, and because of the society we live into today we want a quick fix; instant fitness, instant change. In reality it is hardly reasonable to expect such change considering the fact that it has taken 35 or so years to get to your present–day form. So, instead of rushing into a heavy fitness program and only doing it for perhaps 4 or 5 weeks, seeing no change and giving up, you really do have to take it easy. One needs to take the long view. First, you have to enjoy the transition jog/walk for 15 or 20 minutes around your block, see the houses that you haven't seen even though you have lived in the same block for the past 20 years and you've driven your car around that block without noticing what houses were there.

Set a goal of jogging for 30 minutes and give yourself permission to take two to three months to reach that time. In my world, jog means going at about nine minutes per mile or even slower but the pace will be different for each individual. Jog/walk means jogging for five minutes, walking for four and gradually increasing the jog time while decreasing the walk time. Remember, the body is changing, including all the joints, the knees, the ankles, your arms, shoulders, and especially your breathing where your lungs are taking in five times the amount of oxygen that was normal before you started to run.

The expectations you place on yourself can push you to attempt to do unreasonable things with your body. What I did to myself when I met Peter Barrett on the ship while Bonnie and I were returning to Sydney, Australia, was a good example of placing unrealistic pressure on my body. Sitting in a van and driving 17,000 miles was hardly good preparation for getting on a ship and starting to run with Peter. I was young. I was athletic. I figured that within a few days - presto I'd be fit! Instead, I laboured after just two miles. My breathing was the most difficult thing by far; there never seemed to be enough oxygen.

During that time I would not call it jogging but plodding, as I didn't want to walk. My ego took over and two things got in the way. First, I worried that someone would see me and, as I was only 27, that would be scandalous. Second, was that stupid phrase, "no pain, no gain". If it didn't hurt, you really weren't doing anything substantial. In any phase of your training that is the worst approach to take. Even when you are just starting out on your jog/walk routine don't get caught up in what your neighbours might say. Generally speaking they either admire you or are envious that you have the determination to do something about yourself. And just maybe, you never know, they might be moved to join you. In the case of my shipboard experience, by plodding I was at least able to finish quicker and get back to the serious business of eating. That again is the wrong course of action. Enjoy your jog/walk and take in the scenery, see things you won't see while driving your car, listen to your body, listen to what feels good and what doesn't. Listen and pay attention.

Of course, before you begin you need to buy a good pair of running shoes. Not necessarily the most expensive, but a shoe that fits your personal needs. Go to a running store that has a good reputation, where the owners are runners and know what they are talking about. They will fit you with the appropriate shoe size and width and put you into a shoe that accommodates and compliments the peculiarities of your feet and the way you run. In addition to the knowledgeable people in the running stores, there is an assortment of running magazines that will help you choose the proper running shoes.

Placing expectations on your self is not unreasonable as long as the expectations themselves are reasonable. Don't make the mistake I made when I first started running in Sydney. Running every day was an expectation I placed on myself. When I talked about a rest day back then, it meant running slower than the previous days. In today's language rest means doing nothing or doing something entirely different such as swimming or riding a road or mountain bike. As a result of this approach, I ran in a state of exhaustion most days. The only rest I had was that night's sleep which is not enough. To avoid injury, even at the beginning stages, you must have sufficient rest days, all the while remembering that the body is going through a change for the better.

Listening to your body is important. Think about what is changing; are there parts of the body hurting or feeling stiff? Are you stretching after you finish your jog/run? Has your breathing improved to the point where you feel comfortable drawing that much oxygen into your lungs? Have you reached your 30 minutes of jogging without stopping? You probably think you can graduate to running after only a month or two of jogging and can take on the world and have thoughts of running a marathon.

In Sydney I got caught up in Arthur Lydiard's 100 mile a week program. Arthur Lydiard was **the** authority on running then, as he coached Peter Snell and others to the Olympics and to World Records. If they can get that far I reasoned, why not take his advice and train accordingly? So after running for only a year, followed by three months of 100 miles a week I was certain I was ready for a marathon. What a mistake. I did get to 22 miles, but at that point my body simply didn't want to listen to my mind. It just shut down. When I look back to those days, the marathon was only run by those few who took on the challenge of performance running, as it really was unknown to the masses. It was practiced by a select few, what we now call elite runners.

In 1968 before you could go to the starting line of the marathon you had to be checked by a doctor. In this particular race there were only about 40 of us. The doctor would go to each runner and check his heart rate, ears and eyes and give a nod, as if to say in his opinion you were ready to run 26 miles 385 yards. As I have said, marathon running, not to mention the effects it could have on the body, was really unknown. Of course women were not allowed to enter as it was considered to be too much stress for the female body to endure and would naturally have all sorts of dire consequences. I am so glad that time and sense has proven that theory wrong.

So, there I was at 22 miles with youth on my side, and a year of training under my belt (which I was certain was more than enough). I was completely and utterly exhausted with only 4 miles and 385 yards to go. I had run out of glycogen, a word not used much in those days. We were into protein with meals of steak and eggs being the name of the game. Protein would build muscle and surely it was muscle we needed to run so far. Carbohydrate was another word not talked about much at the time. Meat pies and good Sydney beers like Tooheys were considered great for running. I remember going to Canberra for a 15 mile road race. That Saturday morning, about 10 of us met at a local restaurant in Sydney where we had steak and eggs and toast for breakfast and then off we went to Canberra for the race. I ran my best and the extra food didn't seem to make a difference, but then again, if I'd had a lighter meal my body may have responded differently.

In my opinion, there are two types of runners. The first is a recreational runner who will enter some races to run with friends, or spouse or children. This runner likes running the trails or the sidewalk, maybe listening to some music, and enjoying every minute of the run. Then there are the runners who have a purpose to run best times, run fast and win their age category, maybe the whole event. I must admit I fall into the latter group.

The training programs or approaches for these two types of running are different in so many ways. First, the recreational runner is not really prepared to feel pain on the run. He or she wants to run, sweat a little, enjoy talking to friends or listening to the music, do four or five miles, shower off and feel great about themselves. They watch their food intake and drink alcohol moderately, watch their weight and basically enjoy life. It is a good thing.

The competitive runner enjoys life too, but inside there is a kind of running demon. Such people commonly say that they have to do better than their last race or last training day. Their training includes the speed aspect that is so essential to running fast times. Without speed work the runner is not going to improve his times. The level of performance he or she wants to get out of a race will determine how often speed work is combined with other workouts. In training for my marathons, I included two speed workouts per week. One was on the track running 400 meter repeats, building up the total number of reps over several weeks. The other speed workout was with a group of runners doing fartlek, speed play. We would run a total of eight miles. The first two miles were at a warm up pace, followed by four miles of fartlek. Fartlek is where each runner takes a turn leading the group; he or she would designate the distance and the group would have to stay with the lead runner. The distance would vary, so would the speed of the group, depending on who was leading at the time. Then the final two miles would be an easy pace back to our start place. The rest of the week would be running a few long distances of 15 or 20 miles or so. That was what my "demon" made me do. For me, that was good and the right thing to do. Runners wanting to achieve performance results should consider finding a coach or advisor to help develop an appropriate program of training.

My closing advice to runners of both types is pretty much as follows. Enjoy life. Run how you feel. Do what you must to meet your aspirations. If it is just to keep your weight down, then do that, but enjoy yourself. If it is to run fast and enjoy the workouts, then do that. Life is so short it seems just like only yesterday that I ran my 2:30 marathon in Vancouver in 1982 to set a BC Masters record. I am still running today, but I am also mountain biking and taking Tae Kwan Do classes. I have accomplished my life's goal of passing 45 years of age and that fear I had at 16 is no longer there. Most importantly, I am enjoying life with my wife, our two sons, our daughter-in-law and our two grandchildren.

THE PERSPIRATION ZONE

"Failure is the line of least persistence." [Author Unknown]

"Why couldn't Pheidippides have died here?" [Frank Shorter, at the 25k-mark in a marathon]

Moe "the Eagle" Beaulieu

Moe was born in Nipawin, Saskatchewan, a bit more than 60 years ago and has been doing ultrarunning since he was a teenager. He has a strong sense of spirituality in his life rather than religion and considers Nature to be the one true religion. He is the single father of three grown children.

Moe has worked for more than 25 years in advertising/marketing and sales, but has also been a produce manager and a corrections officer. In other words, Moe has had a varied working life. More recently he settled into his true love, being co-owner with his son Logan, of Eagle Endurance Sports, a Running/ Guided Hiking operation based out of Keremeos, BC (**www.eagleruns.com**). Moe calls Keremeos the "Running Capital of Canada" (although others are awaiting a final and official decision on that claim).

Even though Moe mentions his first long distance experience as having taken place in high school, he maintains that he has been running for just over 24 years, 18 of those on the trails. While he has run in numerous shorter races, Moe concentrates on the ultra distances and has run over hill and dale in four Canadian Provinces, 18 American States and "a few other countries". While he credits himself with just 5 formal marathons and a personal best of 3:14, he proudly points to 97 ultras he has done including the fact that 45 of those have been in excess of 50 miles and up to 100 miles, with a personal best 100 mile road time of 21 hours and 20 minutes.

Moe enjoys spending time with family and friends, reading, music and theatre and trying to survive the ULTRAMARATHON called LIFE. He is always willing to take people out and help them train on his or other courses from Vernon in the North to Manning Park in the Southwest. Moe says that being in the mountains hiking or running is when he really LIVES....VIEWING wild animals like sheep, goats, deer, hawks, eagles and bear; SEEING fast rushing streams, alpine flowers; the sun going down or coming up. Getting back some of our lost senses...."kinda trying to get the PRIMAL feeling".

Persistence OR Non-Existence...

Moe "the Eagle" Beaulieu

I believe the older athlete MUST see success in the DETAILS: small details you COULD have perhaps overlooked a few decades previously. Let me expand on this a bit.

For starters, my son, Logan, really motivated me as he dropped 8-10 pounds, becoming stronger and much faster than he was just two years earlier. I figured if it worked for him to become stronger and faster, it may just work for me to at least MAINTAIN. Realistically, all an older athlete can expect to do is maintain!

The definition of maintain for me is: IF NOT IMPROVE THAT MUCH, at least HOLD ON for as long as possible. My lowered weight and as much, or more, strength, has added benefits. While I always had a good cholesterol reading, blood pressure, etc, I am now way low; like my diet was only dandelion leaves and alfalfa sprouts.

My thing is ultra-distance running and this book is aimed at older runners. So, how did we get here? Skip back to Camrose, Alberta. High School 1961, and I try my first ultramarathon.

Ok, it was really a walkathon. Three friends and I signed up to go of a morning from Camrose, some 51.1 miles to Edmonton. We were an interesting crew: about 150 folks in army boots from the Edmonton barracks, women with baby strollers, a few distance runners (in those days, who knew what those were?) and us. I ran about 22-24 miles and walked briskly the rest. I beat my friends. It seemed important at the time. I had some blisters from my CANVAS running shoes (remember those?) but I was a fit kid. What could it hurt?

My time, and I know runners all want this FINITE thing spelled out, 9 hours: 56 minutes. It says so on the Certificate and the Mayor of Edmonton wouldn't lie! Some U of A student did 7 hours flat. Some said he took a short cut. I don't think so. In fact, this is impossible as he would have ended up in Saskatchewan had he done what they claimed. Well, no one was running 50 miles in 7 hours in 1961 so this guy was hardly human. Heck, I have run 7:33 for 50 miles and that time and much faster is commonplace now for top ultrarunners. Sub-six hour 50 milers may not be common, but they are out there.

Fast forwarding to 1981 and Prince George, I decide one morning that I will start at 5:00 a.m. and just run to the next little town (Hixon) which is 41 miles away. My plan went something like: the family will arrive, see me swimming in the river there and we will all have our picnic and yes, Dad will be available for autograph signing. The time for this was 8:02, all on pavement, to which, as a trail runner,

I now always tell folks I am allergic. Oh yes, I was a little sore, a bit dehydrated but I can remember that run...my longest to that time was a Terry Fox 10 km.

Since then the ultrarun has become my thing. Oh, there were the usual marathons first but then came the 50 and 100 milers, mostly on rocky trails and over mountainous terrain .....my passion! A quote I once heard somewhere and especially like, tells the story:

> *"Our way is not soft grass, it's a mountain path with lots of rocks. But it goes upward, forward, forever towards the sun. "*

My love of nature...away from towns and cities has never left me.

My title for this piece, **"Persistence OR Non-Existence"**, to me means fight the good fight. Live e-**MOTION**-ally. To survive is to move.

My view....there is no finish line only perpetual motion....the constant never-ending journey.

At no time have I personally considered myself a 'real' runner or athlete, but a lot of other folks seem convinced that I am. I guess everything is relative and a matter of perspective.

As a Roadie (pavement runner) you may want to seek renewal of your spirit as well as your body. My advice is head for the hills - literally. On the trails you will never tire, at least not spiritually.

My role models are almost too many to mention. My family and some very good friends as well as endless fellow runners/competitors have inspired me. Role models are important to the older athlete, but naturally those models can be any age. Some of these folks at 50, 55, 59....one 70 and even one over 80.... give credence to what the older athletes can do. At what most would consider an advanced age, they seem to still be improving. The successful ones know it's 80 percent mental, or more: as you perceive...you achieve. They are likely finding the real success is in the DETAILS...

WHY WE DO IT? WHY DO WE CONTINUE TO RUN?

More than the personal accomplishments and opinions I have cited....ask any Ultrarunner, Distance Runner, Triathlete or Cyclist, and you will get a myriad of reasons and explanations. Personal challenge, feeling of euphoria, bliss, renewal, getting back to our true selves......the list goes on. *You come in dead last and you still feel like the winner because...you are!*

Folks have asked me over the years why I run Ultras. I think some believe that this will surely kill me.

Enzo Federico (for trail runners in Western Canada, the granddaddy of the Ultra and the trail), wrote one time on the race info material for the Knee Knackering North Shore Trail Run: *"To the deaf judges the dancers appeared insane...runners run to a music no one else can hear."*

Running may be good; it is not necessarily easy. My friend, Alfred Bogenhuber, says:

> *"Pain is inevitable....suffering is optional."*

Alfred (Bogey) Bogenhuber, aka Wolfie, is still at 65 years young, one of the top US Masters/Veterans in trail and ultrarunning. He knows whereof he speaks!

For most self-styled trail junkies, movement has become MOVING MEDITATON. I am almost saddened when someone tells me they tried trails once and never went out THERE again. Try it again, stay with it awhile and I would be surprised, even shocked, if you don't get hooked.

WANT TO TRY THIS LUNATIC FRINGE SPORT?

Let me suggest that you start with a 25 km trail run. Ask around in your area and make sure you find one that won't discourage and defeat you the first time out. You can also check out the Resource section of this book for some ideas.

Get to the point of all this freaky trail diatribe, Moe!

My raison d'être is simply **action** not inaction. Blind faith, instinct, whatever, Trail running gets you primal again. For me it just is. I feel, in some small way, I am benefiting my peers and general society by personally trying to get and keep in touch with a MORE NATURAL World Order.

Like many other older runners, I sometimes have trouble remembering that I am older. I just keep thinking that I am a runner. Maybe that is because I am. I am a trail runner. I am an ultrarunner. And, OK, I guess I am an older runner. Does the last point really mean anything? Well, at some level it probably does. Here are some things to think about in that regard.

Training Shifts:

The over 50, 60, and 70 runners experience some downshifting....maybe some acceptance of the recognition that it's not quite his or her prime years any longer. I use the word ACCEPTANCE in the sense of perspective. You should never have to stop.....not of your own accord. If you are stopped by circumstances, that is different. But, excuses or rationalizations are just that.....and it doesn't have to be that way. A lot of the time, quite subtle training shifts are all that are called for: like varying the training terrain, OFTEN. Run in different locales....see new routes. Stay fresh.

Don't be afraid to try different, gentler pursuits at times....yoga, tai chi, relaxation response exercises, Japanese tea ceremony. Use creative rest. Try new approaches....AVOID HARDENING OF THE ATTITUDES! Stay fresh...stay motivated. None of us has to train every day, even 5-6 days may be too much.

I have never believed in these "never break the streak at any cost" rationales that seemed to drive people like Jim Fixx. I once tried running only three days per week, now usually four. I've had PR's all over the place using such a regimen. I broke 24 hours in a 100 miler in Virginia that way.

I also water ran in the deep end with an aqua belt for 40-45 minutes once per week. Boring, but nothing better for taper or creative easy non-weight bearing exercise after a hard race. Water running is very aerobic. In 1984, Joan Benoit injured herself just 45 days before her marathon. She never ran outside at all and still after 30 days of water running came out and set a new world record for women of 2:22.

Hills: love 'em or hate 'em!

The Aussies used hill-running repeats years ago with tremendous success. You hear folks talk about how they hate hills and then you meet folks who say they love hills, and THEY are generally strong. The hill lovers have mentally accepted them, which is crucial to your body accepting them. First the mind, then the body.

Here are two or three little tricks that I like for conquering hills in a race:

You are way out there on an ultra or long trail run and just don't know HOW you can go up yet another HILL. Try looking at a spot about six feet in front of you. Don't keep looking at the top of the hill, especially if it's a long way away. This can be demoralizing. But, you can surely make the next six feet and that bit isn't so steep anyway. Step by step you can reach the top without ever looking to see where it is. Works for me, anyway.

My other little trick amounts to never looking back at how far you've come....that's an excuse to tell yourself to slow even more or stop altogether. Remember now, I am talking about trails where the hills can go on for miles, not 500 meters like you often find in typical 10K road races.

Another thing to try if there is a runner just ahead, is to get behind and visualize your weight is on his shoes not yours. Imagine that he is helping to pull you up the hill. Or imagine an invisible string around his or her shoes or hips and that their energy is pulling you up the hill. Don't know what this does Karma-wise but you CAN imagine they are feeling energized as well just to be CHARITABLE. Imagine they are just not getting the total best effect like you. You love them too and wish them well but your JOB in that race is to love yourself just a little more.

Hills in Training:

For 50 km runs some short repeats (50 -200 yards) as well as longer hills are effective. For 50 and 100 milers find a 1-2 mile climb and walk/hike it once or twice per week. Hills will make you stronger no matter what your running potential or genetics. And, although strength with hills may not make your '100 yard sprint' faster, you will hold a pace or tempo longer. Think about it. If you NEVER run hills in training and have to face them in a race situation, especially in a Marathon or Ultra...good luck!

Tactics:

- If a runner is coming up a hill say and is 100-200 yards back NEVER let him see you turn and look at him. They sense you are struggling even if you're not. Looking back once gives the runner behind a little boost. Look back two or more times.....they know they have you! Satchel Page, the great black baseball player who played way into his older years and long before Jackie Robinson broke the color barrier, said: "Never look back. Something might be gaining on you!" I believe he actually meant age, but it works either way.
- And never make eye contact, especially if they are able to read your discomfort. They may also have a stronger force of will....so you make eye contact and cook yourself.
- You can sneakily look out the corner of your eye when you are turning on a trail and you can now tell where they are without you telegraphing that this is even important to you.
- If and when they pass you - you are now thinking, even if only subconsciously - who is going to pass me next? Or how far ahead am I from the next person. That is when you want to remember the very best runners rarely ever look back. Their job is to look and think straight ahead. They are concerned with their own performance, not every one else's in the field. THIS PARTICULARLY APPLIES IF YOU ARE RUNNING FOR TIME OR TO PLACE. If, like the majority, you are running to finish, tactics like "don't look up a hill so often" still apply and can make it easier.
- And, if you happen to be doing the passing, well you can reverse everything. When you do pass, make it count. Be decisive and do it forcefully. There is a good chance you won't see that competitor again.
- There is a little "user warning" that should go with the last tactic. As I was once told by a runner from Texas during a Hood to Coast Relay, " If you think you wanna pass someone ...make sure he's gonna stay passed 'cause if he catches you AGAIN...that good old boy will have you for good."
- In a trail race the other guy can't always see you, so SURGE a bit in the shady or winding areas.....and in the sunny or open areas slow up to

normal so they think you're still just loping along. This won't work too long afore they realize what you're doing BUT mayhaps long enough ? Of course, you could burn yourself up. Only you can judge if it is working.

- Calm your breath (even hold it slightly) when passing as loud ragged breathing makes you appear weaker.
- Conversely, EXAGGERATED ON THE SHOULDER loud raspy breathing may make the person in front of you exhaust themselves to get away from that terrible noise or ....let you by ?
- Likewise try to run TALL when passing ....a great posture, head up, shoulders back makes you look somewhat indestructible ...and a poor running posture will tire you quicker anyway.
- I also have some personal visualization tricks or techniques I use. For instance, tiredness is BLACK or DARK energy that I allow to flow out of the soles of my feet while I simultaneously allow white or sometimes golden light, to pour into a small opening in the top of my head, filling my body and extremities and PUSHING the dark, negative energy and TIREDNESS out. This sort of thing is powerful but pretty much up to the individual.

Motivation:

Run with people slower than yourself and help them train if they want your help. You might be surprised what you learn about yourself.

Run with same pace people. There is a synergy with your fellow man when in stride, in pace or rhythm with someone else.

Run with faster people sometimes and for as long as they don't kill you. Some of this will make you stronger. Too much will put you under.

Read; find other opinions.

Play motivational tapes sometimes. You might think this is humourous...but you may just find it helpful. If you haven't tried it.............

Explore all options; can't learn more if you don't.

I know a runner who took singing lessons and claimed he ran better after a few months.....makes sense - perhaps he learned to breathe deeper?
Oh no...if I go running with Moe he will break into opera!

It is great to think and feel and be alone on runs but it is extremely difficult for most people to NEVER run with others. IF you have slowed down, are older or even if you are younger and just simply in a rut, find someone who is not and run with them. We are social beings. Running with others occasionally is a re-motivator.

Diet:

The following is personal opinion and observation, not trained or professional advice. Eat a variety of foods - a little of everything within reason. Meat and fish eaters are no better or worse off than vegetarians performance-wise as far as I can see. Health-wise may be debatable and for another time and place.

As I see it, if you eat a ton of meat or a ton of lettuce you are still eating 1,999.7 pounds too much at one sitting.

The key is we simply do not practice any sort of portion control. ***But the sign on the restaurant wall says "all you can eat"?*** In a one-helping restaurant meal one would be hard pressed to find less than 1000 calories. More importantly...what kind of calories? We don't know how it's made or what's in it really. Have treats, so you don't feel deprived but again, use portion control. Browse, graze, nibble....just burn as many calories as you take in, unless you are trying to drop weight, in which case, just as simply, you must burn more calories than you consume.

In regard to performance and specific foods, I personally find dairy products to be a cause of phlegm while running if taken even a few days before races. I have heard that for those with the condition, asthma problems are increased as well. Although there is no question that the calcium in milk may be important, there could be other sources you may want to check out if this sounds like a familiar problem for you.

That was just an example related to me. The point is if you find that some food seems to be related to less than great performance for you, it might be real. Do your own research on it. Ask people who should know. Do some reading. But, as with milk, if it weren't for a personal sensitivity, the food itself would be a good part of the diet, maybe even a key component, you may also need to look for a suitable replacement for the important nutrients you may be missing.

Low Or No Carb Diets:

Absolutely ridiculous, in my opinion, for an athlete in training. I mean we have all known forever that complex carbs are a runner's TOP FUEL source. If you think about it with just a little logic, if most "diets" really worked there would then not be a new diet every week of the year on the bookshelves and in the news. The problem is modern society is into the QUICK FIX. There is no such thing. Sorry, but you have to work at it to succeed whether it be diet, or training. Proper diet is commonsense variety, proper portion control and is important for all ages. Running or working out won't cure everything. I believe the older athlete without proper training assessment and proper eating habits could be doomed to failure.

Shoes:

Proper running shoes! I have seen tons of people running in shoes that seemed wrong for them. Deal with a store where Real Runners work and own the place..... not just shoe salespeople.

Spontaneity:

For about 10 years now when traveling anywhere, I take running shoes and running gear suitable for the climate. In this way, it is not unusual for me to stop at a park or wilderness area and run 1-3 hours, change into dry clothes, stretch a bit and carry on again with my journey. I did this while working 45 or more hours per week in advertising/marketing sales. You can always schedule some time if you want to.

I read somewhere that if "you don't take the time for health.....ill health will make the time for you". People have coffee breaks; why not health breaks...even 30 minutes of motion?   Any activity gives you some payback.

There is no easy way to train - not really. It involves some work and your participation. You can't just watch someone else. If it were that easy, everyone would be fit and well-trained. As a trained athlete, you are in 5% or much less of the fittest in the country, especially if you are over 50. If, on top of that, you are into ultra distances, that percentage drops to something so much less than 1% that it isn't worth discussing. Let's just agree it is really small and that this isn't bragging, just a matter of perspective.

I hear people say to me all the time: "Moe - all these extreme distances you do, how are your knees, your feet, your overall health?" Sometimes, I think they expect me to fall to the ground and crumble into dust while they are talking to me. It is pre-ordained as I see it: use your body or lose it. It is like a language skill or anything else, it simply atrophies with disuse.

Fitness and health at any age, but especially for an older athlete with somewhat diminishing returns, MUST be a very vigilant procedure and you never, ever quit.

It is a bit harsh I know, but in reality it is simple....Persistence or Non-existence!

Jane Ballantyne

Jane has run for the last 28 years, adding ultrarunning to her resume only later in her career, but once added it became a primary focus. She has completed more than 25 marathons and 50K runs, not to mention completing several Ironman triathlons. Although she claims many creditable performances, Jane runs now for a different reason and sets her goals for ultras and Ironman competitions because of the physical and mental challenges they present. Each time she undertakes one of these events, she looks forward to seeing how far she can push herself to achieve the goals she has set. She sees each race as different and each one has taught her a little more about herself and the power of the mind. But, she has also discovered the sheer joy and fulfillment of running for its own sake.

She has graduated from the marathon to the 50 km, then 50 mile and 100km ultrarun and, as reported in the following contribution, in 2003 she moved on up to one of the most difficult ultrarunning challenges, the Badwater 135. Jane has let her running take her far and near with runs as far away as the Netherlands where she took fourth place in the Female 40-45 category in the IAU 100km World Challenge (1997) and as close as Vancouver where she has completed the Vancouver Marathon a number of times.

As she describes in the following pages, she considers herself a part of a greater whole when it comes to the teamwork it takes to successfully complete an event like the Badwater Ultramarathon.

A Friend for Life

Jane Ballantyne

As the years go by I wonder why I wasted so much time worrying if I was good enough. Good enough for what? Good enough to enjoy the sun on my face as I settle into a 10 mile run? Good enough to enjoy the wind on my back as I head home from an evening run? Good enough to watch the sun coming up over the Pacific Ocean as I run along its shore? I think you know where I am headed....I was missing the whole point!! I thought running was about being better than others, I didn't see that it made me a better person. Running isn't about beating your competitors; running is about feeling good about yourself and your accomplishments, whatever they are.

I started running after my first daughter was born, because I needed to lose weight and get in shape. I also had a sister who ran marathons in the elite class. She was thin, fast and loved running, and I wanted to be like her. At first, I only wanted to be thin but after a while, I wanted to be fast too.

It worked: I lost weight and soon began to depend on running not just to keep my weight down, but to keep my sanity... a baby will do that to you. At first, I wasn't interested in anything more than getting out of the house and doing my self-prescribed run around the neighbourhood. But slowly, I started to take longer and longer routes until I was running for a couple of hours. My husband was suspicious that I was stopping in for coffee somewhere, but I wasn't. Then I decided it was time to try a race. My competitive spirit changed running from my friend to a fierce competitive challenge. Running was my measuring tape. I evaluated myself based on how well I ran. If I ran well, it was because I was disciplined and committed. If I didn't do well, I berated myself for being lazy, undisciplined and inconsistent. Basically, the luck of the day determined whether I would be happy with myself or disappointed.

Running became work as I made every race a measure of how good I was. Instead of enjoying my improved times, I always compared them to the women that beat me. I was never really satisfied with my races, I set unrealistic goals for myself, and when I didn't achieve my goal I was always disappointed.

I have been running for about 28 years, and just recently I found out that I love running. I know that sounds strange. But at 50, I am finding out lots of things – things that I knew, but didn't know that I knew. It has taken me all these years to win running back as my friend.

There were points in my running life where my focus and determination paid off. Over the years, I have had many successes and I made many wonderful friends. I know at the time I didn't take pride in my accomplishments. I went home vowing to do better next time. Now, as I look back over my running career, I appreciate my accomplishments and long to repeat some of my performances. I no longer run against the other women in the race - I run against myself. I look back to past races and think... I wonder if I could ever run that fast again...probably not. But that's ok, at least now I appreciate those times and hold them dear. Time marches on and takes with it things you didn't even know you had until they are gone. Thankfully, it leaves something better, it leaves peace with who you are and contentment with your accomplishments, past and present.

Although I probably didn't realize it at the time, my change in attitude may have begun about ten years ago when I competed in my first Ultra event. It was a 50 km run, and it introduced me to a new world of running. No longer did I need to worry about how fast I was going, I only needed to worry about finishing the race! That first race has led to an ever-growing list of longer Ultra runs to prove only one thing to myself, that I can finish the race! Ultrarunning has helped me to see that the best competitor is your own past performance and the best measure of your success is monitoring your own self-improvement.

Running is no longer about racing; it's about adventures. It's about dreaming up new and exciting running experiences. It's about sharing the journey with other runners. It's about getting to know the *inner you*. I think that *inner you* only comes out when you are pushed to your limit. If you can continue to push past your limits, it begins to make you wonder, what are your limits? And who sets them?

Overcoming adversity makes you feel good about yourself. When you muster all your courage and determination to overcome an obstacle, you feel competent and gain confidence. You have a greater feeling of self-worth and carry these positive feelings into subsequent activities. It is why I fell in love with Ultrarunning.

I think that I have pushed myself through hard times because my friends and those that I admire thought that I could. They believed, so I believed. This is another valuable lesson I have learned; how influential our words can be to others. Always make them positive!

I didn't find ultras by myself. While I was living in Ontario, some running friends who were old hands at ultras insisted that I come along to the Sulphur Spring 50 km race. I couldn't imagine running a step past a marathon finish line, so I had no idea how I would do it. My friends assured me that it wouldn't be difficult, and foolish as I am, I believed them!

We started out very slowly. It was a two-loop course and as we rounded the end of the first loop, I felt strong and anxious to pick up the pace. My friends all encouraged me to go and run as fast as I could. I did and perhaps misjudged the remaining distance, but I made it! I was the second woman to finish; it was my most treasured race. My first Ultra, my first 50 km race, and second woman...Lori Bowden came first. Lori wasn't the famous Ironwoman back then, but what a great runner!

I couldn't believe that I had finished a 50 km race. I was thrilled! After that first 50 km race, I was hooked. A few weeks later I ran a 50 mile race on the road in Niagara Falls. It was an out and back and I loved it! Next came the 100 km distance. I was fortunate to be chosen for Canada's 100 km team that went to Holland for the World 100km Championships in 1996.

When I came home from the 100 km Championships, I realized I was tired of long distance running. My competitive nature had turned ultras into racing again. It is your mind that allows you to run those long distances; you have to really want to do it. I decided it was time for a change to maintain my newfound appreciation of completion, not competition. I started training for the Ironman triathlon; I hadn't done an Ironman since 1993. This introduced me to a whole new group of friends and I enjoyed the strength that cross training brings.

After doing Ironman in 2000 and 2002, I decided it was time to go back to the long runs again. I missed the solitude, the meditative state that you can reach on those long solo runs. My mind was ready again to focus on completing these long distance events, and I vowed not to let my ego turn them into a competitive arena...this running would just be for me.

I had met Steve King in Holland, when we were both on the Canada's 100 km team. After learning Steve was going to do Badwater 135, I was truly inspired. I set my sights on Badwater. I waited and watched to see how Steve would do. He completed Badwater in 30 hours 30minutes and 51 seconds and was fourth overall, an amazing finish! I greatly admire Steve and it was his inspiration and his confidence in me that propelled me to the start of Badwater in 2003.

Badwater 135 is an ultrarun in Death Valley in California in July. About 70 athletes are selected from around the world to compete in this brutal test of toughness. The race course stretches for 135 miles along the highway from Badwater to Mt. Whitney. Competitors must climb three mountain ranges on the way to the finish line.

The temperatures are about 130 degrees during the day, and the pavement can reach close to 200 degrees. The night is not much cooler, going down to about 100 degrees. Once the gun goes off and the runners start out on the long road to Mt Whitney, there is no escape from the heat.

Badwater 135 requires that runners bring their own crews to follow along the course and provide for the needs of each competitor. I brought six crew members, two vans and endless amounts of odds and ends that mostly just got in the way; I am not known for packing light and we had something for any occasion!

The runners have 48 hours to do the 135 miles in order to receive the cherished **Belt Buckle**. To be an official finisher you must finish under 60 hours.

In July of 2003, I completed Badwater 135 and received my Buckle. It is my greatest accomplishment to date. My greatest running accomplishment? Probably not. My greatest life accomplishment? Most definitely. What I learned in those 45 hours 23 minutes and 46 seconds about myself, my crew and just about life itself was invaluable.

Imagine having friends that would put your goals ahead of their own; friends that would follow you through a searing hot desert taking care of your every need. That describes my crew for Badwater. They were amazing and they were the ones that made it possible for me to finish that race.

I loved every minute of the agony I felt going from Badwater to Mount Whitney. Perhaps the race-course itself best describes what the runner's journey is and what it takes to finish. It starts below sea level and travels over three mountain ranges. I think each runner reaches a point where he/she mentally feels below sea level, the depths of despair....but you rise up and manage to forge on and to conquer what is put in front of you. With the help and support of those around you ...you go on. I think that is why we do ultras: to cross over from what seemed impossible to the possible.

This experience really made me realize how wrong I had been about sharing in someone else's success. My crew taught me that you can rejoice in another's victory and shine with them and through them without diminishing one spec of your own greatness. I now saw my crew as selfless and strong individuals that were willing to go across Death Valley to make my dream come true.

There is a little section of my journal that I wrote about Badwater that I would like to share...I think it illustrates why running is so important to me now and in what context.

"All the preparations, all the training, all the sauna work, could not have prepared me for Death Valley. Nothing but actually experiencing it could make you understand what it would be like.

The race plan that had been mapped out for me went to the shelf after the first 20 miles. The smile that I had embarked on this journey with was fading fast. The heat and the awesome reality of how long 135 miles really was, took over. I was reduced to fast walking after the first check in point at about 18 miles. I could no longer keep up the run portion of my walk run routine - I felt like I was cooking from the inside out and the outside in – I had to keep checking my skin to see if it had been scorched! I trudged on, doing the best I could to power-walk and sometimes run... in what was turning out to be the hottest Badwater race day ever.

Then I realized; this is what Badwater is about. It's like life, you plan, you set goals, you prepare but then it's never quite like you planned – because it's not all in your control... the true test of fitness, physical and mental is to adjust to how things unfold. I had to change the race plan and make it flexible to accommodate the heat and the blisters that were now almost everywhere on my feet."

At mile 72, which I reached at about 24 hours, I was hot, blistered, dusty and exhausted. The sun was just coming up on a new day and I still had the other half of the race left to do... I felt desperate... how could I possibly make it?

I turned to my husband, one of my crew, and said, "Do you think anyone would mind if I quit here?"

He looked at me and said, "I only know one person who would mind... and that person is you".

That is the secret; it's for ourselves that we run. It's a way of proving to ourselves that when the going gets tough, we are the ones that get going!

From my Badwater experience I realized that that is what life is all about too. It is the attitude with which you accept what comes your way that makes you a happy and contented person, or miserable and unfulfilled, no matter what you do or accomplish. Think about it: having a great attitude is not the result of having a great life. Having a great life is the result of having a great attitude!

When I started this, I think my message was going to be that I have become less competitive than I used to be, but as I think about it, I am still very competitive. Yet as I age, I realize that I mostly compete with myself now...or my former self.

As I pass a mirror these days, I am always surprised to see the person looking back at me. The outside shell has grown a bit older, and there is no stopping time, but the inside is growing stronger all the time. I like this new self – actually these days it is a lot easier just being me than trying to be the me I really wasn't. Today I cherish special runs, like the run through Death Valley in July, and special people like the crew that came with me. I cherish family and friends and my good health. I no longer worry if the other runners think I am fast enough... if I am moving forward, if I am out there and if I am doing it, I am fast enough!

I spent years thinking of all the things I wasn't and wishing for all the things I didn't have. I wasted the first half of my life not appreciating me and what I have... and I intend to spend the second half loving who I am and what I have!

I still use running as a measuring tape, but now I am measuring my inner strength and still wondering what are my limits?

Running is my friend again and I intend for us to keep company for a long time to come. I look forward to many more adventures with my friend... just for the fun of it!

Bob Dolphin

Bob Dolphin – Yakima and Renton, WA
Date of Birth - October 4, 1929, Worcester, Massachusetts
1st Marathon – September 2, 1981, Heart of America, Columbia, Missouri
100th Marathon – September 2, 1991, Heart of America, Columbia, Missouri
PR Marathon – April 10, 1988, Emerald City Marathon, Seattle, Washington, 3:00:12

The 1997 London Marathon was his 200th. While in London he met Brian Doherty, secretary of the 100 Marathon Club United Kingdom, who inducted him into this club as the first American to be added to its membership rolls. Peter Graham succeeded Brian as secretary and with his encouragement, Bob formed the 100 Marathon Club North America at the inaugural **Yakima River Canyon Marathon** on March 31, 2001. He and his wife Lenore are co-directors of this marathon and the 100 Marathon Club NA.

His 250th marathon coincided with Rick Worley's famous "200th marathon in 159 consecutive weekends" at the January 16, 2000, Houston Marathon in Texas. In October, 2002 Bob ran his 300th marathon (including 44 ultras) at the Royal Victoria Marathon on Vancouver Island in British Columbia (see the photo).

He spent six and a half years in the U.S. Marine Corps between 1947 and 1955 and chose the October 31, 2004, Marine Corps Marathon in Washington, D.C. as his 350th marathon. After Korean War service, he attended San Jose State College in California and graduated with a major in biology. Three years later he moved to Lafayette, Indiana, to attend Purdue University where he obtained his PhD. in insect ecology. For the next 23 years he had a career with the U.S. Department of Agriculture as a research entomologist, associate area director, and laboratory director in Vincennes, IN, Columbia, MO, Ames, IA, and Yakima, WA. He retired in 1988 and increased his running and racing activities from then until now.

He runs 20-22 marathons each year and an equal number of shorter races and relay legs. His training is frequent 1-2 hour hikes and an occasional five-mile run. He's a member of Marathon Achievers, 50 States & DC Marathon Group, 50 States Marathon Club, three 100 Marathon clubs (UK, Germany, NA) and nine running clubs.

Goal Setting and Adjusting Expectations

Bob Dolphin

For a sport that is as simple as putting one foot in front of another, running/racing is a complex one. Consider how many books have been written on this topic. Joe Henderson, a noted running author and speaker, has written over 25 books, and he publishes one or two new ones each year.

He and Richard Benyo, editor of **Marathon & Beyond**, even co-authored an encyclopedia on the many sports heroes and devotees of running. **Runners World, Running Times and Northwest Runner** are examples of other magazines that nationally and locally influence and inform runners of all ages.

For runners over 40 who are considered masters and for veterans over 50, it has been necessary to rely more on experience. There isn't as much written about and for the older runner. **"Masters Running and Racing for Runners over 40"** by Bill Rodgers and Priscilla Welch with Joe Henderson (1991, Rodale Press) is one of a few on this topic that is helpful.

The book that led me to running in 1979 was **"The Complete Book of Running"** by James F. Fixx (published in 1977 by Random House). A chapter titled "Running When You're Over Forty" was as useful then as it is now.

As we reach our 50's, 60's, 70's and beyond, it's necessary to rely on personal traits and experience to guide our running careers. Many runners are goal-oriented and focused on their family and profession. They transfer these characteristics to their running and racing activities as well.

The goals that we impose on ourselves are limitless. The miles or time segments we run on daily outings or weekly accumulations help us prepare for the road, track, and trail races where the objective is usually set by distance, but sometimes by time (e.g., a 12-hour race on a track).

We all know the stress involved to reach the finish line, with the last mile of the race being the toughest of all. Even a one-mile race is difficult.

Having been through all of this myself over the years, let me tell you how I have progressed over my running career and how I have kept the experience fresh for myself.

When I first started running in the 1980's, I tried everything that involved running: track and field, road running at all distances, cross country, trail running, team relays and endurance runs to 24 hours. Then there were triathlons and biathlons with swimming and/or biking combined with running. Walking was a component of some of this, so I tried some competitive race walks to the marathon distance on tracks or on one-mile loops and endurance walks to 24 hours.

As I advanced from one age division to another, I felt the need to discontinue participation in some of these sports either because I didn't perform them very well or because I didn't enjoy them enough to justify training for them. Over the years I participated in running and distance running from 5K to 24 hours with my main focus on the marathon. Many of my older running friends and competitors seem to have followed the same evolutionary process as they concentrate on those events and distances that give them personal satisfaction.

There are many marathoners who have discovered that they can reduce the intensity of marathon training by simply running more marathons. The implication is that every marathon event finished is a training episode for the next marathon. If a marathoner runs one, two or more marathons per month, then fitness for running marathons can be maintained indefinitely.

As the director of the 100 Marathon Club North America, I am among a group of members in their 70's and 80's who run twenty or more marathons per year. Even at age 75, I find that running 20-22 marathons per year keeps me fit to continue. I can travel to new places, return to favorite marathons annually and have great adventures!

Competing against oneself and trying to better a personal record at certain race distances is always a challenge, and it's a reason to focus on the training to improve performance. Runners new to the sport quite often see their finish times improve with training and experience.

I started running in 1979, and my times kept getting better until they peaked in 1988 when I was 57-58 years of age. The marathon personal records (PR's) went from 3:57:00 to 3:00:12 in seven years.

Veteran runners can still reach for modified PR's even if their original ones are no longer attainable. From the **Masters Long Distance Running Committee** of the USA Track and Field and the World Association of Veteran Athletes (WAVA), there are age-graded tables available to adjust times to a runner's age. Using these tables, some of us can achieve sub-three hour marathons or 38 minute 10K's. (See further discussion and examples in the Resource Zone.)

Age-class competition is one of the most satisfying aspects of running contests. A second place "50 and Over" trophy in my first race, a 10K road race, was a big factor in my becoming a racer. Initially, I would finish in the first 15% of the field of runners. Now, in my mid 70's, I'm at the back of the pack. However, with its inherent successes and failures, the thrill of competition continues.

By staying with competitive running, the rewards increase and standings improve as the division gets smaller. Twenty years ago when I had a certain place in the pecking order, I had no idea that I would move up the ladder as superior running peers dropped out for various reasons.

While the reduction in age-class numbers may not improve one's running ability, the remaining veterans who race will be called to the podium more often for an award at the conclusion of an event. Because of this phenomenon, when I turned 70 years of age, I finished first in all of my races for 18 months. I had never done this before in 20 years of running!

In the larger races, there may be more competitors in my peer group. For example, at the 2003 Marine Corps Marathon in Washington, DC, I finished first of 47 in the 70 and over male division. But at Boston and Honolulu where there were large contingents of 70-year-old runners, I didn't fare as well.

Every runner needs to find something that challenges him or her. Marathoning is my specialty, so I will cite how to establish some marathoner's goals.

For starters, you could run a marathon in every state and attain the rank of "finisher" when a marathon or ultramarathon has been run in all of the lower 48 states, Alaska and Hawaii. Clubs that foster these quests are the 50 States & DC Group and the 50 States Marathon Club.

And, just to show the reader that I am not alone in setting some very interesting goals, I will share with you some of the amazing goals and accomplishments that a few other older runners have established. Some club members do more than one cycle. Ray Scharenbrock, age 71, of South Milwaukee, Wisconsin, has run 500+ marathons and has finished **EIGHT** state cycles. He's now running half-marathons in all of the states (a 50 and DC Group activity).

If 51 marathons isn't enough, become a "megamarathoner" and join the 100 Marathon Club North America. This club is patterned after its United Kingdom counterpart where all it takes for membership is *the completion of 100 marathons/ultramarathons!!* My wife Lenore and I started this club in 2001 at the request of Peter Graham, secretary of the 100 Marathon Club UK, and membership has reached 150+.

Norm Frank, age 73, of Rochester, New York, is the member who has run more marathons and ultras than anyone else in North America. His total of **800+** is amazing and makes my total of 352 modest by comparison.

Run a marathon on every continent. Some runners have goals to run one in all of the European countries, in all counties of Great Britain, in all of the Canadian provinces and territories, and the list goes on and on.

Some marathoners have "strings" of running marathons in a particular race, many times from the inaugural one to the present. Runners Pat and Sylvia

Quinn, Mac Bohlman, and Russ Akers are veterans with a "string" of all 25+ Coeur d' Alene (Idaho) Marathons.

My own strings came about after I moved to Washington state in 1984. My three different marathons with 20 consecutive years are the Seattle Marathon, Capital City Marathon (Olympia, WA) and the Portland Marathon.

John Bozung of Orem, Utah, has a different kind of string going. He has run a marathon/ultra every month of the year for almost **12 years!** David Jones and Ron Fowler, both of Seattle, have run every day for **20 or more years!!** Other veteran runners across the country have similar strings going.

Some marathoners keep track of how many "different" marathons they have run. Others run all of the marathons that are available in certain states. California and Washington have more marathons available than the other states in the nation, so this is a challenge, especially if the ultras are included.

Many of our marathon friends are also race directors of marathons or events of a shorter or longer distance. This adds another dimension to marathoning and is a year-long function for those of us who take on this role. As co-directors of the **Yakima River Canyon Marathon** in Central Washington, my wife and I could probably be known as the "oldest marathon race directors in the world". Our goal is to give the runners the best marathon experience imaginable! We do our best, and many runners come back every year and bring along their friends.

If you really want to set some goals, join the **Marathon Maniacs**, a club for runners who aspire to run many marathons **often**. There are ten levels of "mania" based upon marathoning accomplishments. My six-week string of marathons was good for four stars, but 20 year old Brenton Floyd of Harrison, Tennessee, has top billing with 10 stars for running **52 marathons** in 2003.

I think it is easy to see that there is no limit to what one can do in setting objectives and finding satisfaction in the ensuing accomplishments. And, if it isn't clear from the examples given, I should point out that time and placement need not be a part of a goal to complete a specific set of runs. I am the first one to run more than 350 marathons/ultras in the Pacific Northwest and this has resulted in some recognition from the regional running community. My long-range goals are to run/walk 500 marathons, finish the 50 State and DC cycle, and be active in running activities for the rest of my life.

Don Lang, in his early seventies, is from Glendale, California, and is nearing his 400th marathon completion. He "collects" new marathons that he hasn't run before and rarely repeats one. Even so, he has run more marathons than anyone else in the Western United States. He runs about **50 marathons** per year, every year.....always without injury and usually with long distance air travel involved.

While many of us love to build up our totals or set string type goals that are not necessarily based on finishing times or placements, we should also recognize that there are some amazing older runners out there setting times that runners decades younger would envy.

There are many veteran runners whom I emulate and admire. John Keston, 80, of McMinnville, Oregon, runs races from track events to the marathon. Whatever his age, he sets world records for that age! He makes the most of his current year and looks forward to his next birthday. He's a friend and I've enjoyed "competing" with him in several marathons. It's indeed humbling to finish an hour *after* someone who is five years older than I. When he was 69 years old, he ran a world record 2:58:33 marathon. As a further example of his remarkable abilities, at age 71 he set another world record by running a 3:00:58 marathon.

At the Portland Marathon in 2002 he ran a 3:22:59 for a 76-year-old male world record. When we ran the Bend Marathon in Oregon on a warm day in August of 2003, John ran a 3:19:01, another world record for a 77-year-old runner. At age 80, John ran a 3:51:07 at the Napa Valley Marathon in California on March 6, 2005. When certified, this, no doubt, will be another finishing time that no other 80-year-old male has accomplished.

Records are made and then meant to be broken. Ed Whitlock of Milton, Ontario (near Toronto in Canada) has an amazing list of accomplishments. When he was in his 60's, he had some sub-three-hour marathons and hoped to run others as a 70-year-old. When he reached that age in 2001, he ran the Toronto Waterfront Marathon in 3:00:24 to set a world record but missed a sub-three hour time by a mere 25 seconds.

Because of an injury he had to wait until 2003 to try again for a sub-three-hour marathon in Toronto. This time he was successful and established a new world record of 2:59:10 to become the first person over 70 to run a marathon in less than three hours. The saga continues. In 2004 at the age of 73 he ran an improved time of 2:54:45, again at Toronto, for his remarkable third world record in the marathon as a 70 year old.

To get to his running potential, Ed had a rigorous training program. On most days he ran three hours on a 2.5-mile loop around a cemetery near his home. This in itself is hard to comprehend. It reflects his tenacity and dedication to meeting his goals as he established an international reputation and received celebrity status as a marathon runner.

On March 16, 2005, Helen Klein, 82, of Rancho Cordova, California, won her age division at the Napa Valley Marathon with an excellent time of 4:57:12. She was ahead of over 200 younger runners who made the 5:30 cutoff. She has had a marvelous record of running accomplishments. In 25 years of running and racing she has set at least 17 world records in the age groups from 60-64 female to 80-84 female. She has run over 150 marathons and ultramarathons with two-thirds of them being ultras. While she was in her 70's, she set a world record for a "6-Day Road Race" (373 miles) and for a 24 Hour Road Race (102 miles, 1300 yards). She ran five 100-mile trail runs in one year at the age of 66. In all of these she was the oldest woman to finish these races at the time. She is a former co-director with her husband, Norm Klein, of the Western States 100 Mile Endurance Run in the California Sierra Mountains. She has completed this race four times in her 60's, finishing in less than 30 hours. When you factor in her gender and her age at the time of her many accomplishments, she may well rank as the finest endurance athlete ever!

Regardless of whether you run to set time/placement goals, multiple event goals, or even just run because there is no better thing to do, it's a rare runner who doesn't get injured on occasion. Nothing can be more demoralizing than to be a runner and not be able to run because it is too painful to do so. It's a challenge to accept the down time, lose fitness and miss scheduled races. However, it must be accepted that the body needs time off to heal, so it is prudent not to rush things and delay the healing process. To do so risks making a temporary injury a permanent one, sometimes necessitating surgery. Most runners are aware that as they age, the healing process takes longer and the time to retrain to one's original fitness level is lengthened.

While recovering from an injury, aerobic fitness may be maintained by cross-training. There are alternatives such as swimming, biking, cross-country skiing and rowing to name a few. My preferred alternative is brisk walking that includes hills and mountains. Walking has helped me maintain general aerobic capacity, muscle tone and optimal body weight. I have walked races from 5K to marathons while injured rather than not compete. However, this doesn't always work. Several years ago I had to skip two events during the fall marathon season when a calf muscle was too sore for distance walking. Running in place or with a flotation device in a swimming pool is also beneficial.

As we get older, our motor skills slow imperceptibly, but in a cumulative fashion. While we can see the aging in our faces and bodies, we can only imagine the internal changes that we cannot observe. Popular media reports fill our minds with concern about muscle atrophy, diminishing heart rate, bone-loss, arterial plaque buildup and more.

At a certain level runners can clearly measure the summation of the aging processes. All that we have to do is compare our race results from one year to the next! This works well on a race that is run each year on a course that doesn't change. Occasionally, we may improve our times over a previous year due to training, the weather, weight loss or any number of factors that support a faster race. We're elated with the change of fortune even if it is temporary. We all know deep down that aging and slow-downs will continue. Ultimately, while we may be able to slow the rate of change, we can't stop the process. So, we should just ignore it and go on, thankful that running contributes to good health and feelings of well-being.

With the reality that time affects our physical capabilities, there is an important part of running and racing that is happily independent of the physical. This is the mental aspect, the power of positive thinking. The mental control of one's body is independent of aging. That which is learned from race experience, the drive, mental toughness, and strategy may even help the older runner improve over a period of time. Regardless, these qualities can be drawn upon in future races and at any age to handle new challenges. In a race there is the same perception of effort no matter what your age. The same feelings of fatigue are prevalent, and the same desire to get to the finish line as quickly as possible constitute the "Runners High" for most of us.

When running becomes difficult, it may be worthwhile to consider having a running partner. Some of my best training runs involved running and talking with a friend. It was relaxing and pleasurable to talk about common interests. This made the miles and time fly by, and there was less fatigue at the conclusion of the run.

Some running clubs have fun runs where the emphasis is on social exchange while jogging along at an easy pace. This kind of activity often leads to group discussion as the group follows a pre-arranged, easy and often familiar route. Focus is removed from the act and strain of running and placed on communication and community. Depending on the size and nature of the club, the group runs may be offered at different distances at one outing to accommodate all participants, including the slower runners and the walkers.

To persist as a runner, it pays to have running heroes whom you admire and endeavor to emulate. There are many individuals who affect one's running career, but there are always a few who stand out. These are some of the runners who have inspired me.

When I ran my first marathon, the Heart of America Marathon, in Columbia, Missouri, on Labor Day in 1981. Sy Mah was introduced as a special, respected runner. He had run several hundred marathons and was the pioneer megamarathoner. At Columbia he ran his third marathon of the weekend, including two in Michigan. In 1983, I ran the American Medical Jogging Association Ultramarathons with him at Chicago, Illinois. By the time he died in 1988 he was the first person ever to have run 524 marathons and ultramarathons.

Norm Frank of Rochester, New York, is the current standard bearer among distance runners. He has run more than 800 marathons and ultras. Between 1998-2000 Rick Worley of Kingwood, Texas, ran 200 marathons in 159 consecutive weekends and is listed in the Guinness Book of World Records for this feat. During this time he completed three 50 States & DC cycles and one tour of the Canadian Provinces and Territories.

At my first Boston Marathon in 1983, Joan Benoit set a woman's world record with a time of 2:22:43. I watched her on TV as she won the women's marathon at the Los Angeles Summer Olympics in 1984. She has been my role model ever since.

While it may not always be possible to reach quality goals such as new PR's as we age, there is no reason why we can't have new quantity goals. In my 50's and 60's I set a goal of racing 52 times per year, which is an average of one race per week. Some years I made this goal and other years I did not, settling for 40+ races.

Another aim that I have enjoyed pursuing was increasing the number of marathons/ultras run in a calendar year. Starting with 18 in 2001, I raised the number to 21 in 2002, then to 22 in 2003. My goal of 25 was on schedule in 2004 until I was injured in November and had to be satisfied with 22.

My "six marathons in six consecutive weekends" goal was accomplished once in the spring of 2003 and twice in 2004 during the spring and fall "marathon seasons."

A aim that I pursued for years was to run more marathons/ultras than anyone else in the Pacific Northwest. At the end of 1995 I had run 177 marathons and ranked 6th in the Marathon Achievers Club. The leader had 221 marathons at that time. Since 1995, my position moved upward on the list until I came into first place in 2003, a position I still retain with 352 marathons/ultras as of March 2005.

Avid runners can also review personal records and log books to count races and set reasonable goals. Road runners who have been racing 20-25 years may endeavor to reach a grand total of 1,000 competitions. Travelers can set geographic records for countries or continents. Some enjoy "collecting" unusual events.

These examples show that there are many different kinds of goals and records that can be pursued in running that don't involve speed. This sport of putting one foot in front of the other provides so many goals!! Those that are personally important and satisfying are the ones that should be pursued.

THE CONTRIBUTION ZONE

"You only live once and if you want to get something done you have to do it while you have the chance." - [Terry Fox]

Rob Reid

Rob Reid took up marathon running in 1979 as a physical education student, and has since run 27 marathons, winning 5, with times from 2:22 to 2:46. He has posted a masters PB of 2:27:35 and turned in a 1:22 half marathon in his fiftieth year. Rob is the Race Director of The Royal Victoria Marathon on Vancouver Island. Rob founded a charity running group called Runners of Compassion (**www.runnersofcompassion.com**). He is the owner of The New Balance Store and Frontrunners Footwear (Victoria, BC) and has partnered with staff to open the Nanaimo Frontrunners and WestShore Frontrunners, both on Vancouver Island. Rob won the Victoria Businessperson of the Year Award presented by the Victoria Chamber of Commerce in 2004 after his Frontrunners Footwear store was recognized as Business of the Year in 2003. Maybe this recognition arose from the attitude behind the following Rob Reid quotation: "We need to be more than a store, we need to promote a healthy lifestyle."

Rob is presently spearheading a project to pay permanent tribute to the memory of Terry Fox in the City of Victoria as part of the 25th Anniversary of the Marathon of Hope. A monument at Mile Zero of the Trans Canada Highway will honour the achievement and dream of Terry Fox on the 25th Anniversary of the Marathon of Hope (September 2005). Rob has assisted the Canadian Broadcasting Corporation on preparations for a two hour live broadcast of the largest participatory run, ever in Canada for the Terry Fox School Run, September 16, 2005.

Rob confesses that his joy in the sport has been the wonderful friendships that he has made, and the difference charity running makes for people in need. Rob lives with his overly supportive wife Joan Geber – a Director of Maternal and Women's Health for the Province of B.C. and his sons Nathan and Keegan. Rob's older son Jeremy and daughter Braden live in Calgary, Alberta.

Putting Your Heart and Soul Into Running For the Most Mileage Possible

Rob Reid

Because of their experiences on the road and trail, I believe seasoned runners can now prioritize all the vast benefits running can bring. Running is more than a movement that benefits its participants. It has real legs in making strides for the human race on a global scale.

Can there be a movement afoot where runners collectively change the world with their healthy and giving hearts? Many of us have so much to share when we look at the small planet around us. How can we best continue to spread giving to others in our community, our country, and the rest of the world?

As runners we value the economy of effort, the ability to improve not just our own physiology, but with the perspective of age on our side, the innate ability to value the bigger picture of life. There have been global leaders we have all learned from over the years. They have changed the world with their giving hearts: Mother Theresa, Mahatma Ghandi, Martin Luther King, Nelson Mandela, Stephen Lewis and one of the greatest Canadians, Terry Fox. I think also of the lone protester who stood at the front of the tank at Tiananmen Square. All of these unselfish people were put into a situation that defined their calling and by accepting their personal challenge, became heroes of change, heroes of giving. The mature runner has peaked in his or her athletic pursuits, and can now run forward setting philanthropic personal bests.

Why do we only imagine John Lennon's song "Imagine"? What can we do to live it? Can we as runners harness our energies by training our attitudes as well as our bodies? Am I only a lowly shoe retailer who is meant to grovel at people's feet due to a past life experience?

I do believe I have found an answer to the questions I have posed, at least for myself. Before sharing these thoughts I believe a little background is required. Our attitude and behaviour appears to have something to do with our genetic pool, and the environment in which we are raised. The saying that to be an Olympic Champion means we must choose our parents wisely does carry some truth. Our genes certainly do play a part; however, other sayings that have touched me over the years continue to affect my attitude too. I will always remember Ted Kennedy speaking about his brother Bobby Kennedy: "Some people look at things the way they are and ask why, others dream things that never were and say why not". For me, growing up in a large Canadian city, Toronto, seemed normal enough until a turning point would change the course of my life at the tender age of six.

My Irish immigrant dad was a successful, hard-working life insurance salesman. It seemed to me that he cared about people and wanted to help in whatever way he could. Ironically, he did not qualify for a life insurance policy himself because of a genetic heart defect. He worked long hours, socialized hard, but sadly in those days the medical profession did not educate or promote a healthy lifestyle to heart patients. He smoked and he drank.

At the age of 38 his condition was serious enough to warrant a new type of surgery. I visited him at the Toronto General, sitting on his bed, not really understanding what was happening. The patient in the next bed made me laugh. Why I remember being amused and not being extremely saddened seems to be the human essence of living with memories that haunt you and make you sad. The hospital handled crowds of his friends, his clients who came to see him before the surgery. I remember coming home from kindergarten the next day to a house full of friends and family. Was dad having another party at the house and making everyone do silly things so he could use his movie camera? A close family friend, "Uncle" Jack took me down the street to sit on the steps of a neighbour's home and told me that my dad was in heaven now. Mom sold the house to pay the doctors, and at the age of six I went to live with a family I did not know. My time with a new surrogate family was strange and not welcomed by me. I missed my mom that is certain, and all my friends and familiar surroundings were suddenly gone too. This time is a real blank except I do remember tempers, my schoolwork suffering and only being able to see my mom on weekends when she would sneak me into the Women's College Nurse's Residence where she lived and trained for a profession she once had practiced. Luckily, this did not last longer than a year. We found our own apartment, and I changed schools. We had stuck it out together and started a new chapter in our lives.

Many people were kind and giving to me during this time. These kindnesses made such a difference and came in many forms. Being a six year old Canadian in Toronto meant being a Toronto Maple Leafs fan. The Leafs were a child's heroes, like a dad. I remember how much it meant getting a letter and tickets from one of the greats of the game one day. He actually wrote me! This gesture stayed with me and over forty years later a local Member of Parliament who knew me and my story, was breakfasting with this hero of mine. He mentioned how his heartfelt kindness so long ago had given me hope. Meeting Frank Mahovolich, the one time Toronto Maple Leaf, later that afternoon and fitting him with shoes was a real honour. It was an added pleasure and more than a little humourous that he later sent me a thank you and a photo of him in a Montreal Canadiens jersey - from when he played with Toronto's arch rivals - Go Leafs Go?

Going back to the early years, let's just say I did feel an emptiness for my dad. How would I fill this? Is not a parent, a mentor for his children? So what did I take away from this? How did the heart he had, really make a difference to mine? It did instill in me the fact that life can be so short for so many. While running on a desert trail to a summit in Arizona I came upon a saying on a plaque:

> *"The clock of time is wound but once, and no one has the power to say just when the hands will stop, on what day or what hour. The only time you have is now, so live it with a will, you never know when the hands may soon be still."*

I have always felt that we are living for those who lived before us too, and their struggles are what make us tick. We must attempt to learn from history and those mentors around us that we admire and emulate. We as a species do have to learn from those who have gone before us for they have not lived and suffered for naught. It is all too easy to be lazy and forget this as we rush from task to task failing to properly evaluate and prioritize what counts in the long run for mankind, and our children's children.

It was while I was at University that a Phys. Ed. professor, Jerry Gonser, gave me a gift. He allowed me to gain confidence in finding out what I could be, to believe in myself. He did this by inviting me to go running. I laced up my 1973 Chuck Taylor basketball shoes and joined in. As an ectomorph, I had a pain threshold equivalent to a firm hand shake (no body contact sports, thanks) and running was something simple I could do for my heart-health and self-confidence. Completing the 1979 Boston Marathon was my Everest and from that point forward I would live, and work at the lifestyle.

Exploring different careers meant teaching, counselling and working for a large sporting goods company, The Forzani Group, which has become the largest in Canada. It offered a great training ground for dealing in the future with staff and suppliers. I later hooked up with an individual who was well recognized as a Canadian running great, and we partnered to open a running store in Victoria, B.C. When we expanded to another city I then learned the lesson about being an absentee owner. It struck hard, meaning we would dissolve our partnership. Though not all ideas work out, the life lessons and the reinforcement you gain in your own convictions, on reflection, make those experiences not an impossible hurdle but a step up in educating yourself for a successful future. As in running a marathon, enough can never be said for the unsung supporters with whom you surround yourself, whether they be accountants, business allies, or of course, family. These are the people who help you back on your feet when and if you ever hit the wall at mile 20. It will always be your reputation by which your friends judge your success. So, as with running, my reputation in business was defined by my ability to exercise my will to succeed in serving our local and global communities.

Our training as athletes involves a disciplined routine in balancing the easy workouts with harder sessions of fartlek, hills, intervals, and tempo as well as maintaining a good diet as we strive to reach our own personal goals. Our bodies may be our temples, and running our yoga, meditation, and for me my morning coffee. However, as an offshoot of all this concentration, do we become too selfish, and self-centered after a certain amount of time?

To me, it made sense for runners not just to develop healthy hearts, but also to exercise compassion and giving, in becoming truly balanced human beings. I believed there could be corporate responsibility no matter how small a company was, and possibly others would volunteer to make a difference on a individual basis.

Reading a series of articles in a national publication moved me into action, as it had others. Since 1949, a culture, a religion, a country had been overrun by a much larger power. The people of this country continued to flee the oppression. It seemed like a marathon of freedom over the Himalayas. Their leader, who spoke of compassion and giving, had won the Nobel Peace Prize. He is a leader who speaks of the values of concern for our fellow human beings in a peaceful way. That attitude has been forgotten by too many of our global leaders of today. Maybe world leaders need to be screened for giving hearts. Politicians Without Borders? Imagine. The issue of Tibet is an acid test for our world as we choose which path to follow.

What began as a plan to raise money for The Tibetan Children's Village in Dharmasala, India became a service club for runners wishing to do the right thing locally and globally. I approached like-minded runners who wanted to balance their running and giving goals. Runners of Compassion was born. It now has two chapters and raises monies that go out to many charitable groups, sometimes left off the main screen of funding. We assist with a breakfast program, carry out a Shoes For Youth Program so young people needing footwear for sports can participate, assist a women's shelter, and try to cover everything from street youth programs to sponsoring Tibetan refugees, and medical students, schools in Central America, and an AIDS orphanage in South Africa. We put on events and receive monies as a chosen charity of the Royal Victoria Marathon. Runners of Compassion is my church and it allows me to flex my muscles with regards to the giving values I hold important as a local and global citizen. (**www.runnersofcompassion.com**)

While running allows us to train both our bodies and our minds to succeed athletically, it has of late become a way to express ourselves in other ways. The growth of runs geared to raise funds for charity, and the number of runners who now enter events for the sole purpose of bringing awareness to a certain cause has changed the profile of our sport over the last twenty-five years.

So, do runners who have been known as a lonely, self-possessed lot only worry about their next personal goal? Training on a daily basis for many has not changed. The goals of a 10 km or marathon are still there. But, it seems that for whatever reason, we are increasingly motivated to take up activities for more than just self-centred reasons. As athletes age, it seems natural for them to give back to the sport and to the community. As this retrospective sensitivity develops, it becomes a time for us to fit into the shoes of others, and leave a legacy.

In honour and memory of our great Canadian hero, Terry Fox, who could not continue his run across Canada to raise research monies for cancer, many of us lace up our shoes to help. When his run ended, I made my first attempt at an ultra distance run, having secured sponsors from local Calgary neighbourhoods where I lived at the time. Terry moved us, and our proactive response could also assist others needing our help. The annual Terry Fox runs were born and held around the world to celebrate Terry's giving spirit. The event every September as we walk or run defines our generous Canadian spirit.

Special-interest charity running groups are booming at recreational centres, stores, businesses and clubs across the country. An added feature of today's running scene is the charities that link the fundraising and travelling to international events. The main three in this category are, The Leukemia Lymphoma Society of Canada Team in Training, Team Diabetes, and The Arthritis Society Joints in Motion Training Team. All these groups offer entry, travel, accommodation, coaching, and outfits for runners. These groups attract a majority of novice runners who experience a social outlet where they can feel good about helping others while doing something new for themselves.

Holding a run for fundraising is a mainstay in communities across the country now. The strongest event of this type is the annual national Breast Cancer Run that attracts tens of thousands. They have recently added a 60 km. walk held in a number of large urban centres. These mass events have become a part of a pop culture environment that many citizens want to belong to for the intrinsic values it represents. We tend to wear our giving on our sleeves with bands that show our support, whether for Lance Armstrong's cancer charity, or the Breast Cancer Society.

What drives these charity events? All the charitable interest groups are getting plugged into high tech online gifting, making the dollars raised a key component of the success of the event. Also, the fact that they promote participation over athletic achievement has reshaped the format. The priority has changed whereby the athletic achievement is surpassed at the finish line by the giving that takes place. Runners in these events wait at the finish line for friends, but are not motivated so much by their results. And those responsible for organizing such groups, clinics and events should hold their heads high and take credit for the sport of running where the playing field offers many benefits for those participating. Our sport has succeeded in reshaping the lifestyle we live to include giving. Running in North America in its amateur sense is a pleasant change from the stories of strikes and drug abuse that plague professional and some Olympic sports. It is about what you are doing, not about what you are going to get for it. There is a "purity" in it that is good for the soul.

Existing events like 10 kms and marathons, which were originally set up for athletic performance are now partnering with charities that enable corporate sponsors to buy into the giving that takes place. Giving a portion of their operating monies to charitable causes in their communities has become commonplace. This philanthropic new approach by business allows an outlet for company morale and teambuilding where everyone wins. These sponsors can feel good that their companies and employees are involved in a value-added sport that combines both fitness and giving.

The saying or religious law stating "Love thy neighbour as thyself", is a central message of every major religion, and building from that the Dalai Lama states exercising love and compassion is the only true religion. Let us as runners celebrate the evolution that has taken place in our sport. As a seasoned runner, I will continue to remember my dad, and keep living a dream that he cannot share in body, but I can celebrate his spirit in me. Our running community has a great opportunity to become mentors, and leaders in fostering a heartfelt attitude of generosity for a healthier future. It will have immeasurable benefits for both our local and global communities.

Evan Fagan

Evan entered his first running event at the age of 49 in 1986 and entered first triathlon at the age of 59 in 1996. He ran his first marathon in 1988, but has picked up the pace since then and so far has completed 122, as well as two ultramarathons. Since 1996 he has completed 47 triathlons, including two Ironman Canada events. Evan is an active member of the Team West Coast Running and Triathlon Club, in Victoria, B.C.

He participated on the Triathlon Canada National Age Group team to the Triathlon World Championships at Cancun, Mexico in 2002, and at Honolulu, Hawaii in 2005.

Evan has volunteered at various running, triathlon and charitable events and is Race Director for two annual running events.

As a Certified (IAAF) official run course measurer, he has assisted many event directors, including directors of several charitable events, by establishing very accurate race courses, from 1 km to the marathon distance. As a Level 4 Track Umpire, Evan has participated for over 10 years in numerous local and national track and field events, including the 1994 Commonwealth Games which were held in Victoria, BC.

Evan assures us that he has experienced most of what has been written in this chapter and can hold his own in a marathon, recording a personal best of 3:39 in 1992 (Napa Valley Marathon), when he was 55, but his greatest personal satisfaction came from completing his first Ironman at age 67.

Time and Knowledge: The Experienced Athlete's Gift to the Community

Evan Fagan

"The September game demands the very best. It allows for no excuse, it provides no opportunity for redemption." - George Sheehan

Millions of dollars are raised annually through running events organized by local, national and even international charities. Virtually every week from May to October one can find events, whether "Fun Runs", or serious competitive runs, ranging from 5 km to marathon distances.

It seems that many older runners, who have abilities and time, lend their expertise to these kinds of community events. Charity organizations rely on assistance and expertise from the running community for direction and advice on how to organize and conduct running events as fundraisers for their particular cause.

Many of the runners who volunteer their time and expertise may well be beyond their working days and have retired – from working five days per week at a job - but not really retired – not from life. That is to say they may have left a job, but have not withdrawn from society. With much more free time these people are ready, willing and able to perform volunteer work for charity organizations. What a good way to stay active in a sport they love. They not only participate in the sport but also greatly contribute to events for runners and walkers – they stay involved!

"The spring is for the young, but when the shadows lengthen and the leaves change and everywhere there are hints that time is running out, when the import of everything that is done is raised to epic proportions – it is time for the veterans, the older men in the league, tempered by time and season after season...So it is with life, the best of life comes in life's September. Life is played best by a veteran, understood best by the master. Life is the supreme aging game." - George Sheehan

One should not underestimate the contribution a veteran runner can make to charitable organizations. In most cases, the staff and other volunteers are not runners. They do not have any knowledge of how to present a running/walking event, even though they are very keen to employ such events as a means of raising sorely needed funds to support their activities and services. We are all aware of the effects of cutbacks in Government funding and today, more than ever, many charities rely heavily on direct financial support from the community.

Most charities are worthy causes and deserve support. For personal reasons and experience, it may be that for a given individual, a particular charity is more attractive than others. Seasoned runners are in a unique position to assist, especially those who may be retired from the world of work. It is often the older runner who has the time, experience and know-how that charitable organizations depend upon. Their personal contribution to the wider community reflects favourably on the running community. It's something the running community can do for the greater good of those most in need. The unselfish use of time and talent by the experienced runner is very valuable and worthwhile. Through their good example, others may be encouraged to participate and become active and involved.

A specialized area of expertise held by some runners is that of course measurement technique. Such trained individuals can greatly assist charity organizations, (and the running community as a whole), by accurately measuring the run/walk courses. There are numerous annual charity "Fun Runs/Walks" organized as fundraising events. Often, and for a variety of reasons, the course will change from one year to the next. While it is unlikely a participant in these "Fun" events will ever set a world record, the fact the road race course is the exact length as advertised, is nonetheless important. For a course to be distance certified, the measurer must also be properly certified through successfully completing a recognized course measurement seminar. While many runners are interested in becoming qualified, it is often the veteran, possibly retired runner that has the time to respond to requests from charitable organizations to measure courses.

Volunteering their time, while remaining fit and competitive, gives experienced runners new avenues of opportunity to make valuable contributions to their chosen sport. Volunteerism keeps people involved, perhaps even more involved than they were before (because of their increased leisure or discretionary time). They can offer an extremely valuable service to the community. Within these activities volunteers encounter new challenges in attempting to meet the needs of the organization they serve, where the primary goal is centered on fundraising and the cause, rather than solely on the running. Those in the running community who volunteer time and talent serve to establish respect and value in the community on behalf of other runners, run clubs and related organizations.

Seasoned runners are often looked upon as community-minded citizens because of their ability to generously serve. Their interaction with other non-runner but like-minded individuals enhances their sense of community involvement and camaraderie. This is a great motivation factor for anyone, but particularly for the older runner. They can continue to be active in the sport they love, perhaps long after they themselves are no longer competitive, even in their own age class. Involvement at the level of the charity Run/Walk often leads them to take on other areas of responsibility within charitable organizations, further enriching their volunteer experience. Generally, the veteran runner becomes involved because it is a good thing to do; it's a "giving back" to the sport of running, which gave them so much; it's to help worthy causes for the greater good of the community; it's unselfish giving of time, talents and expertise; it's showing a fine example for others who may be so inclined.

Some older runners have developed different ways to contribute to our sport. Many, with or without a track and field background spend years volunteering in a variety of roles such as event organizers, officials and coaches. Each season they spend countless hours assisting with elementary and secondary school track and field events. In Canada that may include other local, city, provincial (BC Summer Games), Western Canada, national (Canadian National Championships), International, Commonwealth Games and other high performance track and field events. The pattern will be the same regardless of where one calls home. Some represent their sport through local, national and international sporting organizations which include local track and field clubs, and at Regional and National Athletics Associations, as well as International Federations. What a contribution these individuals make to the youth of our country. Some are former regional and national record holders; others are former educators; and most of them still remain active in running, either as participants or as volunteers.

While most of the contributors to this book may be better known for their performances as runners, most, if not all, have a parallel involvement as volunteers in every imaginable field of support from coaching and mentoring to event organization and everything between. Although tempting, it is hardly possible to mention every contribution of every author, but a quick read of the biographies will tell the reader a lot about how these active and involved senior runners give selflessly of time, energy and talent.

A unique sub-group among the event volunteers and organizers is the brotherhood of race announcers. Such individuals, though rare due to the huge effort needed to be good at it, make a tremendous contribution to the sport of running and triathlons. Once again, these few special individuals tend to be older athletes who, based on their experiences, share their expertise and knowledge by making such high profile contributions to our sport. Participants very much appreciate hearing the announcer as they approach the finish line. Hearing their name and something about them as they actually cross the finish line just adds so much to their experience and memories of the day.

With the proliferation of running clinics sponsored and organized by running clubs, retail running stores, YW/YMCA, and local recreation centers, the elder runners among us are often called upon to volunteer their time to be clinic run leaders, guest speakers or club coaches. They willingly give of their time, share what they have learned and provide insight from the perspective of their accumulated years of experience in the sport of running. The majority of attendees to clinics are beginning runners who are very keen and appreciative audiences. With a noticeable increase in new runners, some experienced runners are offering their services as personal coaches. Although some charge fees, there seems to be no shortage of clients.

Much of what has been stated thus far will also apply to the triathlon athlete who participates in events ranging from sprint triathlon to Ironman. It is noticed that the longer the triathlon event, the more participants seem to rely on coaching from those experienced in the sport. Generally, the coaches come from the ranks of the very experienced and usually older athletes.

> "In September, the runner has become what May and June and July taught him to be. He knows things that were a mystery when the season began. He has developed a concentration that was absent earlier in the season, and he no longer has time for nonessentials. The game has become all. In the September of my life I am all that the past has taught me. I know things that were a mystery before. Every year has become an asset, every experience a treasure. I am no longer a rookie, no longer a neophyte. And I no longer look to veterans for guidance – I am a veteran, a master at my own game." - George Sheehan

Most people are aware of local, provincial/state and national organizations which rely on run/walk events as major fundraisers for specific worthwhile causes. Almost every weekend, charity organizations sponsor run/walk events. All of the volunteer contributors are owed a large debt of gratitude by their communities. Seasoned runners involved in this way are a great source of inspiration to all of us. They have done their best. For those no longer able to post the athletic achievements they used to, their active involvement within their community keeps them connected with their sport. Even those who are still active benefit from a different perspective through involvement at the organizational level.

For all runners, old and young, a key aspect of the sport is in the friendship, fellowship and camaraderie of like-minded people that is otherwise lost to the individual who drifts away from running entirely. People who remain active, concerned and involved usually lead a more enriching life. Their self-esteem and self-worth are greatly enhanced, something so important to people in transition from a life of work to that new existence called "retirement". May all of them carry on with such good work and by their fine example encourage other runners to become involved in some way so that this fine tradition may continue. We who believe must ensure that those in the running community continue to give their special contributions not only for their own benefit but more importantly for the benefit of others where we all live, play, work and enjoy life together.

<u>Bibliography</u>

Sheehan, George, M.D. *Personal Best*, 1989, Rodale Press Inc.

THE PARTICIPATION ZONE

"I still bother with runners I call hamburgers. They're never going to run any record times. But they can fulfill their own potential." [Bill Bowerman]

Dan Cumming

Like others, at around age 40 Dan realized it was time to make some changes, especially regarding the amount of exercise he was getting. At that time, British Columbia was looking forward to Expo '86 and an ambitious group in the Okanagan Valley created the "Okanagan Express Relay" as a special event which would see 26 runners go nearly 450 km from the East Gates of the Expo site to a park in the middle of Summerland. That was how it all started and twenty years later, he's still going.

Born (1945), raised and (mostly) educated in Vancouver, Dan's career gave him many opportunities to travel and live abroad. He never passed opportunities to run (at least 16 countries, including nearly two years in the tropical climate of Malaysia). Having earned a PhD in Food Sciences in 1974 from the University of BC, Dan has lived and worked throughout Canada, in Europe and Southeast Asia. His career includes being a research scientist, inventor, research manager, diplomat and business manager.

From age 40 when he started his "second" running career, he improved performances at all distances over the next few years, hitting a personal peak in 1988-89. In 1988 he ran his first marathon, and while he readily admits the time of 3:25:19 was not spectacular in the greater scheme of things, Dan saw it as a small miracle because as recently as 1985 he could barely run a mile. He states his second marathon was almost more of a personal miracle than the first. In 1990 Dan underwent disk surgery in his lower back. While recovering in the hospital, he set a goal to run another marathon someday. It took 10 years for all the elements to fall into place. The second wasn't as fast as his first, but that was not the goal anyway. It was the personal challenge of seeing if running another marathon was possible.

Dan's running is far less goal-oriented than in his younger days. He is a member of the Pacific Road Runners, and has just become Deputy Race Director for the "First Half" half marathon, a major fund-raiser in support of Variety.

Dan is co-editor with his wife Judi of "Points of Light: Life Defining Moments" (Trafford Publishing, 2004), a work of love that eventually involved 34 contributors who share personal stories about powerful, life-altering experiences. One of the contributions is by Dan. It is about running.

Meditation for Runners, or
Getting to Know Your Inner Runner

Dan Cumming

I am certain the term **Meditation** brings all sorts of things to mind, but probably not running. At one time my personal image of meditation was of somebody sitting in the lotus position, the sound of tinkling bells or gentle Asian music, perhaps the soft burbling of running water, the scent of incense and maybe the flickering light of a few candles. Sounds OK, and I'm sure you could get into some fine meditative thought processes in such a situation. However, I don't believe there would be much argument if I were to say that no part of this image sounds like you would be moving particularly fast or getting much exercise. So, what is meditation for runners?

It is probably many things to many people, and I know for sure that I didn't invent it. To some extent, a former physician and old friend formally introduced me to the concept although I was probably already essentially doing it myself. I suspect many people who are reading this are also doing a form of *runner's meditation*, whether they see it as such or not.

A second question that deserves an answer is: "What place does this subject have in a book for older runners?" Well, it has as much place here as in any book about running, but maybe just a bit more because of the nature of running that many older runners will do, or be able to do.

What I have in mind, whether you want to call it meditation or something else, is getting to a free state of mind where you can let your inner self take over. If things go really well it will sometimes even tell you what's what in other aspects of your life. Almost always, you can count on the exercise to relax and refresh your body and mind.

Most long-time runners will already know that when you go for long easy runs, it is easy to slip into a state of mind where everything is just flowing and you are concentrating on nothing in particular. In this state, I have personally been able to come to an understanding of important issues and even solve a few problems. This tends to happen not because I am somehow actively trying to think about these matters, but because they are on my mind in a general way. When my mind is freed to take its own course, it always amazes me how the "answer" just seems to come floating to the surface. If not, then certainly a feeling of calm and peace will replace agitation and stress, should they be there.

I can already imagine some people saying, "But, isn't it dangerous to just let your mind wander while you run?" Well, yes, it could be if you are running on busy streets or over precarious mountain trails. However, I find that in my own case (and I doubt that I am unique) there is a part of my brain that is looking out for rocks, curbs, roots, puppy-dogs and stray children even while the rest of it is in another realm. This could be a good place to get into a discussion of "Left Brain" vs "Right Brain" function, but this is not intended to be about theories or deep psychological matters. So, we can leave such discussions for another time and place.

I am simply suggesting that you can let your mind float into a meditative state while you are running and that within reason, another component of your brain will take care of business. If you think about it, this is really no different from a hard workout where you may be concentrating on technique, speed or control. Are you also concentrating in the foreground of your thinking on where each footfall is landing? I think not. When pushing toward the end of a hard race or workout, are you concentrating on running or on your detailed surroundings?

If you can run safely while concentrating on a strong finish, why can't you run safely while your mind has a little workout of its own? In fact, I know people who run as much as anything, because they find this kind of mental state is a wonderful place to be and running lets them get there. I know people who feel running can sometimes be an almost spiritual experience. Sometimes, I am one of them.

It may be difficult for a beginning runner, still struggling with developing his or her fitness to the point where running is easy and pleasurable, to imagine that you can slip into this contemplative state. Nonetheless, many people do reach that point surprisingly quickly. Obviously, this kind of thing works best for lone runs in quiet surroundings. That does not necessarily mean open fields or deserted beaches. It can just mean early morning or later in the evening when there are fewer people, pets and cars around, and naturally being in a safe place that you know reasonably well. There is no reason you can't do this in the company of others, but while you may be able to run and meditate, you can't run, talk and meditate.

There are clearly differences between what we may consider classic meditation and what I am talking about, but maybe not so many as it might initially seem. First, forget the lotus position. Second, you are going to have to breathe comfortably and evenly while you run, so the studied breathing exercises of meditation require some modification, although the principles remain essentially the same.

Much of the rest of your preparation is similar. You must be relaxed. That is actually a goal to work on while running at any time. Just as with some of the preparative exercises for classic meditation, you can run while mentally working your way up and down your body ensuring that except for the muscles being used to propel you, everything is relaxed and flowing. Even the working muscles can and should be as relaxed as possible, just for good running technique. Sometimes this all happens naturally, but if you have never done this or thought about doing it, you may have to make a deliberate effort to get into the right physical and mental state.

So, here comes a bit of the 'how to' on meditation for runners:

> It goes without saying that you have to get into the rhythm of your breathing and your stride. This process of meditation is going to be part of an easy run, and probably a longer run, although the latter isn't a necessity.
>
> When you have warmed up and reached a steady easy pace, start working on becoming fully relaxed as you stride along feeling good and sensing yourself part of everything around you. This is where a nice park, early sunny morning or a soft warm summer evening can help, even though they aren't an absolute necessity for the process to work.
>
> Start with your hands. Make sure they are relaxed and open, not clenched in some kind of tension building fist (*they shouldn't be anyway*). Feel the air moving smoothly in and out of your lungs and imagine the oxygen flowing out to your limbs, letting you run effortlessly at an easy pace. If it helps, this can be a good place to pause in the process. Really feel the oxygen coursing into your muscles and the blood flowing smoothly, bringing the energy to your strong confident stride.
>
> Concentrate now on your arms swinging effortlessly, helping your legs do their work, but know that part of the easy swing is a relaxed feeling from top to bottom. Consciously sense this and stay with hands and arms until you know every muscle group is fully relaxed and without tension. *After a time, this sort of 'inventory' won't be a studied thing. You will just do it as a quick mental check of all systems to make sure no tension is building where it shouldn't.*
>
> The next natural place to go is your shoulders as an extension of your free-swinging and fully relaxed arms. Let off any tension you feel and while you are at it, see that your neck is held comfortably without any strain or stress at all. Take your time with this. Make sure you know that each part is truly flowing in a relaxed motion, totally in harmony with your body. *You will be surprised at how quickly it all comes together if you let it. Just as tension building things like clenched fists and high shoulders can transmit that tension to other parts, so too can the relaxation process flow quickly to other parts. This will be especially true once you have done this a few times and know what it all feels like.*
>
> Mentally feel your back, working down toward you buttocks. This area can be bad for being tight and eventually being part of a breakdown in your form on a long run. Any time you feel you need to run your 'inventory check', work through the parts again that you have already

relaxed, just to make sure. It won't take long and you will probably be glad you did.

As you lope along, your breathing is deep and steady, your stride and arm swing are natural and rhythmic. Your body is in synch and the loose, relaxed feeling is starting to be a full body sensation.

Work down your legs. Obviously they are doing most of the work, but they should feel powerful and loose, fully capable of what you are asking. If they are not, then slow down a little. This isn't a race. Feel the oxygen flowing from your lungs giving power to your legs as they stride along in an easy gait.

It is up to you how long it takes to reach an overwhelming feeling that your whole body is one fluid part working together in total easy harmony. *At first it may take longer. Once you are familiar with the technique and the feeling, it can happen quite quickly.*

When you know you are there, relieve your mind of the responsibility for consciously managing this preparation program and let it begin to float where it wants to go. Try to clear everything from your mind. Do not start trying to problem solve. That is not what this is about. Let things come to you naturally. *Even though this isn't a problem solving exercise it is amazing how many times the solutions to problems will float out of the warm and gentle mist you have created as you attain this relaxed state of mental and physical being. But, I must stress that this will be a fortunate bonus that you may realize from time to time. It is not the object of the exercise.*

It might take a few tries if this doesn't just come naturally, and remember, as I said, a lot of people already do something like this without any conscious effort. If it sort of sounds familiar to you, it probably is.

Once you get the hang of it, you mostly just have to make sure you have the right atmosphere, the right pace and a good relaxed technique. Most of the time the rest looks after itself. *I must admit that on a cold rainy night this might be harder than on a bright spring morning or a soft summer evening, but you will know when it is right.*

Just let it go on as long as you want, floating from thought to thought, but remember these are the things your "inner runner" wants to tell you. It isn't a Q&A session. If nothing else, the stress relief that comes from this kind of running is worth it, all by itself. A run of this kind is very refreshing and can send you back to the rest of your life with new energy and a calm approach that seems to get things into perspective faster so that you can deal with them effectively or maybe just have the patience to wait out something that you can't do anything about for the moment.

Back to the matter of why this is in a book for seasoned runners. The main reason is that older runners may be doing more of the sort of running that lends itself to this kind of contemplative or meditative running. Some mature runners have more time and more flexibility as to when they run, as they may be retired or semi-retired and probably don't have kids around that need their attention and support. In some way it is one of the rewards of the grace of getting older. This subject could fit in very well in any comprehensive book on running, but we veteran runners tend to have a natural advantage of not having to get anywhere or prove anything.

I know that I run, mostly because I love to do it and love the feelings it produces, both physical and mental. Although there was a time when I could claim to be a fairly decent runner, I have never been fast enough to really challenge anybody other than myself and now that I am in my sixties, I can no longer better my own personal bests. That doesn't really matter if remaining involved and active is the goal, and for me it is. This meditative approach is part of what makes running special and a reason that, while I enjoy social interaction with my running, I also enjoy long solo runs.

So, if you don't already know about this secret of running, give it a try. It may take a few times to get it working, but stick with it; it's worth it. If nothing else, the relaxation techniques may even improve performance when you get into a competitive situation.

So .... On your Mark!   Set!   Oooooommmm.

Maurice Tarrant

Born 1930 in the town of Paignton, on the south west coast of Devon, England. Married in 1950 to Phyllis Scoble; five children Gail, Philip, Claire, Mark and Lisa all living in the Victoria area. Ten grandchildren.

Maurice started into sport at the age of seventeen, playing rugby union and rowing coxed fours for Paignton until the age of twenty-three.

Achievements included representing the Devon select team in rugby 1949, and junior champions of Great Britain rowing in 1950.

In 1955 he was three miles champion of Devon, and represented the county in all England cross country championships and inter-county track meet at the White City Stadium, London, England. Best track times 3 miles – 14:10 mins and 6 miles 30:07 mins.

Maurice emigrated to Canada in 1957 and became Canadian citizen.

He returned to the sport of running in 1985 at the age of 55. He recorded best times: 5k 16:54 (58), 8k 28:01 (58), 10k 34:26 (57), 15k 53:34 (58) 20k 75:25 (55) and the half marathon 72:56 (59).

Maurice holds or has held more than forty Canadian age class records. (To date)

Running for FUN in Retirement - Fitness/Understanding/Nutrition.

Maurice Tarrant

Staying fit is a key ingredient to having fun in your life and being able to carry out many physical activities whether walking, running, swimming, cycling or other pleasant pastimes such as gardening or home projects.

My first introduction to the running scene came about in 1951 at the tender age of twenty-one, during "National Service" days in England, while I was taking a basic training course with the Royal Air Force. Carrying a rifle over a cross-country obstacle course, I found myself running easily with the drill instructor while the rest of the recruits struggled in our wake. The instructor suggested I could be successful at the sport of running and soon after I entered my first race. This was a half mile event on a grass course where I finished second.

In 1955 as the three miles champion of Devon, I participated in a six-mile race at an inter-county track event at the famous White City stadium in London. My "advisors" suggested that I should run hard at the start to avoid being "boxed-in". At the sound of the gun I set off like a hare. I found myself in the lead going into the first bend and continued in front of the pack for the whole of the first lap. For several laps thereafter, runner after runner passed me. I passed the three miles mark in 14:14, with a finishing time of 30:07! This was my first lesson in how not to run an efficient race. Even-pace running has always been more successful for me and in particular, it provides a better level of comfort throughout the race. Some of the names that gave me inspiration in those days were Bannister, Chataway, Brasher and Pirie.

In my early years as a runner, from 1951 to 1961, there were very few aids available such as the books written by Joe Henderson, Dick Beardsley, or Jeff Galloway. Also equipment available to runners did not have the technical advantages that we now find easily at our favourite store where we can also find knowledgeable staff willing to fit us with the "right" pair of shoes or clothing.

Towards the end of the fifties I had lost much of the "fun" that I had previously experienced in racing, and with the responsibility of helping with our growing family it was time to spend more time with the children and their development. However, I did stay fit in other ways such as refereeing soccer for the younger players and helping with the development of junior soccer teams in the Ottawa area. What I did specifically is less important than the fact that it maintained an effective level of fitness.

When I returned to competitive running in 1985 at the age of fifty-five I had the first ingredient of fun, <u>fitness</u>. Now I needed to <u>understand</u> the physical boundaries of my body, which was no longer that of the 25-30-year-old, and find the best state of mind to maximize my potential.

I believe this is best achieved by having regular workouts. By following a sensible program of training, it is possible to define your own limitations and work to improve them. There are many good coaches available in the community and it would serve one well to join a club and follow the advice of successful runners and leaders in the group.

I was fortunate in the eighties to be coached by Mike Creery of Victoria. Mike was able to observe and advise me in many aspects of track training. This includes a very minimum of ten minutes warm up prior to group training and a sequence of drills around the track. One of my personal favourites is the "ladder workout" involving a series such as 200/200/400/800/400/200/200 metres, with emphasis on the downside of the ladder being of equal quality and time as the ascending distances. At that time I was the oldest runner on the track and Mike would advise me to miss a sequence if necessary to maintain the quality of work. This all gets into the area of aerobic and anaerobic training which is really not a topic for discussion here. Arthur Lydiard has written some great articles on aerobic and anaerobic training. Well worth reading. Reference - *Athletic Training: A guide to the Lydiard Running Lecture Tour* (1999).

From the age of fifty-five to sixty five I was able to train five or six days a week and fully recover from a race within a twenty-four hour period. During the past decade I have reduced my training schedule to three or four days a week and now need up to forty-eight hours after a race to begin the training phase again. I also find it helps to include walking in my recovery phase, and it is easy to find a willing training partner in our pet dog, Seamus.

A typical training week now includes; a run of forty to fifty minutes at 60-70% effort on Tuesday, up to an hour tempo run at 70%-80% effort Wednesday and then on the following day I like to join up with our Thursday Morning Gang for up to an hour of group running. On the Saturday between races I normally carry out an endurance strength run of up to two hours at 60-80% effort. That is what I do. It is what works for me to be fit and enjoy what I do.

Starting in January of each year I compete in the New Balance Island Road Series on Vancouver Island. This is a set of nine races from 5km up to the half marathon, which is held up and down the island from Courtney to Victoria. This series and others like it, provide excellent opportunity to find out your "best" distance. This year is my twenty-first consecutive series. Keeping the string going is part of what is fun for me in running and may be something to try when those personal bests are but happy memories.

There is an excellent "age grade indicator" available on the web site of the World Athletics Veterans Association where you can record your age, gender, distance and time (**www.howardgrubb.co.uk/athletics/wavalookup.hml**). This calculator then provides your percentage performance for that race. I use this on occasion to find out if my running is up to par, for better or worse. Over the past twenty years my percentage has stayed fairly constant even though clock times have slowed a bit. Of late, there are a good many tables and calculators available to aid in evaluating and managing your running. Some of these are mentioned in the Resource Section of this book and I recommend having a look.

A particular calculator that I like and use, is a race calculator which provides your average pace for the run, and can be used to forecast a pace over a different distance. Even-pace running is most efficient especially in the longer distances. A good example could be two cars of the same model, power, etc. having the same amount of fuel in the tank. One car is driven with the pedal to the floor and the other at an average speed. The car driven faster will not go as far as the car driven at an even pace! The longer the distance, the more important this becomes.

The following is my own best performance percentage for a 10 km distance over the past twenty years, and how I apply the race calculator for even-pace running over a different distance and subsequent results:

Age Category	Year	Time	Percentage %	Race Calculator Projected		Actual
55-59	1987	34:26	92.55	5km	16:25	16:54
60-64	1990	36:41	89.29	½ mar	81:29	80:52
65-69	1995	37:29	91.86	½ mar	83:15	84:11
70-74	2000	41:51	87:06	5km	19:57	20:15
75-79	2005	43:47	88.83	5km	20:52	20:42

Comparison of these performances indicates that although the raw clock times for 10K have slowed over the twenty years by more than nine minutes or approx 27%, the performance percentage reduction is less than 4%. In relative terms, that is probably no more than the variation within any given season and a series of similar races.

The use of the race calculator can be an important tool for subsequent races. For example, for this year the 10 km time of 43:47 translates to a projected 5 km time of 20:52 with an average pace of 4:10 per km. This then becomes my target time for each kilometre of the race and is most critical in the first kilometre and for subsequent even-pace running. Bear in mind these charts are only tools that may help, always try to keep the "fun" in running.

The last, but not the least part of this equation is <u>nutrition.</u> Plenty of fruit, vegetables, and home made soups and baking keep me fueled for training or racing. I shudder to think about the choices I made in my early years of running. Hydration wasn't even a part of my vocabulary back then. Now water goes everywhere with me. At that time too, I would partake of a steak about two hours before a race. What was I thinking? Red meat is not in my diet these days, and although fish and chicken are, most of my meals are vegetarian, a personal choice.

Well-balanced meals that include carbohydrates, proteins etc are the way to go:

1. Grains, bread and cereals, pasta and rice.
2. Dark green leafy, yellow or orange vegetables.
3. Citrus fruits, tomatoes.
4. Milk, cheese, yogurt, food made from milk.
5. Meats of choice, eggs, meat substitutes.

Use these five food groups as a guide, but the bottom line is eat sensibly and don't get hung up on fad foods or drinks. Good eating habits can be acquired, it's never too late and your body will thank you for it. Your health will improve and so will your running times.

If I may, let me share with you a small glimpse at what "FUN" means to me in my running program these days. What follows is typical of what might happen during any given week or two while the Island series of runs is going on. I hope it shows that training is so much more than workouts and drills and that it is part of my life, and I suspect, were you to ask, an important part of most active runners' lives, young or old.

Wednesday: Last Sunday was a race day, so today is a recovery run to include a few light pick-ups at 70% effort. I like to eat a very light breakfast, at least an hour prior to my run. Whether training or racing, I start my routine with a five minute walk. Starting from home, this takes me into the nearby countryside. Following the walk I jog for another ten minutes, along a road with fields on either side in which the daffodil pickers are hard at work. Today is cloudy so I am unable to catch a view of Mount Baker in the States. But I am able to view the sea, which flows along the Juan de Fuca Strait.

At this point you might ask what has this to do with running. For me, relaxation is a part of preparation for a race and I am fortunate to have this sort of running route. Once the walk and jog is completed, I stop to carry out a set of light stretching exercises for five minutes, then I am ready to train or race!!

For the past couple of years I have had sore calves or hamstrings during and following running. Since carrying out the walk, jog, and stretch routine I have not had this problem.

In training I use telephone posts to measure distances for my pick-up repeats. I speed up for about 120 meters (three telephone posts) then jog for the next 120 meters. Today I repeat this a dozen times. The last "sprint" needs to be at the same pace as the first repeat. The warm-up took about twenty minutes, the repeats almost that length of time and I complete the workout with a twenty minute tempo pace to my home, followed by more light stretching.

Earlier I mentioned the Thursday Morning Gang (TMG). When we started this group a little over five years ago, there were six of us. We now have a regular turnout of over thirty runners and walkers keen on keeping fun in their lives while keeping fit. There are over eighty on the mailing list. Each week we meet at a different location but always close to a café that can serve a noisy group for coffee, muffins or breakfast. We have newcomers to running and others that hold Provincial and National records. If there is a fun group near you, it will reward you by finding some ease from busy schedules that we all seem to have these days, even in retirement!

Thursday: This particular Thursday the leader for this month has chosen to meet near the start of the 5 km course that will be the next race in the Island Series. I arrived prior to 8:30 a.m. in order to go through my fifteen to twenty minutes warm-up drill followed by stretching. By 9:00 a.m. there are over thirty runners and walkers gathered, ready for up to an hour of "fun" exercise. There was much talk of our last race together among the runners who were planning to participate in the next event. We jogged along the route to get a feel for the course. Knowing the course and being able to jog the whole route provides a certain amount of confidence for race day. The last 200 meters we made a final "burst" across the finish line to our own cheers! We then ran back to the café for a hearty breakfast, coffee and muffins.

Friday: A day of rest and time to visit the garden centers for new plants.

Saturday: This is my day for an endurance run of up to two hours. I carry liquid for any run lasting over an hour, usually a sport drink mix that I plan on using about every twenty minutes. I started out as usual with a five minutes walk, ten minutes jog, followed by light stretching. Heading into the open countryside I can see snowdrops and daffodils by the side of the trail with the hedgerows showing their blossoms and the feel of spring is in the air. Cyclists and other runners are out in force, all with cheery greetings and smiles on a perfect day for training. There are kilometre markers along the trail to provide an idea of pace. About every twenty minutes I walk in order to have a good drink and avoid dehydration. I see several groups of young children playing soccer, bringing back happy memories of days with my own family. The first hour has come all too soon and it is time to retrace my route to home.

Feeling some fatigue at the hour and a half mark, I ease the pace and give more thought to my style of running and relaxation movements. Arriving home almost on the two hours mark, I am ready for breakfast and the rest of the day.

The week prior to the race: Tuesday and Thursday involve easy runs.

Day prior to race: Take it easy and pack my running kit.

<u>Race Day</u>:   Before any race I like to be up and about early for breakfast (two slices of toast with honey) and to drink plenty of water (up to a litre). I also like to arrive at the registration to collect my race number at least an hour or more prior to the start of the race. Around forty minutes prior to the start I carry out my walk, jog and stretch routine. My projected finish time according to the race calculator will be 20:52 for this 5K, at a 4:10 pace, as per the above table.

There are almost 900 runners and walkers in the race, so I line up as close to the start line as possible in order not to be blocked too much during the first kilometre. When the gun sounds, I run hard enough not to be trampled by anyone and try to stay within my own limitations. During the first part of the race many runners pass me but I work on staying relaxed. At the 1 km marker my time is a little under four seconds faster than the planned pace but this is not so critical in a short race. By easing up slightly I find it more comfortable and am able to keep a better stride length and breathe easier. At the 2 km mark I no longer check my time and find that I am now catching runners and passing some of them. Heading for the 3 km and 4 km markers I concentrate on keeping pace with other runners around me and not chasing any that pass at a much faster pace. Into the last kilometre now and knowing the course, I am able to keep a fairly good pace and look for the finish line. I push the final 200 meters and check the time of 20:42! 10 seconds better than forecast by the race calculator and a personal best for this course.   And there you have a typical period in my personal running life, a bit of an insight into what "running for fun in retirement" actually means to me.

Bruce Deacon, Olympian, wrote in his column; there is something in the human spirit that attracts us to a physical challenge. It brings out the best when we push ourselves to do something that is hard. It feels good to push ourselves further than we thought we could go. Keeping the fun in retirement - Fitness, Understanding and Nutrition has helped me in the "golden years". I seek new goals each year, try new methods and having a running program as part of my life helps me feel good about myself and others around me.

Keeping fit, understanding my limitations and maintaining good nutrition is helping me to enjoy running and life to its fullest potential.

Lorne Smith

Ironman Triathlon World Championship
October 18, 2003

Lorne Smith is 72 years of age. His athletic background is canoe and kayak racing. He was North American Champion in 1,000 meters singles kayak in 1955 and competed in the Olympic Trials in 1956. He was inspired by Terry Fox and started running in the early 1980's when he was in his late 40's. He competed in his first Ironman (Canada) in 1989. He currently holds the record for Ironman Canada (70-74) with a time of 13:26:07, breaking the record by 1 hr. 50 mins. Lorne has also competed in five Ironman Hawaii, seven Ironman Canada, several local 11.8 km swims, various local marathons, trail runs and triathlons, as well as the Nanasivik, NU, marathon.

Lorne met his wife, Isabel, in Flin Flon, MB, and after teacher training in Winnipeg, he signed on to "Teach in Canada's Arctic."

In 1962, Lorne and Isabel went to Baffin Island where Lorne taught school in the isolated settlements of Arctic Bay, Cape Dorset (joined by baby daughter Linda) and Pond Inlet. Living on Baffin Island gave Lorne a great deal of respect for native people. In Arctic Bay, he did some travelling by dog team to teach in outlying camps on weekends.

After seven years in the Arctic, in 1969 (when son Tom was born), Lorne finished his B.A. and undertook a Masters Degree in Anthropology at the University of Manitoba, Winnipeg. Following graduation, in 1972, they spent two years in Churchill, MB, and then moved to Yellowknife, where they remained for 18 years. Both Lorne and Isabel retired from the NWT Government and arrived in Penticton in October of 1992.

They still miss the North in many ways, but both feel so very fortunate to have settled in the Okanagan Valley!

Age Group Athletes And The Search For Fitness, Enjoyment And Better Health

Lorne Smith

To be human is to participate and to compete. Societies all over the known world have included "sports" in their activities, in addition to the daily need to survive and to forage for food, water and shelter in a hostile world.

From the earliest times, humans have had to compete with other humans, other animals and the elements in order to survive. Many human activities have been centered around games of skill which were often related to hunting, in the case of men, while the gathering of foods and the raising of children was normally relegated to women.

The resources that were available to various groups varied from place to place and depended on a whole complex of resources, including access to shelter, food, water, wood for making fires and a host of other natural resources.

As the human population grew and spread out of Africa, the adaptability of humans enabled them to "be fruitful and multiply" and survive in some the most hostile places on earth. From the deserts of the Sahara to the jungles of Borneo, the mountains of the Himalayas and the most isolated islands in the world, human societies have established themselves and have survived.

We need to remember, that the spread of humanity was initially a result of walking, swimming, floating on rafts, logs, boats, and domesticating various kinds of wild animals as beasts of burden as well as using them as a source of food.

Now with our gas guzzling SUV's and our dependence on automobiles, ships, trains and planes, we are more likely to drive to the corner store than to walk a block or two. Many of our children are obese - the effects of which are reflected in the health system as more and more children become less and less active. Meanwhile studies have shown that families are eating more and doing less to use up the calories that they are taking in.

Notwithstanding the general situation noted above, many of our children are fit, active and engaged in a variety of sports and the arts as well. It is essential that we encourage our children to enjoy activities, which are beneficial to their health, and their parents and other members of society should actively participate in keeping fit. There are also those mature individuals who have got the message and are making sure that they exercise enough to at least delay the onset of old age to some extent. And then, there are the "jocks" who seem to revel in their physical activities and fly in the face of the myths of aging and what it is supposed to mean. So, all is not doom and gloom.

We all need to keep fit. The benefits are enormous and add to the quality of life. Over the last many years, the fitness boom has been promoted extensively by many "so-called" disabled athletes, who are fierce competitors in wheelchair road racing, bob sledding and other types of sports such as wheelchair basketball. What an example they set for the rest of us, regardless of age!

"Old Soldiers' Philosophy"

Don't stand up when you can sit, don't sit when you can lie down.

I suppose there is a practical reason behind this "philosophy". In a way, it is a short term strategy of survival. If you don't know when you must stand and fight or run for your very life, your best strategy is to conserve all the energy you have. Luckily, most of us are not caught in such conflicts today and as older athletes we have other battles to fight and win.

So, why do we run? The reasons are valid and a part of human evolution for centuries, born of necessity. More importantly: why run, when not so long ago people in their "declining years" were supposed to slow down and take it easy?

Simple explanations

1. It is good for you.

2. You need to exercise to aid in keeping your health, regardless of age.

3. It can and should be fun,

4. You get to be with a lot of great people who are fun to be with and running with a group is a nice change from running alone.

5. Running is a great way to forget your daily cares

6. It beats being at the office or sitting in front of a TV watching someone else be physically active (well, OK, not always).

7. It is good for you.

Where to start

1. Check your local running stores.

   a. Many of them provide running clinics and other advice on how to get started.

b. Do their staff members run themselves? Most of them do! Why? Lots of reasons, but not least of all, because it improves their chances of being fit and healthy.

c. Find a knowledgeable staff member for good advice on how to start. Make sure it is someone who understands your special needs.

d. A good running store will be able to guide you in selecting shoes that are right for you! People with foot problems may need special cushioning or custom shoe inserts in their runners in order to stay injury free.

e. There are specialized shoes for just about any kind of running. Many of the long trail runs are held in mountainous or hilly terrain. Trail shoes are specially designed to provide stability and comfort in very difficult terrain. There are also hiking shoes, cross country shoes, track shoes with spikes, super light weight track shoes and so on. It can be hard sometimes to decide what shoe you should buy - again, a good running store can make it a lot more likely that you will be pleased with your purchase.

2. Find yourself a clinic.

a. Many running stores, community centres and running clubs hold clinics. These regular running programs are a good way to get off on the right foot, (no pun intended).

b. In Canada and many other countries there are a multitude of training programs that will get you up to competing in races of all types: speed walking, jogging, half and full marathons, cross country running and trail runs starting from a few miles to 50 and 100 mile events.

Age Grouping Makes the Playing Field Even

At one time, before the current popular interest in running developed, runners would sometimes show up at an event and find that they were competing against national champions and world class athletes. Even when there were few or none of these super performers, older runners were always faced with the younger athletes performing at their peak. The result was that a lot of runners would end up eating the dust of a few well-trained and experienced athletes who, as noted above, might even be champions at their particular distances.

The introduction of an "age group" classification has created a huge contingent of runners who compete in runs, which are graded by age: 40-44 Male, 65-69 Female etc. The "age groupers" are men and women, boys and girls who would like to race and compete in track and/or road races covering the distances from 50 meters to marathons and ultra-marathons - (anything over 26.2 miles is an ultra-marathon). Competition means many things beyond out and out winning of any given event.

One can compete against the clock or against a previous best performance. One can even run against the calendar, trying to maintain performance levels as long as possible and age-graded performance tables will help a person keep track of his/her own abilities and compare times over many years. But, at the first and simplest level, age-class events allow older competitors to pit themselves not only against the field but against athletes who fall within the same age range.

The idea of introducing age-graded classes for competitive events has been a godsend to the sport of running. This wise idea has provided a great incentive for seasoned runners to continue doing what they enjoy - competing with other athletes - while making the "playing field" a lot more level. In most events we find five-year fields for both male and female competitors with prizes and recognition at each level. For those who crave competition, this format brings life to each event.

Lest one think that older runners are doddering old men and women, the Masters World Records would indicate something very different. One record for Canadians to be VERY proud of is the Marathon World Record for the 70 to 74 year old age group.

Toronto resident, Ed Whitlock, was the first person in the 70+ category to finish a full marathon in a time of less than 3 hours. He had attempted this goal when he turned 70 but fell short of the mark by just a few seconds. However, two years later he was successful when he was under the three hour mark by seven seconds and has repeated the feat several times since then. As late as October of 2004, at the age of 73 he has reduced his marathon time to 2:54:45! His training involved running around the local grave yard, usually doing 14 -15 miles per session! At well over 70 years of age, Ed Whitlock is recording raw times that would place him in the top 100 finishers in most marathons other than the very largest, such as London and New York, without consideration of age and in most Canadian marathons, within the top 20.

There are many role models like Ed in all senior sports, but Ed Whitlock is the Master of the Marathon! At least he is for now. I say for now, not to diminish Ed's amazing accomplishments in the marathon and a good many shorter distances, but because records are made to be broken and I imagine even now there is a 65 year-old man out there somewhere, maybe even one of the contributors to this book, who is looking at Ed's time(s) and planning his own assault. That is what the competitive heart is about and how the age-class system works to give us older runners a goal for the future, even when our best absolute times and performances may be behind us.

May the achievements of all these dedicated, remarkable athletes, men and women, inspire you to achieve your own form of greatness!

THE COMPETITION ZONE

"Doctors and scientists said that breaking the four-minute mile was impossible, that one would die in the attempt. Thus, when I got up from the track after collapsing at the finish line, I figured I was dead." [Roger Bannister - After becoming the first person to break the four-minute mile, 1952]

Paula Fudge

Paula Fudge is a world level athlete, who has represented Great Britain on the world stage, held a world record and brought home gold medals for her country from international events. She was born in March of 1952, and was accompanied into the world by her twin sister, Ann, who has played a prominent role in Paula's life and running career.

Paula began her running career at the age of 12 with her local athletic club and proceeded to win various events through her teen years. As she became older her distances lengthened out from sprints to include 1500 m and 3000 m events and cross country. As her running career moved into the international sphere she began to show her mettle, becoming the British and Commonwealth record holder at 3000 m and 5000 m on track, and collecting a gold medal for the 3000m at the 1978 Commonwealth Games in Edmonton, Canada. Paula continued on to become the World Record holder at 5000 m on track. In 1982 she was the bronze medallist at 3000 m in the European Indoor Championships. As an older runner (50 Plus), Paula has set the British Veterans record for 5 km on track (17:47.8) and World Veterans record for 3 km on track (10:08.83).

With time, she continued to increase the distances run, representing Great Britain in the World Championships in the marathon event. Her marathon career was topped with a time of 2:29:17 at the Chicago Marathon at the age of 36, placing her third.

Paula has represented her country on track and road numerous times and around the world on the international competitive stage. She continues to run and to enjoy the sport to which she has dedicated such a large part of her life. She currently lives in Surrey, England with her husband Robert and daughters Rachael and Abigail.

Competing At The Top – A Personal Perspective

Paula Fudge

IN THE BEGINNING

Having had the privilege of being an elite runner and a moment of recognition on the world stage, I find myself at a new and interesting stage in my running career. Now that I have joined the ranks of the so-called "older runner", I find myself taking a different approach, even though running is no less important in my life than it ever was.

As a relative youngster I had my share of both good and bad races. Sometimes I felt like giving up, but the next training session or race had to be done, so I would get on with it. In truth, I suppose I didn't really want to give up. Having a twin sister enabled me to look up to her when she was successful and encouraged me to 'plod' on past my own challenges. My twin sister Ann won All England Schools gold [classed as mini Olympics for school children] at age 16, something I never achieved, generally exiting in the heats. At 20 she represented England in the International Cross Country Championships. I managed travelling reserve. Ann finished as high as 4th and no lower than 13th in the seven World Cross Country Champs she ran in. My sister also had many trips abroad representing England or Great Britain on cross country and track in her early twenties, something I didn't achieve until a couple of years later. My first World Cross was in 1979, seven years after Ann's first representation. We both competed at international level regularly and she won Commonwealth bronze when I got the gold medal. I was always pleased when she raced well and achieved age records and fastest relay legs. I dreamed of one day achieving the things she had. Patience was worthwhile as eventually, like her, I represented my country, got selection for major games, won our National Cross Country Championships and was brave enough to try the marathon.

At any age, injuries have been the hardest things for me to cope with, as they always seem to happen when they are least wanted! Frustration was the worst aspect of injuries when there was no rehabilitation work that could be done to aid recovery. Missing out on qualifying times for finals of races and for major championships were a real disappointment and tears were certainly shed, but I always tried to focus on the next aim, the next challenge. Over the years, I've had a couple of injuries which took so long to get better that I was wondering if it was worth carrying on but in spite of those doubts, something within me kept me focused. Many times, because of the competitive spirit I hold in my heart, I have been disappointed with my performances in World Cross Country championships. It seems that in those days the British were not prepared for the speed at the start of the race; hence we would die. I hated reading my results in our athletics magazine and vowed to try harder next time.

When I was running at my best and what could be considered the height of my career, I was competing in the World 10K road championships in Lisbon. Every time I went round a corner I had a sharp pain in my foot. I learned later that I was actually running with a piece of detached bone below the inside of my ankle. Not surprisingly, this prevented me from running at my best and afterwards I was bitterly disappointed as I knew I could have done much better.

Recently I have been injured for two months and although I have tried to keep basically fit I'm finding it hard to 'get back'. My motivation is to just keep working hard and stick at the training. Hopefully, with this approach I will get back to the level of performance I was at before the injury. My present day running group are really encouraging and I'm doing it for them as well. They have been cheering and urging me on through the sessions for which I'm very grateful – it makes the pain easier to bear. I may not achieve my times now but it's the buzz and friendships that keep me going.

At this point, one might ask why dwell on frustrations and relative failures instead of reporting the highlights and winning moments of my career. That is coming, but I believe it is important to understand that we who are seen as high achievers have our trials and downtimes just as others do. If there is a message from this then it is that we must keep going in spite of the challenges and disappointments until we achieve the goals we have set for ourselves.

Achieving Commonwealth Gold (3000 m, Edmonton, 1978), European indoor bronze (3000 m Milan 1982), World Record 5k on track (Knarvik, Norway, 1981) and going under two hours thirty minutes for a marathon (Chicago, 1988) were my highs. At the Commonwealth Games I dreamt the day of the race that I was on the top level of the podium. When I took the lead in the final 300 metres, I was determined no-one was going to overtake me and I just kept working hard to stay in front. I was over the moon! I had never thought I would get a gold medal from a major championship. It was a fantastic feeling standing atop the podium hearing the English anthem.

My 5K World Record came out of the blue, as I had been injured with Achilles tendonitis. From the start of the race there were really only three of us. Ingrid Kristensen went ahead and I was second. As the race progressed I overtook Ingrid and churned out a string of hard steady laps to leave her behind. With just one lap to go I was told a world record was possible so I hung on as best I could, fighting the weariness and the knowledge that I would win the race regardless of whether I let off a little or not. It was a wonderful feeling afterwards as so many people were cheering and congratulating me. When I phoned my mother to tell her the news, she thought I was joking and told me not to be so silly!! Not the kind of response I expected, but I wasn't about to let it spoil my celebrations. In the evening it was great to celebrate with my fellow athletes from so many different countries. Even at the highest levels of competition, this sense of community is something that makes running special for me.

My first and last marathons were very memorable. In my first marathon I was very unsure of what to expect but it was a great experience. It was rather scary though as I found myself in the lead, hoping nothing would stop me from finishing. As the race progressed the weather changed from frost at the start to high humidity. The last six miles were unbearable. Still, I ran through it and it was a fantastic feeling crossing the line, breaking the tape with arms aloft and shouting my delight for all to hear. In Chicago, at my last marathon, I was feeling really good throughout the race. At twenty miles I worked out the mile splits needed to give me a time under two hours thirty minutes. I kept pounding away and had to concentrate hard as once again I was approaching the finish with no-one around me to force the pace. With the finishing straight in sight I reached down and picked the pace up, going through the line with a time of 2:29:47. I was thrilled with my result and was literally jumping for joy. As my husband and daughter weren't at the finish to celebrate with me (they were in the hotel) I ran up to my agent and gave him a big hug. I was completely shocked by my performance. I never thought I could run that sort of time.

THE OLYMPIC DILEMMA

Selection for Olympic marathon had been finalised, my sister Ann being one of the runners. However, a subsequent injury prevented her from taking part. Veronique Marot and I would have to do a run-off for the place. While warm weather training in Lanzarote to prepare for the run-off, I received a fax to say a decision had already been made. I wasn't selected. Even though further preparation for the now cancelled run-off was unnecessary, I decided to run the half marathon in Oxford, as planned, when I returned home. It was a scorching hot day and I finished second overall (men and women) in just over 73 minutes.

I decided to enter the Great North Run, a half marathon, run from Newcastle to South Shields where I recorded a PB of 71min 37sec. Since I felt ready for the marathon challenge, I made plans to compete in the Chicago marathon. In the meantime, as fate would have it, Veronique Marot had dropped out of the Olympic competition and I had been asked to run in Seoul. I turned it down. I had committed myself to another race and even more importantly, I realised I could not leave my four-year-old daughter for three weeks. She was a very important part of my life and I couldn't upset her or myself. I had done the world championships the year before and I had satisfied myself at a major championship. To this day I have had no regrets about my decision. It seemed the press and public had trouble coming to terms with my decision. As much as it pained me to disappoint my supporters, it was and is more important to me to be true to myself and to my values.

That was then and this is now. While I am hardly "old", neither am I young, at least according to the calendar. Running remains important in my life, but with new perspective. Perhaps I can share some of my thoughts on the subject.

Setting Targets

I don't set any targets because at my age and family commitments it is difficult for me to be positive about fulfilling them. Maybe when I reach 55 and my children are independent I will be more positive about European and World Master Championships which are meetings I would like to do.

Challenges

Each year I set times I would personally like to achieve, mainly on the track. For me, the challenge is personal even though I have been able to retain a significant level of performance. The times I set are realistic but challenging goals that encourage me to keep training hard. I have no idea what the British Masters records are and obviously, that being the case, don't build my year around them. If I achieve a record then I am delighted.

Having Company For Training

I enjoy having company for training as it helps me relax and work harder. It is also a good way of feeling comfortable with people running around me, as in a competition. However, I also like to run on my own. I find it helps with learning to concentrate on running to form (we are not always surrounded by other competitors in races) and to run through bad patches. It makes me mentally stronger as well and just proves that we can continue to learn and improve our technique regardless of age.

Track Sessions

For me, these are the hardest workouts for which to get motivated, so I get my long time coach of 35 years to set the sessions. He knows my ability and mental and physical strength. When I see the programs he sets, I am ready to do them and prove to myself I can complete them. Luckily for me there are plenty of people of all ages to train with and we keep each other going. It's great running on the track because we all encourage each other through sessions providing motivation to work hard and strive to meet the objectives we have set. Afterwards, we discuss how the session went and congratulate ourselves on what we have done. It is hard to say too much about the importance of support from those around us and who hold first-hand knowledge of what we do.

Running With Younger People

I enjoy running with younger people and I hope in turn that it will motivate and encourage them to achieve their ambitions. I'm there to encourage and help them realise what they are capable of achieving in a training session as well as competition. It keeps me going and helps me to understand what they want from running. At my age it is great to know I can still keep up with them. I'm pleased that I am able to pass on my wealth of knowledge, experience and advice and can help them with anything they want to know about what it is to train and race to a high standard.

Achieving Aims

In the past, achieving the aims I set out was a wonderful feeling.   Now if I manage to get into the British rankings for distances I'm really pleased with myself and it helps me set my aims for the following year. Some of my goals, especially my half marathon and marathon times were a long time in coming and I achieved them when I least expected to do so. They also happened after the birth of my first daughter. After having six weeks off I was really keen to get back jogging and then to competitive running. As I my fitness returned I was starting to race again and getting the 'buzz' again.

Friendships/Camaraderie

Over the years, having travelled throughout my own country and the world, I have made many wonderful friendships.   It has been a amazing experience travelling around, meeting fellow athletes and race organisers for whom I have a great respect. Their friendship, advice and encouragement have been invaluable. The after competition get-togethers were great too, an important part of the whole experience.   The seriousness disappears and everyone joins in conversations reflecting on the day and talking about plans for the future. One can learn so much from listening to the stories of other people's experiences. I have been fortunate to have experienced this at a national and international level but I am sure that this kind of sharing can be experienced by almost any participant in our sport. Without doubt, the topics of conversation may differ and the times and performances, but the personal camaraderie is pretty much the same.

Encouragement From Others

I have been very fortunate throughout my career to have the full support of my husband, my long time coach and all my family. My children have been an inspiration and encourage me while I'm doing the hard track sessions.   My parents were a help in supporting me at races and helping with baby/child sitting. So that I could compete abroad, my coach and women team managers would look after my daughter while I was training and racing. We had a good relationship and luckily my daughter was very well behaved. As I got older my agent and Steve King were key advisors and supporters who were great for encouraging me to keep going in the face of various challenges. Having a twin sister to train with and share experiences has been a tremendous help. I was lucky to have company for many years and even now we still compare notes as to how each other is doing although we live apart.

Motivating Others Through My Own Racing

I know that I have been encouraged by other athletes, including older runners, so I hope that seeing me perform at a reasonable level would encourage others to keep training and help them set challenging goals for themselves. I trust I can show them that whatever a person's age, it is still possible to compete.

Keeping Fit

As I get older, over and above any competitive goals I may have, I want to keep fit, as I feel it's important for a healthy lifestyle and hopefully a longer life. If an injury occurs I try to walk every day and if possible, work out on a static exercise bike until I can get back to running. I try to keep a basic level of fitness as I find it is harder as I get older to regain my full fitness level or recover as quickly as I once could. However, it is also important to have rest periods to help the body to recover from the intense training regime.

Biking And Running In Water

I am very impressed by the results achieved by fellow athletes who bike and/or run in water. Running in water helps maintain cardiovascular strength and also takes the strain off body joints when training hard, while allowing a high level of fitness to be maintained. With biking, the strain in mainly through the knees but cardiovascular work is again possible as well as the benefit of strengthening the thighs. In my opinion, this is best achieved by using a bike with arm movement, which gives the same action as running. Using a static bike and running in water, it's possible to incorporate repetition sessions, which is very beneficial in a strengthening or recovery program.

Physio And Massage And Their Importance

With high mileage and intense track and road sessions necessary for performance athletes, looking after the body is very important. Legs and backs take a pounding and in later years the body stiffens up very easily. Massage is a great help to relieve tired or tense muscles and re-circulate the blood. I have personally also found that reiki is a good treatment. It is very relaxing and helps loosen my back and for me is a very good alternative healing treatment. Regular massage can also prevent strains, tears and tendon injuries from occurring. However, if there is a persistent problem then physio advice is important and it's advisable to seek help immediately when it is clear that one is dealing with an injury and not just normal stress and strain. Physiotherapists are able to detect the source and basis of the injury and give rehabilitation exercises and treatment thus enabling the athlete to take as little time off as possible. As we get older it is much more important to listen to our bodies and rest before having a major problem.

MEETING THE QUEEN AND MEMBERS OF THE ROYAL FAMILY

A most pleasant part of my career as a British runner has been to experience first hand, the support and interest of the Royal Family in sport and athletic endeavours.

Throughout my athletics career, I have been very honoured to be introduced to the Queen, the Duke of Edinburgh, Prince Charles and the late Princess Diana. I, along with other elite athletes, was presented to Prince Charles and Princess Diana before the start of two London marathons. They were very charming and of course wished us all good luck on our runs.

While relaxing in the grounds of the University of Alberta, Canada (host of the 1978 Commonwealth Games), I was one of the fortunate athletes to be introduced to the Duke of Edinburgh who was 'wandering' through the athletes' village.

As a result of my Commonwealth Games Gold Medal, four years later I was chosen along with two more gold medalists, to start the 1982 Commonwealth Baton relay from Buckingham Palace. Before the official start, I had the honour of being introduced to the Queen who said a few words to us.

In 1984 I was invited to Buckingham Palace along with our World Record Breakers to receive my World Record Plaque from the Duke of Edinburgh. It was a memorable and wonderful experience. Seeing part of the Palace and meeting royalty again was something to treasure.

I also had an official invitation along with many other sports people to attend a garden party at Buckingham Palace in celebration of 'Forty Glorious Years of Sport.' It was great to meet so many other famous and talented people and to once again be in the company of the Queen and Duke of Edinburgh.

CONCLUSION

I feel athletics has been very fortunate for me - making me richer in friends, knowledge and fitness. All the above episodes helped to keep me focused on what I had achieved and what I wanted to achieve.

Herb Phillips

At age 65 Herb is living proof that age is nothing to stop you from attaining excellence. His running interests cover the gamut from short to ultra-long distance. Herb hasn't stayed at home while doing these races, having completed some of the World Class marathons in Boston and New York, travelling to Finland, France and the Netherlands to compete. He does seem to be a bit stuck on doing the Royal Victoria Marathon, with his running count already at 18.

Herb was voted Athlete of the Year (Male) by BC Athletics in 2004, based on a stellar year of running capped by a 2:47:02 Marathon time at Victoria, which was a single age (64) World Masters Record, which bettered his own time set earlier in the year at Newport.

He is one of these people who didn't even begin running until in his forties, when he recognized the need for life-style change and then went about it in a big way. Herb enjoys the challenge of the ultrarun as well, having competed both nationally and internationally at the 100K distance.

A Question of Retiring At Age 65

Herb Phillips

The wheels are going to fall off one day! So the question is, should a distance-running competitor reaching the age of 65 be planning and looking forward to retirement?

This year I will be 65 and I would like to think the answer is no. I believe the motivation level to train daily and to compete in races on a regular basis can still be there after one becomes a senior citizen. However, this is also a very important time in life to be working hard at enjoying each moment. That is, it's time to run every race like it may be the last and get the most fun possible out of each effort.

There are many rules and guidelines established for successfully motivating competitive runners. It seems to me however, that to stay motivated, there are certain adjustments required for older athletes and particularly those that continue to compete past the age of 65. The most important element of success for older aged athletes should be measured by the degree to which we are having fun and staying healthy.

Aging athletes with a burning desire to run fast every time they run, often have difficulty accepting the principles of moderation. Athletes who have been involved in competitive running for a number of years and who continue to focus on goals that would have them forever striving to train faster in order to run faster will sooner or later end up facing failure. Certainly the focus has to be changed. Eventually this desire for that ever-increasing speed will lead to problems.

Rules such as never run full speed in practice become very important. Now is not the time to experiment with training efforts that end up being too difficult to be accomplished. So if today's not the day for it, then the new rule is, " just don't do it". Although older athletes can still strive to do as close to their plan as they feel is possible each day, the more important thing now is that they continue to enjoy their running. Some days there will be no motivation for extra effort; other days there is an abundance of motivation. Regardless of the results on any given day, that day's effort should still be considered a success. Rather than trying to take pleasure from speed that has long since left a 65-year-old athlete, the enjoyment should come from the realization that each day you have become one day older and that you are still an active runner.

Only death stops us from growing older. With good luck, even at age 65 there can be a great deal more life left to enjoy. Most senior age athletes will have recognized the fact that rather than getting faster, they are getting considerably slower. This slowing of pace has likely been a reality for a number of years. It now becomes important for us to understand and focus on what running will do for the rest of our lives and in particular what will happen if running should no longer be an enjoyable part of our life activities. Hopefully there is still plenty of other enjoyment in our lives besides our running.

SOME THOUGHTS ON TWENTY-TWO YEARS OF COMPETITIVE RUNNING

How did it get started?
What kept it exciting?
How to stay motivated?
What was the plan?

Getting Started.

I had already reached the Masters age category in athletics before running my first race. Having spent over twenty years neglecting good health and fitness, at age 42 I realized that a change to a healthier lifestyle was in order. I started running as a means of getting into some sort of reasonable shape. This meant trading a comfortable seat at the cocktail lounge for an uncomfortable jog around the track. The search for a good martini became a search for good running shoes. Heading to the bar became heading to the track.

Like so many others in similar situations, I looked to recreational running for a route to better fitness. I committed myself to getting out and running a minimum of five days each week. Unknowingly, I had begun what has proven over time to be one of the most certain paths to becoming a lifetime runner. After running almost daily for three straight months, running became my addiction and with it came an enjoyable new lifestyle.

I continued running with a goal to do the local marathon and what I thought would be my only race. I had almost secretly stretched my running distance and training pace to the point where I was thinking I could possibly run a 3:30 to 3:45 marathon. I surprised myself by running just under 3:15. At the time I said I was happy to have successfully run a marathon and to have got that out of my system. However, four months later I was at the start line for my second marathon. That ended up with a 2:49:51 finish and a month and a half later I ran my third marathon finishing in 2:44:29.

At age 42 and after nine fairly intensive months, I had become a marathoner. As the mileage increased my weight decreased and 185 pounds became 130 pounds. Skinny was okay.

Keeping It Exciting

With a dedicated effort towards improving my running, over the next few years my success at running distance races became very satisfying. My performance peaked in my early fifties. While I am very proud of my accomplishments, I do apologize for the need to list them here, but it is precisely these accomplishments that give weight to the ideas I feel are so important to share with fellow members of the older running community.

At age 52 I ran the mile in 4:45, the 5K in 16:21, and the marathon in 2:35:28. At age 53 I ran 8K in 26:42, 10K in 33:52, and the half marathon in 1:12:29.

My most consistent marathon racing performance was when I was 53. In back to back marathons I ran the Sacramento marathon on December 5 1993 in 2:37:39 and the Napa marathon on March 6 1994 in 2:37:40.

Where could I have lost that one-second!?

But, as inevitably happens to everyone, by my mid-fifties I could no longer run personal bests at any distance. At that point my times began to slow down. I got in about a dozen years of steady improvement, a good run by any standard. However, even to this day my age-graded performances continue to show periodic improvement.

Twenty-two years after running in my first race I still enjoy running and particularly as a marathon competitor. In those 22 years of running with a total distance close to 80,000 miles, I've averaged over 9 miles a day. My largest single week was 151 miles and my highest month total was 532 miles, but that was back in 1994 when I was at some kind of peak in my performance.

I have run in 790 races, including over 50 sub-three hour marathons as a masters athlete (over age 40).

In my current age group (60–64) I've had four marathons that I deem to be particularly successful and satisfying from a performance perspective. They are:

> 2000 San Francisco 2:52:40 placing 19th overall, first M60-64, and first age-graded

> 2003 Tucson 2:51:13 placing 22nd overall, first M60-64, and first age-graded (91.03%)

> 2004 Newport 2:47:28 placing 4th overall, first M60-64, and 93.07% age-graded

> 2004 Royal Victoria 2:47:02 placing 14th overall, first M60-64, and 94.3% age-graded

Apart from these personal performance highlights in my senior years, I have also had the enjoyment of participating in a number of half marathons, marathons, and 50k's with my daughter. I recall a marathon, one of only two that I've ever dropped out of, where she toughed out extreme weather conditions to the finish and proved that she was a better runner than me that day.

Horrible weather won't always get the best of me. As a 60-year-old I was the overall winner of the Haney to Harrison 100 K for the third straight time under the worst wind and rain conditions in which I have ever run. In that race my 8:07:09 finish was 25 seconds faster than my 60-64 age-class World Cup win of three months earlier. However, the most exciting race I've ever been in and the one I'm most proud of was my seventh place finish in the 1500 metre, 55-59 age-group final at the World Masters Track and Field Championships in Buffalo New York. It wasn't the fastest or the best age-graded result I've ever run but it was what I believe to be my best effort. I was so emotionally high the next day, I recorded my only other DNF marathon. I simply couldn't stay focused on the marathon.

Staying Motivated

Fortunately, with the use of age-graded tables older runners can still remain highly motivated to remain fit and competitive athletes. Year over year comparisons of effort can be measured with these easy to use age-graded tables. As an example, my best marathon time of 2:35:28 at age 52 is a 90.8% rating. However, at age 64 my 2:47:02 marathon time is a 94.3% rating. Therefore the marathon at age 64 is a greater achievement by a considerable margin if we ignore the actual times.

For a variety of reasons, there are often not a lot of competitors in the older age groups of races. Not everyone 65 or older is fortunate enough to be able to run regularly. Nor is running the choice of exercise for everyone. Many seniors can find plenty of other ways to stay healthy and happy. So in some races with a limited number of upper age group athletes entered, simply striving to place in your age group can short-change the motivation needed to excel. Knowing your current age-graded percentage fitness level and striving to achieve that calculated time could be considerably more motivational than just trying to medal. Having actual clock-time goals and some fantasies of great performances can keep the older runner motivated. Still, it is important to understand that as you age you will reach some of your objectives but you will miss plenty of them.

Another beneficial way of using the age-graded tables is to calculate your percentage at one distance to set your goal at a different distance. In other words, a good % rating at 8K can be very motivational for setting a projected marathon result. Here are some examples.

- In early March I ran 17:40 in a 5 K, which is age-graded at 92:33%. On March 28th I ran 1:21:37 (90.65%) on a fairly tough half marathon course.

- A week prior to the Newport Marathon I ran 29:48 (89.61%) on a hilly 8 K. This indicated a good fitness level and proved very motivational for that (93.07%) marathon.
- Two weeks prior to the Victoria marathon I ran 37:30 (90.88%) in a 10 K, so again I was very comfortable with my fitness level and ran at a 94.26% age-graded effort.

Striving to set race age-group records, or regional, and even national age-group records can provide that extra lift as well. In all sports, setting new performance records at any level establishes new motivation for other athletes. This holds particularly true for those of us mature runners where most of our existing records were set with a somewhat limited number of competitors. These records should fall quickly now. More and more of the really good runners are finding the time and enjoyment to continue running and are entering new age groups. The existing records set new challenges and are there to be bettered. The pride of establishing any new mark will also bring the personal reward of not only motivating others to meet that goal, but also being able to enjoy seeing it surpassed.

The Plan

These days I basically plan to run 10 miles one day then 15 the next. If I don't feel like doing the 15 miles I just don't do the full 15 and if I don't feel like running at all some days then I don't. Of course I do have to put in some twenty and twenty-five milers now and then. I'm pretty good at telling when I'm just lazy and when I'm really worn out so I get out early when I'm looking for an excuse on a lazy day.

Are those distances in some way magical? Only to me. This is what I do in context of who I am, how I got here and what I still want to accomplish. Each individual has to find a balance that fits with his or her own plans and goals.

My training now has few if any track workouts. My daily runs are often on trails one day and on the road the next. I have a one-mile section marked out on my trail run for the times I feel the need to run a mile fast. I don't take a watch so I only measure how I did by how I feel. Basically, I use races for speed work now. I stopped doing any two-a-day running about five years ago.

For the nine-month period leading up to the 2004 Victoria marathon I ran 3,053 miles, not because it was specifically ordained as necessary for that race, but because it is consistent with the pattern of what I do, and have done for years. That works out to a daily average of 11.14 miles, 12.6 miles per run day when you subtract the 32 rest days. Over those 274 days I took 32 days off. Therefore my average run during that period was 12.6 miles. Ninety of those days I ran 10 miles, fifty-five days I ran 15 miles, and thirty-two days I ran 7 miles. In addition, I would add in longer runs, up to 25 miles, and raced approximately every 15 days at various distances.

It may be of interest to note that, other than when racing, almost the entire running program regardless of the distance was at an eight to nine minute mile pace. For comparison and to put my training pace in context, my race pace for the 2004 Victoria marathon was 6:22 per mile.

My 2004 plan consisted of a list of relatively simple rules.

These Are The Rules That Made Up The 2004 Running Plan

Keep it simple.
Run lots.

Run 10 miles one day.
Run 15 the next.
Add some long runs.

The Two main Principles of the Plan are –
Keep it <u>Healthy.</u>
Keep it <u>Fun.</u>

<u>Health Rules</u>

Eat well.
Eat a big breakfast every day no matter what time of day it is.
Sleep long. The earlier to bed the better.
Burn the TV schedule.
Running injuries are not allowed (falling down injuries will happen).
Most runs are easy – some runs are tougher.
The plan is the plan – the actual doing is very different.
The plan has holes in it – Days Off!
The days off are not predictable.
There is no make-up for days off.
If today is not the day, don't do all of it or any of it.
10 miles is sometimes 7 miles and occasionally 12 miles.
15 miles is sometimes 10 miles and occasionally 20 miles.
Realize the difference between tired (ok) and lazy (not ok).
No hard runs on tired days.
Training is practice – practice is never full speed.
The watch only goes to races.
Race at least once every month.
Stretching is what sprinters do – distance runners do warm-ups.

<u>Fun Rules</u>

Regardless of the results every day is a successful day.
Enjoying the daily run is as important as the overall results.

Training has at least six different running routes on roads.
Training has some trail routes.
Running can't use up the best part of the day.
It's convenient to miss the race awards but do attend some.
Go to races you are not running in.
Volunteer at some events.
Fill your life with much more than running.
The family has veto right to any part of the plan any day.
At age 64 memory starts to fail – the first thing to forget is your age.

The marathon is the hardest race of all distances to run well. It has some additional rules.

Don't train specifically for a marathon.
Stay the course – no big changes to the plan.
Continue to race all distances.
Inject more long runs.
Ignore the time of long runs.
The only important rule of long training runs is to run the last 5 miles well.
The legs should be sore after the long run but fine the next day.
Get excited about the marathon you plan to run – fall in love with it.
The legs can't do what the mind can't do.
Don't plan to run every marathon faster than the last one.
Never pay attention to another marathoner's plan.
Don't even listen to another marathoner's race day strategy.
Marathons are not run in temperatures over 70 degrees.
Plus 70-degree marathons are always converted to fun runs.
Three marathons a year is one too many.

Note:

This was my plan.
It's not a recommended plan.
It works for me. It won't necessarily work for anyone else.
It definitely won't work for the inexperienced or elite athlete.

THANK YOU TO MY FELLOW COMPETITORS.

You have kept me going. Without you being there I would never have run my best. No matter what pace I ran, I have always enjoyed competing with you. Without your competition, there can be little fun. Over the years I have found that I cannot race well without picking up the synergy of the other athletes in the race. I will certainly count on your competition to enable me to carry on.

Jack Miller

Jack Miller is a runner, coach, and educator. He has been a competitive runner since 1975 with PRs of 2:31 for the marathon, 1:12 for the half marathon, 54:27 for 10 miles, 32:47 for 10 km 15:52 for 5 km, and 4:33 for the mile. The 10 km and mile times were both recorded as a masters runner. Jack has run a total of 54 marathons since his first one in 1977, and all of them have been sub-3 hours. Personal worsts were 2:59 in Athens, Greece [The Original Run] and 2:57 in the Big Sur Marathon. Having recently had his 60th birthday, Jack was first in the 60-64 category at the 2005 Flora London Marathon in a time of 2:55.

One of Jack's "most memorable moments" in running occurred in 1988 (age 43) when he beat the legendary Bill Rogers (age 40) in the Johnny Miles Half Marathon in New Glasgow, Nova Scotia. Not to diminish the accomplishment, but Jack was in peak form (1:13:01), while it was obvious that Bill had an off-day (1:13:26).

Jack has been a track, cross-country, and distance coach and mentor for recreational athletes, young elite athletes, university runners, as well as national and international calibre runners in the Canadian Armed Forces. Jack recently completed his Education Doctorate (Ed.D.) at the University of British Columbia and is currently a faculty member in the School of Education at Thompson Rivers University in Kamloops, B.C. where he hopes to be coaching the cross-country running team in future years.

The Competitive 50+ Runner:
Setting Goals, Training, and Racing

Jack Miller

INTRODUCTION

Being a competitive runner is not something that is simply based on one's winning accomplishments or records, although having a few of the latter certainly helps. Rather it is a state of mind on the part of the athlete that is then reflected in the way others view the individual.

A case in point is the routine or ritual that most competitive runners practice in the final minutes before a race. For these athletes, this is a time for physical preparation for an event, a time for introspection, and a time for focused mental preparation. This is the time to put on the "race face", shut out the rest of the world and focus on achieving just the right level of pre-race "activation". This type of competitive runner is very much focused on his or her pre-race preparation, has well-established goals for that race, and is usually aware of whether or not (age-group) rivals are also entered in the race.

Other individuals, who may not overtly exhibit this very focused approach to racing would rather let their performances speak for them. Such individuals, at least on the surface, are very self-effacing, quiet about their accomplishments, and usually appear to take a much more "casual" approach to racing and competition. It is not that such individuals wish to lull their competitors into a false sense of superiority prior to competing, it is just that they don't outwardly exhibit the intensity and focus that others do. Instead, it is fellow competitors, who are aware of the performance levels of these people and what they are capable of in any given race, who contribute to others' perception of those athletes as "elite".

Of course, there are other athletes who do not fit neatly into either of these two "categories", who could be considered to be elite based on the way they approach competitions and by the results they achieve. A case could be made for this "model" to describe a competitive runner as a continuum rather than a dichotomy. Some of my fellow contributors to this book certainly fall within the parameters of this continuum.

The Competitive Personality

As someone who has been a competitive runner for some 30 years, it is my opinion that the "competitive personality" endures with age. Any runner who has enjoyed the success of winning a race, winning an age category award, or setting a course, provincial, or national record, can attest to a feeling of accomplishment. Add to that a sense that all the training behind that achievement was worth the effort. The more success one achieves, the greater the reinforcement of the feeling that you are capable of a level of performance that will result in either a winning effort, an age category placement, or a personal best for that distance. The more this occurs, the greater the assurance that you are capable of being competitive in any given race.

Age notwithstanding, the competitive "edge" or desire to win does not die easily. Of course with advancing age, one does slow down, but to the competitive runner, this is a matter of degree or perception. Sure, your clock times are slower and your finishing place overall in the race diminishes. Even so, the desire to compete against others in your age category often remains as strong as ever. In a way, the desire to win can be replaced by the desire to do better. Witness Herb Phillips, who at age 63 and then again at age 64 lowered the existing Canadian record in the marathon twice in the span of 4 months to 2:47:32, and then 2:47:02. Why did he wait until he was that advanced in the 60-64 age category? Who knows, but it was likely his desire to continue to strive to be the best he could be in a given race, knowing that if one trains hard enough and smart enough, that eventually training, absence of injury, and good race conditions will all come together on a given day. Likewise, many of Ed Whitlock's age group records (in 2004 at age 73, he ran 2:54:45 for the marathon) have been set well past the younger end of the category, adding credence to the hypothesis that even as one ages, the desire to compete, the desire to win, and the desire to do better, "sticks" with you. And, as anyone can see, people like Ed Whitlock and Herb Phillips are not just hanging in and outlasting the competition, they are recording stellar results.

The Importance of Training

Juma Ikanga (noted Tanzanian runner, who won the 1989 New York City Marathon in 2:08:01) is quoted as saying "The will to win means nothing without the will to prepare." His message, I believe, is that no matter how hard you will yourself to win in a race, it will not happen unless you put the supreme effort into your training and race preparation. As a coach, I have frequently told my athletes that if you pay attention to your training, train hard when it is required, and prepare for a competition, the race can be much more enjoyable than if you are ill-prepared on race day and attempt to win by absolutely thrashing yourself. Sooner rather than later, such methods will catch up with you. It will only take one or two races of trying to "will" yourself to win without sufficient training and race preparation for you to realize the benefit of proper training and the wisdom of Ikanga's words.

Effort-based Training and Racing

As "younger" elite athletes, many of us have utilized methods of training such as intervals, hill repeats, tempo runs, cruise intervals, fartlek, etc. In fact, many older runners still use one or more of these methods as part of their pre-race training preparation. Of course, with advancing age comes a decrease in ability to post the same times for 400 metres, that 300 metre hill, or tempo runs of 20 to 30 minutes at sub-6:00/mile pace. What does not change, however, is the perceived effort required to engage in those types of training on a regular basis. In other words, even for aging athletes who still consider themselves to be able to perform at an elite level, it still "feels" that just as much effort is required to maintain what used to be a more leisurely pace. This has important implications for training and racing. Runners who have begun to see steady declines in their race performance need to adjust their thinking to be satisfied with results that are less related to absolute time and more closely related to age-based performance standards. Not that time isn't important, it just shouldn't be the only gauge with which to measure your race performance. In addition, planning and following training routines that involve quality training sessions on a regular basis ought to be guided by principles of perceived effort (on the part of the runner) as much as by the actual time it takes to complete an interval, a hill repeat, or a given fartleck component. By judging the quality of a workout based on perceived effort rather than actual time, aging athletes will be combatting the aging process. At the same, they will also be developing a more realistic approach to training, enhanced recovery from training, and more realistic racing expectations.

The Purpose of Training

In recent years, running coaches who work with a variety of athletes from novice to elite, have developed training programs that begin with "training to run", progress to "training to compete", and for the most advanced athletes, "training to win".

The "training to run" level of training has as its focus an introduction to training and running. It emphasizes learning about the various types of training, focuses on making the training fun and enjoyable, and de-emphasizes the competitive nature of the sport. This approach also has as an aim that through regular progressive training, athletes will gradually improve their ability to run and race. The emphasis is on slow and gradual improvement under non-threatening conditions, with a gradual and fun-based approach to competition.

"Training to compete" takes the approach to training and racing up a notch. The mind-set that the coach is trying to get the athlete to adopt is one that is much more focused on being competitive in races, while at the same time trying to de-emphasize the necessity of winning. The focus is on establishing personal best times for various events and improving results in a variety of ways (best result on this course, finishing within 1 or 2 places of another athlete known to perform well at that distance, etc.) and beginning to focus on top-three finishes in age category competition. For the senior runner, the major shift in emphasis is to progress from running to just finishing in the top half of the age category to competing for medals. For some runners this can require a huge shift in thinking and a significant change in the way they approach their daily training. Some of what follows may help in achieving such a goal.

Finally, "training to win" is the approach taken by the majority of elite runners, young and old. The main purpose for the training is to win. Although most older runners don't usually think of winning a race outright, it does occasionally happen. Sometimes, maybe not often, the conditions are just right and suddenly you find yourself in the front of the pack, wondering if you will have enough stamina to last but having the time of your life nonetheless! However, training to win for elite older runners usually involves competing as a top masters runner, being satisfied with finishing as the top over-50 runner and winning your age category. Once again, moving up a notch on the training scale involves a shift in thinking and a subsequent increase in training variety, volume and intensity. It means that better planning is required for training. All of the associated methods of training such as getting professional advice or coaching, regular massage, weight training, plyometrics, and mental preparation become part of the elite athlete's program. These enhancements are all necessary when winning is added to the list of goals.

For the older runner – the aim in all three of these approaches, but most particularly "training to compete" and "training to win", is to try to retard the slide down the slippery slope of declining times and discouraging race results. In other words, for the older elite athlete, these two training methods are designed to slow down the process of slowing down.

SETTING GOALS

One of the most important activities that a competitive runner should regularly engage in is goal setting. This is particularly important for those athletes who are self-coached. At least two to three times a year you should look ahead, pause to review, refine, and otherwise modify your training and racing goals. If you don't, you will be in danger of entering races that you are not prepared for, either physically or mentally. For the elite athlete, paying close attention to goal setting is very important. It is only by setting racing-related time and performance goals that competitive runners can determine if their training and racing strategies are appropriate. Setting goals involves setting long-term goals, setting short-term goals, and setting realistic goals.

Long-Term Goals

Ultimate long-term goals might involve the rest of your life. Shortly after turning 45, I decided that my (very) long-term goals would include being the best Canadian at the marathon distance in my 50's, being the best in North America in my 60's, being the best in the world in my 70's, and still running marathons when I am 90. These might seem like lofty and unrealistic goals to some, but it keeps me looking forward, eager to get to that next age category, and serves as a template for my shorter-term goals. At a minimum, long-term goals should be at least three and preferably five years. I say five years because that fits nicely into the master's age categories and provides a sufficient length of time to cover the full spectrum of race lengths and types if that is part of your training plan. It also provides an ideal "window" within which to plan for and set goals in that particular age category – from entry into the category, to mid-range, to preparing to exit one category and enter another.

Short-Term Goals

Short-term goals will usually be set for a period of from six months to one year. Of course these shorter-term goals are based on your long-range goals, and will be more specific and in greater detail. Short-term goal setting will likely include specific weekly, monthly, and seasonal training details. It should include these elements, particularly if you are fortunate enough to have a certified and knowledgeable coach who can work with you to include periodization as a component of your approach to training. (*Periodization* involves a detailed one-year plan that specifies the volume, intensity, and duration of training over a full 52 week period, including details on race dates, the specifics of "quality" training sessions, mental training, as well as rest and rehabilitation, all of which are integral parts of a detailed training plan.) Even for the majority of us who are self-coached, it is important to plan appropriately in order to meet your racing goals. (For the athletes I coach and for the students I teach at university, I advocate the 8 "P" approach – **P**rior **P**lanning and **P**roper **P**reparation **P**revents **P**iss-**P**oor **P**erformance!) By using the periodization approach to training and racing, it becomes much easier to adhere to your day-to-day training requirements if you know your plan includes a well thought-out approach that includes the right amount of training, rest, taper, and mental preparation leading up to all of your planned races. It also helps to compartmentalize your approach to training for a variety of different race distances or types over the 52-week period.

I would like to emphasize the importance of adding variety to your racing goals - something you should consider in setting your long-term goals. If you have developed at least a mental long-range plan for racing, it is wise to include in that plan the type(s) of races and race distance(s) you will focus on in any given year of the plan. For example, the first year you might train for a marathon in the spring and then shift gears and focus on cross-country running in the fall; the following year you may adjust your training to focus on a few fast 10 k races in the spring and then run a marathon in the fall; then you may do a half marathon the following spring, some track races in the summer, and then a marathon in the fall; and in the final year of this plan you may choose to race for the first eight months of the year and then take three or four months at a significantly reduced volume and intensity of training in order to be "fresh" when you enter the next age group.

Realistic Goals

Goals must be realistic; that is, attainable. Setting goals that are way beyond the capability indicated by recent training, is to set yourself up for failure. There is nothing more disappointing than setting a goal that is obviously out of reach and then running an excellent race, only to fall short of an expectation that was unrealistic. It may well be that you would have been capable of achieving that goal on a given day, but the weather conditions, your recent injury, or the unknown difficulty of the course may have mitigated against achieving your goal for that race. This also underlines the necessity of adjusting your goals to meet conditions on race day. This does not mean "softening" your goals just to make yourself feel good because you don't really feel like "going for it" on race day, but rather making realistic adjustments based on day-of-race conditions that differ from those on which you based your original goals. Weather is an important consideration here – an element over which you have no control – and to ignore wind and/or temperature conditions is to jeopardize your chances of achieving intelligently adjusted goals. Additionally, setting conservative, realistic goals will also give you an opportunity to achieve your pre-race goals without an unnecessarily high risk of injury.

"BIG-PICTURE" PLANNING

Once you have set (or adjusted) your long-term and annual goals, it is time to do some "big picture" planning. For example, if your goals include running a sub-40:00 10 K in the spring, racing in two or three short races (such as a 5 K and a 1500 m track race in the summer), and then running a sub -1:30 half marathon in the fall, you will have to first engage in the appropriate planning that will help you to focus on the finer details of training later on. In order to develop these plans, you might ask yourself the following questions:

- How many weeks lead-up to each of the races should I plan for?
- What length and type of taper should I plan for before each of the races?
- How much and what type of rest should I take after each race?
- What components of "quality" training should I use to prepare for each race?
  - tempo runs
  - hills
  - cruise intervals
  - track intervals
  - fartleck
- Should I try to do some of my training with a partner or club?
- Should I have regular massage and if so, how often?
- Should I do any cross-training, and if so, what activities?
- Should my diet and/or food intake change when I shift training for the next type of race I plan to run?

Training

I have already mentioned that periodization of training is advisable for all competitive runners. Not only does it force you to plan for a year of training and competition, but once the plan is completed, it gives the runner a good visual representation of the overall annual plan. If the plan is developed properly, with one glance runners can see what phase of training they are currently working on, how many weeks remain until the race, when the pre-race taper begins, and what other training and race-related activities to expect. Each part of the periodized plan leading up to a race will involve different training strategies, differing amounts of "quality" training, and various other considerations relating to a specific race. I have selected four race distances as examples of the various aspects of planning that must be addressed in developing your training plans.

a. *Marathon* – the main emphasis in planning to race a marathon is inclusion of sufficient preparation time. I would recommend at least 18 to 20 weeks lead-up to race day. This might typically involve 8 to 10 weeks of distance build-up, including a weekly long run that is two to three times the distance of your other daily runs and a minimal amount of "quality" training (possibly some easy tempo runs or fartleck once a week). This initial stage would be followed by 3 to 4 weeks of a mix of medium tempo runs and hills workouts twice each week; 3 to 4 weeks of a variety of interval sessions twice weekly (an equal balance of track intervals and "cruise" interval on the road is advisable); and the program will finish with 2 to 3 weeks of gradual taper before the race.

b. *Half-marathon* – planning for a half-marathon is similar to planning for a full marathon. The major difference is a reduction in the overall volume of training. The lead-up to the race can usually be done in about 10 to 12 weeks (depending on the runner's base fitness level). The weekly long run need only be from 18 – 22 kms unless a longer race is planned in the few months after the half-marathon. Because the race is shorter in distance, speed and strength will play more important roles and therefore more attention should be paid to the "quality" training in the last 6 to 8 weeks prior to the race. The pre-race taper can usually be a bit shorter (10 days to 2 weeks) than for the marathon and should involve short sessions of race-pace speed work at least two to three times during the taper.

c. *5 K to 10 K* – planning for races in the 5 K to 10 K range requires emphasis on speed rather than distance and stamina. However, if the race is an important race, the lead-up should be about the same as for the half-marathon (i.e. 10-12 weeks). This will allow sufficient time to include 4 to 6 weeks in which "speed work" is a training focus twice each week. Speed work for this racing distance should be short, fast intervals with minimal rest which can be done on a track or on measured distances on the road. "Ladder" or "waterfall" intervals can add variety. The taper for these short road races should involve a week in which the volume of training is substantially reduced and three or four consecutive days in which leg speed or turnover rate is emphasised, with significant recovery period between these short, intense intervals. For example, if preparing for a Sunday race, try the following:

Day	Warm-up	Intervals	Recovery
Monday	15-20 Min. jog	4 x 400M slightly faster than race pace	3-4 minutes between each 400M
Tuesday	Same	3 x 400M	Same
Wednesday	Same	2 x 400M	Same
Thursday	Same	1 x 400M	N/A
Friday	Easy 20 minute run	None	N/A
Saturday	Day Off	None	N/A
Sunday	30 minutes	Race	

By doing this workout the week prior to the race, you are "training" your neuro-muscular system to become accustomed to the race-pace you want to run, while providing enough recovery between intervals to minimize the chance of excess fatigue. If your training leading up to the race taper has been done well, you should feel like you are "floating" through these workouts!

d.   **Track** – planning for track races is substantially different from training for any of the road races already discussed. Here, the principle of *Specificity of Practice* really has meaning. If you are going to race on the track, you must train on the track. Races of 1500 m to 5000 m on the track are fairly common for masters runners and proper preparation is essential if this is your desired mode of competition. Training for track racing is comparable to training for 5 K to 10 K races. The main differences are that more speed is usually required (particularly for 1500 m) and you must be comfortable running on the track. In the final 6 weeks leading up to the race, plan on training on the track at least twice a week and plan on running fast during those workouts. Racing on the track is usually more congested than on the road and therefore it would be to your advantage to do at least some of the training with a small group of runners of about the same capability so that you experience running the corners surrounded by other runners. This style of training will better mentally prepare you for this much tougher style of racing.

Racing

The number and type of races that you enter in a given period of time should depend on the goals and annual plans you have made for yourself. Since your periodized training should set which races you will compete in over the 12 month period as well as the rest and recovery that should occur between races, you should not be tempted to do too much "spontaneous" racing. That is, entering a race on a whim at the last moment. Too much racing can be detrimental to your overall racing performance, just as too little racing may leave you unprepared for the rigors of top competition. If your annual training and racing plan is well conceived, the appropriate ratio (for you) of training, to taper, to racing, to rest and recovery, will allow you to reach appropriate peaks for the most important races of the year.

Injury Management

Without doubt, one of the biggest obstacles to top-level performance for the over-50 runner is injury. As we age, we seem to become more susceptible to injury. The injuries are often more serious, and it seems to take much longer to recover than it did when we were younger. Injuries can result from falls or other dangers encountered on the run; they can result from other activities that you regularly engage in; they can result from over-training; or, (and this may be the most common type of 50+ injury), from a gradual degeneration or wearing out of connective tissue or joints. As runners, we know that this is bound to happen for most of us and through a preventative approach to training and racing, we can hopefully minimize these effects.

Injury prevention as a key approach to training and racing is not new to most of us, but deserves emphasis. One of the most important injury prevention measures, particularly in a build-up to a half-marathon or marathon, is gradual increases in mileage. There is nothing that can bring injury on more quickly than dramatic increases in volume. The commonly accepted maximum increase in weekly mileage is approximately 10% over previous distance. If you are currently training for a marathon and putting in 90 – 100 kilometres per week, your total weekly increase should not be more than about 10 kilometres. This same principle applies to the weekly long run common to marathon and half-marathon preparation. Increases should not exceed approximately 10% of the distance you normally run. For example, if you are currently doing 20 miles for your long run, you should add 2 miles to that distance, and 22 miles would be a reasonable increased distance.

Another important injury prevention strategy is to use the hard/easy training principle. A "hard" training session (this could be an interval session, a tempo run, a hill workout, a fartlek session, or a long run) should always be followed by an easy run – a run that is not necessarily shorter than the previous day, but certainly a run that does not involve a great deal of effort or strain on your body. As a 50+ runner, you should consider taking two days of easy running following a quality workout. Typically, if I do a long run on Sunday, I do an easy run on Monday, a "quality" workout on Tuesday, easier days on Wednesday and Thursday, another "quality" day on Friday, a very easy day or a day off on Saturday, before returning to the long run on Sunday. Of course, the options are endless, but it is very important not to neglect the easy training days following the tougher workouts.

Active rest and recovery is another important aspect of injury prevention. Rest and recovery is particularly important following very strenuous workouts or races. Racing puts enormous stresses on your body and system – the adrenalin rush associated with competing allows us to push beyond what we would normally be able to achieve. This "over-achievement" takes a toll on muscles, joints, and connective tissue. Before returning to active training, your body needs a good period of rest in order to rejuvenate. Coming back too soon after a race invites injury. The generally accepted "rule of thumb" associated with the return to training following racing is one day of "rest" for each mile that has been raced. For example, if you have just completed a 10 K race, take 6 to 7 days of rest. This "rest" period does not necessarily mean do nothing at all (although you may wish to take a couple of non-running days after a long race). Active rest can mean walking for the first few days after a race, followed by very easy running. There should be no attempts during this one-day-per-mile-of-race recovery period to perform any type of quality training whatsoever. To do so will invite injury. In this relatively short period of time you will not be losing any fitness or racing ability. In fact, just the opposite will occur – if you take sufficient rest during this period, your performances are much more likely to return to "normal" or even better than if you attempt to return too quickly to regular training.

The common cold is another type of "injury" that runners often succumb to. Colds and other such viral infections affect the body's immune system and should be treated with care. It is not advisable to "run through" a cold or flu at your normal rate of training. Your body is in a weakened state and is very susceptible to further injury at this point. It is advisable to insert three to four days of very easy running into your training schedule in order for your body to recuperate from the added stress of the virus. In the end, you will come out of a cold stronger, if you pay attention to the appropriate amount of rest that your body requires.

If, in spite of diligent use of the preventative measures stated above, you still manage to develop a soft tissue, connective tissue, or joint injury (the most common running injuries), the use of an ice pack and tensor bandage is by far the cheapest and most reliable (in my experience) method to control the injury and enhance your return to active training. Immediately upon sustaining the injury, icing 2 to 3 times each day for 10 minutes at a time is best. After about 48 to 72 hours alternating cold and hot applications can be used. For approximately two to three weeks after the injury occurs, I would also advise icing after each training session. I also advocate preventative icing following strenuous workouts for extended periods following serious injury.

I have known many runners who have developed an innocuous soft tissue injury such as a slight muscle pull or a "stiff neck" developed from a variety of causes. They immediately use heat to ease the discomfort. This is absolutely the wrong thing to do! Adding heat to a soft tissue injury immediately after the injury occurs, only inflames the area and worsens the injury. Again, use ice or a cold compress for the first 48 to 72 hours and then alternating cold and hot treatment. Remember, ice FIRST!

Once the injury has been stabilized, I would highly recommend you follow-up with at least one massage session. Even one or two massage sessions will substantially increase the rate of recovery following injury. Massage speeds the expulsion of damaged tissue from the area, increases blood flow, which in turn quickens a return to normal use of the affected area. The added bonus is that it also feels good!

As a final note regarding injury management, remember that self-diagnosis and treatment should be used only for minor injuries and conditions. At no time should you attempt to treat an injury the cause or ultimate effect of which you are unsure about. When there is any doubt about the type of injury you have and how it should be treated, you should be consulting your physician. To do otherwise will jeopardize your recovery and long-term health.

Be SMART

The "SMART" approach to training is one that all runners should take. The acronym SMART stands for a goal setting process that involves setting **S**pecific, **M**easurable, **A**ttainable, **R**ealistic, and **T**ime-sensitive goals. This SMART approach can apply to your approach to work, to running, and to life in general. Another way to see it is that if you look after your automobile by having it maintained regularly (time-sensitive and realistic approaches), if you pay attention to your family financial situation (specific and measurable quantities of money), and if you set (attainable) goals for your retirement years, it makes sense that you would also want to take a SMART approach to training and racing.

So, how can you apply the SMART method to your running and what does this mean? First, a **S**pecific goal is one that you can readily identify as pertaining to some particular aspect of training or racing. For example, "I want to train in order to get fitter" is NOT a specific goal. What is fitter? Fitter for what? You may argue that fitter for you means being able to run a faster 1500 meters. Well, if that is the case, state your goal that way. "My goal is to run 1500 metres on the track in 5:30 within the next year." It is only through setting very specific goals that you will be able to determine whether or not you have attained those goals.

This leads to the next step in setting SMART goals. In order to measure whether or not a goal has been achieved, that goal must be stated in measurable terms. Using our example, there are three measurable aspects to this goal: the distance is 1500 metres, so the race has to be that distance; there is a time goal which will be easily measured by having the race timed and the results published; and there is a specific time period within which the goal is to be achieved. Stating your goals in this way may seem to be an over-statement, but if you truly want to determine whether or not your goal has been achieved, it must be stated in specific and measurable terms.

Next, is this goal attainable? Attainability may have as much to do with "outside" factors as it does with your actual ability to meet the goal. For example, if you live in a relatively remote location that does not have a track, training and preparation may be a problem. If there are no track competitions close to where you live and it is not feasible for you to travel to locations where track races are available, this also mitigates against being able to meet your goal. So setting goals that are attainable involves determining in advance if all of the necessary conditions are right for you to be able to reach those goals.

Similarly, what makes a goal realistic? Well, that is only for you to decide. If you ran 5:35 for 1500 meters last year, but you know you were not in top form, or you were racing with an injury, or there was a 30 k/hr headwind during the race, then setting 5:30 for a goal to be achieved within a certain period of time would be realistic. If, on the other hand, you have never run faster than 7:00 for 1500 meters on the track, you have not raced on the track for the past five years, and you have recently sustained a serious injury that would preclude training at a high level for the next year, that goal, under those conditions, is not a realistic one for you. Of course, in setting realistic goals, you must take into consideration those factors over which you have no control: the weather, course conditions, and other competitors in the field. Setting realistic goals usually means setting goals that take into account all of the possibilities you may encounter along the way. Set your goals based on what you might reasonably expect to achieve, NOT what you hope you might be able to do (in your wildest dreams).

It is important to keep your goals time-sensitive. The setting of specific goals should be embedded in your periodized plan. Setting specific goals too far in the future diminishes their immediacy as well as their importance. By setting a goal that you want to achieve by one year from now, you have put reasonable time constraints on that goal. The goal is close enough in time for you to keep it in mind when planning and carrying out your training, yet it is far enough in the future to give you adequate time to plan, train for and make attempts at the goal. The time-sensitive nature of the goal(s) also involves reasoned responses to the questions "Do I have enough training time available between the date when I set the goal and when I will race?" and "Do I have sufficient time each day to do the training required to enable me to attain this goal?"

THE TRAINING CYCLE

Based on my extensive experience in training, racing, and coaching, there is a definite "training cycle" that I associate with typical distance-training regimes. This cycle involves: development of an aerobic base, strength training in a variety of forms, development of speed and speed endurance, and rest. Integral to this cycle is an understanding of what constitutes "over-training" and the advisability and appropriateness of cross-training. A more detailed discussion of each of these components follows.

Aerobic Base

The aerobic base phase of training is characterized by a gradual build-up of the cumulative distance or time that you run on a weekly or monthly basis. As previously mentioned, a safety guideline is to increase your weekly mileage no more than about 10% of the previous week's distance or time. I mentioned some specifics earlier in the section on training for a range of events, if you want an example. There are various ways that are effective in building up your aerobic base – the trick is to find one that suits your needs. The overall length of building the aerobic base depends on the distance you are preparing to race. If you are a proponent of weight training to augment leg, core, and arm strength, it is best to do this during the aerobic build-up phase of your training. Because building the aerobic base is usually associated with easy running in ever increasing volume, weight training can be accommodated without unduly stressing your body. Weight training three times per week on your shorter and easier days is best.

Strength

There are two main ways to build strength in running. One is by doing runs that incorporate frequent hills or doing hill repeats. In a typical marathon training program, you may wish to follow the aerobic build-up phase with a series of hill repeat workouts. The hills need not be steep and the repeats need not be overly long. I suggest starting with 8 repeats of 1 minute uphill running. Recovery is an easy jog back down to the start point. Running these workouts on dirt or grass surfaces is best, particularly the down-hill recovery. The effort for these hills is not excessive. You should not be totally "bagged" when you reach the turn-around point; moderate exertion is sufficient. The idea is not to train the anaerobic system, but rather to strengthen the quadriceps and calf muscles and work on good running form, including appropriate arm swing.

The other way to develop strength for running is to engage in "bounding" and/or plyometric exercises. (Plyometric exercises consist of two foot jumping up onto and off boxes or steps of varying heights. Professional guidance should be sought from a coach or mentor if you wish to include plyometrics in your training program.) Bounding is best done on a grassy area with a slight upward incline. By exaggerating the running motion and pushing off the ball of the foot, bounding is accomplished by trying to "spring" up the incline, getting as much "air time" as possible. Once you have established a rhythm and feeling for this activity, it will reap benefits in building running strength. During the strength phase of your training, if you wish to continue your weight training, it should be a maintenance program. Twice weekly weight training sessions should be sufficient to maintain a good level of strength.

Speed-endurance

Speed-endurance training and speed training can both be added to your training regime at the same time. Which of the two will be emphasized in your training depends on the length of the race you are preparing for. For longer races such as the marathon and the half-marathon, speed-endurance should be the training focus. There are many ways to develop speed-endurance and I will highlight the ones that I feel provide the most benefit.

Tempo training or pace training is perhaps the most ignored, yet most important of all methods of developing speed-endurance. A "typical" tempo run consists of a 10 to 15 minute warm-up run followed by a certain period of tempo running, finishing with 10 – 15 minutes of easy cool-down running. The speed and duration of the tempo run should be gradually increased over about 4 to 6 weeks, again depending on the distance of the race you are preparing for. Tempo runs should begin at about 20 minutes duration and gradually increase until you can run 40 to 50 minutes at the sustained pace. The pace of the tempo runs should begin at about 10 – 15 seconds per mile slower than 10K race pace for the first run (consistent pace throughout each individual run) and gradually get faster until you can sustain the target race pace for the full tempo run. These runs can be combined with other speed runs during this phase of training and should usually only be done once per week.

Cruise Intervals are another form of speed-endurance training and can be done in an endless variety of creative ways. Typically, a cruise interval workout involves a 15 to 20 minute warm-up run, a long interval run of 8 to 14 minutes, followed by a very short recovery period of 60 to 90 seconds. Usually only three or four intervals are attempted during each session. The intervals can be done using either time or distance, and can be done on a track, on trails, or on the road. The speed of the cruise interval is usually at about aerobic threshold level, but not "all-out", since the recovery period is very short. If you are preparing for a marathon or half-marathon, the speed of the cruise interval is about 15 – 20 seconds per mile slower than your anticipated race pace. Cruise intervals for 5 K or 10 K race preparation are similarly about 15 seconds per mile slower than race pace. These quicker cruise intervals will tend to be a little shorter and have a slightly longer recovery period, but within the ranges noted.

Another form of speed-endurance training is **medium-hard fartlek** workouts that emphasize longer periods of "up-tempo" running during the fartlek, with shorter than usual periods of recovery. The biggest difference between this kind of workout and cruise intervals, is that in doing the fartlek workout, there would usually be much less attention paid to your watch and more emphasis on "feeling the effort" rather than tracking it by distance and time.

The final type of speed-endurance training that I have found particularly effective is combining **mile repeats** with a long run. This type of workout would usually only be done once every 3 or 4 weeks and would begin with a long warm-up run of about 50 – 60 minutes. The warm-up is followed by 5 or 6 mile repeats at your target race pace, with an equal recovery period. So, if you plan to race at 6:30 per mile, run your repeats in 6:30 followed by a one mile easy jog recovery. This type of workout involves some long range planning. In building up to a marathon for example, you would like to try to increase these repeats by 1 mile each time you do the workout until you are able to do 10 repeat miles. Once you have completed the mile repeats, finish off the workout with a 30 - 40 minute cool-down run at an easy pace. As you look at this and add up the miles, you can see the total distance will likely exceed 20 miles, so this is not a workout you would try to accomplish at the beginning of a training program, but is one you could handle as a very effective way to prepare for the demands of a marathon.

Speed

The "need for speed" in racing is obvious. If you want to run a little faster than other competitors or a little faster than you did in the last race, you have to develop the ability to cover the same distance in less time. As with speed-endurance, there are many ways to develop speed in preparing for a race. I will illustrate only a few.

Probably the most well-known and widely used method of increasing your speed is interval training or simply **intervals**. This involves running a measured distance in a pre-determined time, followed by a rest period of easy jogging, walking, or simply waiting until it is time to run fast again. These workouts are usually done in "sets" – that is, a set of 400 m intervals might be 8 or 10 times 400 m, usually at slightly faster than target race pace. Each interval is followed by a period of rest. The length of the rest period (distance or duration) is usually the same as or as little as half the speed portion. As levels of speed and speed-endurance increase, the length of the speed portion can: a) be increased, or b) the time to complete the distance can be reduced, or c) the rest period can be reduced. In this way speed, or the ability to run at a certain pace for a longer period of time, is increased. An alternative to "regular" intervals is a workout called **ladder intervals**. For example, a runner could do

200M/rest/400M/rest/600M/rest/800m/rest/1000M/
rest/800M/rest/600M/rest/400M/rest/200M.

Once again the rest interval is determined by the individual and will depend on fitness levels at the time the interval workout is done. A "rule of thumb" for the rest periods for an experienced runner is half the previously run distance and for a novice runner, the same distance as the previously run interval. Still other alternatives might include doing only an "up" the ladder interval workout, or "down" the ladder workout (the latter are sometimes called waterfall intervals). As you can see, interval workouts can be varied, with as many combinations available as there are runners to run them.

Another type of speed workout that can be done without having access to a 400M track is a high intensity, short duration **fartlek** session. Instead of a free-form, medium intensity workout, an interval-like fartlek session that focuses on 8 to 12 "up-tempo" periods of 30 to 90 seconds followed by 30 to 60 seconds of easy recovery jogging will provide similar results to those of a regular interval session. This workout can be done on trails or on the road instead of a track. Although the distances are not pre-determined, the same benefits will accrue if you know your own pace and the effort required to run at a certain speed.

Speed can also be enhanced by concluding a regular workout with between 6 and 10 "stride outs" or "striders". These striders are usually from 60 to 150 metres in length and are not timed, but rather the emphasis is on good running technique – good arm swing, good posture, and good leg turn-over. The pace is fast, but not "all out". Doing these striders two to three times each week after longer, steady-state runs, helps to remind your neuromuscular system that speed is an important component of training.

Rest

One of the most neglected components of any training program is rest. We tend to think of training as only that part of our preparation for a race that involves running. But without rest, our bodies would not recover properly from the stresses involved in training and eventually would break down. This is particularly true for older runners, whose ability to recuperate after more strenuous workouts is not nearly as efficient as for younger runners. Regular rest is also important as a preventative means of avoiding staleness (see the next section). Rest should be planned for and included in your annual periodization as well as in your weekly and monthly schedules. To not include rest as part of your program invites meltdown and/or injury.

Staleness

Staleness is a condition that most of us have experienced in our running careers, although some may not recognize it. Staleness results from the cumulative effects of continuously training at too high a rate with insufficient rest periods. In a word, staleness is over-training to the point where your body cannot handle the levels of stress it is being subjected to. How can you prevent staleness? Ensure that you have planned and implemented regular periods of rest in your program. This may mean taking an occasional day off, it may mean doing some form of mild cross-training, it may mean doing a week of reduced volume and intensity in your training, or it may mean taking more easy days between quality workout sessions. Whatever you do to reduce the stress that comes from high intensity training must be planned and done regularly. You may ask, "How can I tell if I am over-training? Are there any symptoms that might tell me I could be setting myself up for a "crash?" The answer is yes; however, the signs may be different for each individual. There are three signs that tell me that I might be nearing over-training. The first and most effective predictor is an elevated resting pulse rate. My normal resting pulse is somewhere between 38 and 44, depending on my current level of training. If my resting pulse goes up to 58 or 60, I know that something is happening with my body that is abnormal. Time to back off for a couple of days! If I'm not getting stale, I might be on the verge of catching a cold. The next most accurate predictor is having difficulty getting to sleep or having a sleep in which I toss and turn or wake up three or four times during the night. When I am in a heightened training mode, I usually go to sleep very quickly and sleep straight through for seven or more hours each night. If this is not the case, for me it is a sign that I may be over-training. The third and less certain indicator is, if I walk up a couple of flights of stairs and I am breathing more heavily than normal, I might be heading toward staleness. This is a more subjective judgement of whether or not I might be getting stale. I may have walked up the stairs immediately after a workout or first thing in the morning, I might be a bit tired from a hard workout the day before, but if the condition persists, it is yet another sign that I might be approaching a state of staleness. For you the signs could be different, but body awareness and the will to pay attention, will direct you on this matter. Be sure to listen to your body!

Cross-training

Personally, I have mixed feelings about cross-training. I know that some runners and other athletes swear by it and to some extent I agree with the principle of doing cross-training. I will say that it is a good form of rest from the rigors of training based solely on running. Furthermore, most cross-training activities that runners engage in do have a strong aerobic component and are therefore somewhat beneficial.

The reason that I am not too keen on cross-training, is because of the principle of specificity as it relates to running. If you want to be a better runner, then you have to run. Having said that, I believe that for the competitive or elite runner, a little bit of cross-training can be effective. As a coach I would encourage it during the "off-season" or that portion of your periodization that is non-competitive. Cross-training is also appropriate when you are recovering from an injury. The most effective cross-training activities for runners are water running (not swimming), cycling (either stationary or actual cycling), walking and/or hiking, and soccer. I would always recommend moderation in your cross-training activity; otherwise, you are a soccer player, cyclist, or hiker who runs occasionally rather than a runner who occasionally plays soccer, cycles, or hikes.

MENTAL PREPARATION

Mental preparation has long been the domain of sports psychologists and thought to be only for international calibre and professional athletes. Although to some extent this may be true, many of the principles and methods of mental preparation have practical applications for most competitive runners.

The first aspect of mentally preparing for a race is planning. If you have planned for every aspect of the race, you will be more mentally ready to run the actual race. Planning involves more than training, including a proper taper - all of which prepares you both physically and mentally for a good race. Planning for a race means: ensuring that all of your transportation and accommodation requirements have been attended to if you have to travel some distance to get to the race; having at least looked at a map of the race before getting to the site; knowing if you can drive to the start and/or finish line of the race; knowing where to park and whether or not you have to pay for the parking; knowing whether or not traffic will be blocked off in certain areas and if so, what time the closures will happen; knowing where you will meet someone after the race; preparing your race equipment and clothing well in advance of your travel date (making sure that your favourite racing shorts and singlet are packed, that every conceivable article of clothing suitable for all possible weather on race day are also packed - it is better to have articles of clothing that you don't use than to realize too late that you should have brought those gloves after all); remembering to bring your race number or the confirmation paper that you require to pick up your number; and making sure you have packed all the pre-race and during-race nutrients and fluids you usually use. Doing the pre-planning necessary to ensure you are ready to race when the gun goes off keeps your mind on the race before as well as during, and not on worrying about whether or not you have sufficient quarters to put in the parking meter!

Another part of mental preparation is visualizing the race course. This is rather difficult if you have not run the race before, but if you arrive at the race location the day before and are able to drive at least parts of the course, it can serve the same purpose. If you have run the course before, it helps, during periods of rest and relaxation leading up to the race, to mentally rehearse how you will run the course. Close your eyes and mentally run the race, feeling the differences in terrain, seeing other runners, seeing the finish line and feeling the effortless running you will be doing on race day. In the event that you are not familiar with the course, part of your pre-race preparation on race day should be to run the first mile or so of the course from the start line and then, if possible, run out from the finish line approximately one mile and run back to the line, all the while paying attention to your surroundings so they become familiar to you and so you can key off familiar sights when you are making the final push to the finish. Visualization is designed to familiarize your mind with the race and make you feel relaxed as you await the start of the race.

Another strategy that I use and encourage those I coach to use, is to develop a motto or slogan that describes some affirmative action you can associate with your training and racing and to have one or more mantras to use both in training and in racing. For example, a few years ago I was coaching a few runners who frequently came up with excuses why they couldn't train at certain times or were not able to "fit things into their busy schedule" – as if we didn't all have busy schedules! I suggested they use the phrase, "If that's what it takes". So when they said they would have to get up at 5:00 a.m. to get their run in that day, I simply said, "If that's what it takes"! In fact I have used this same phrase myself as a means to manage having to get up at 4:30 a.m. to do a workout because I otherwise would not have had the opportunity to train. If I have to run 35 K on my treadmill because it is dark outside and there are no street-lights where I live, then I simply say to myself, "If that's what it takes".

I also suggest using certain key words or phrases that describe how you want to run in certain situations. I may say to myself over and over, "run smooth" when I know I have to push to keep the pace in a race without getting into oxygen debt. Or I may say to myself "run strong" when there is a hill in a race and I do not want to lose my racing tempo. These words or phrases may only have meaning for you, but that is fine – using a mantra is for yourself and doesn't have to make sense to anyone else. It serves to keep you focused on the task at hand during training or during a race and most often it serves to bring your focus back, should it begin to wander in a long race.

One of the most important aspects of mental preparation prior to a race is adjusting your pre-race thinking to match race conditions. First of all, I encourage those I coach (and try to convince myself) that it is important to train in all types of weather. It is important to train when it is windy, when it is raining, when it is snowing or when it is very cold, simply to prepare yourself for all possible race conditions. I have run marathons and other races in 50 k/hr winds, in absolutely torrential rain, in very cold and very hot conditions, in fog, and in every other condition imaginable. If you have trained in adverse conditions, it makes racing in those same conditions that much more bearable – not fun, but bearable. And, you will have an advantage over those "fair weather runners" who only train when the conditions are ideal. (Of course some of those people don't even show up for the race when conditions are less than ideal, so you have already beat them before the race starts!) The second important aspect of mental preparation is to adjust your pre-race thinking to match the actual race conditions. If you anticipated ideal conditions, but on race day it is so windy or hot that it will likely affect your ability to run the time that you have planned, make the necessary mental adjustments and shift your goals so that they are realistic given the conditions. If you do not make these adjustments and start the race with expectations that are unrealistic given the conditions, you are highly likely to fail to meet your own goals even though you may turn in an otherwise amazing performance under the circumstances.

RACE PREPARATION

All of what I have suggested up to this point has, in some way or other, been designed to get you to the start line well prepared. There are, however, four points that deserve repeating.

First, you must have done adequate training. If you have planned and prepared well for the race, then give it your best shot – carefully planned and executed training usually results in good racing results. If, however, you have trained well, but not really with the intensity you would have liked or without having put in the distance that you planned to do, don't try to outrace the training you have done. Run conservatively, be patient, and then push in the latter stages of the race if you feel good.

Second, and this also applies to your training in preparation for a particular race, you must apply the principle of specificity to your training. This means ensuring that at least some of your training has to approximate the race pace you expect to run and the conditions that you anticipate will exist on race day; (i.e., don't do all your training on grass and trails if your race is going to be on the roads). As I mentioned before, the majority of your training has to be running and not some aerobic substitute. And, your training must be specific to the distance you are racing – if you are racing a marathon, you must do the long runs, including even the occasional "over-distance" workout as well.

The third point is adequate planning and preparation. I have already mentioned the 8 P's. Need I say more?!

The final point to emphasize in race preparation is to set conservative and attainable goals for each race. Be realistic – review your training and match your race expectations with the training you have done. Also, allow for conditions on race day and if necessary, amend your goals accordingly. If race conditions are poor, back off your predicted results. You will live to race another day!

CONCLUDING REMARKS

I have attempted in these pages to provide you with the essentials of training and race preparation. Most of the information is based on my extensive experience as a competitive runner, coach, and life-long learner. Much of the information is common sense, some of it is based on technical and coaching research, and most of it has been used extensively by competitive and non-competitive runners alike. There is not much here that is new, but sometimes if you describe things in a different way or look at things from a different perspective, it can open up new ways for you to train and race. Now is the time to apply a few of the suggestions and strategies to your current training and look for the resulting improvement in your race performance.

Bart Yasso

Runner's World columnist, Bart Yasso picks the best races to run around the country every month.

Bart has competed in over 150 marathons around the world from the Boston marathon, New York City marathon, Antarctica marathon to the Mount Kilimanjaro marathon. He won the 1998 Smoky Mountain Marathon.

He has completed the Badwater 146 miler through Death Valley. Badwater is considered the toughest run in the United States. The run is held in July, starts at the lowest point in the U.S. and finishes on the top of Mt. Whitney, the highest point (14,496 ft.) in the 48 states. The race is run in temperatures of 125°F and more.

Over the past 25 years, Bart has competed in over 1,000 running and multi-sport events including triathlons, biathlons and eco challenges. In 1987 Bart was crowned the U. S. national biathlon long course champion. The championship race was held in New York City. He has completed the Ironman five times.

He completed two solo unsupported bicycle rides across the U.S. in 20 days, averaging 155 miles per day.

Bart is the inventor of the Yasso 800s, an amazingly simple and effective technique for marathon training.

Bart notes that: The Surgeon General has declared that it's OK to smoke the competition.

How to be a Faster Master:
The Perfect 10 or the Bo Derek of Running

Bart Yasso

Recovery is the most important part of a training program. Runners try to accomplish everything in a calendar week. As a masters runner you need to allow more time for recovery. Getting in your quality workouts with subsequent easy days and rest days usually cannot be accomplished in a seven-day cycle. And why should it? Clinical studies have shown that because running utilizes the same motions over and over, excessive workout intensity and duration does not allow for proper physiological adaptation. Muscles and tendons fatigue easily and as a result, overuse injuries occur. Failure to allow for easy days and rest days between quality workouts is the most common training mistake. As masters runners we must use our knowledge to keep up with the younger generation.

The Perfect 10 program I designed has more emphasis on rest and recovery, so the quality workouts become more beneficial. If you follow a 10-day cycle instead of a seven-day cycle, not only will you run faster, but chances are you will also stay injury-free, even at more advanced ages.

Has the Seven-Day Week Cycle Ever Been Interrupted?

There is no record of the seven-day cycle ever having been broken. Calendar changes and reform have never interrupted the seven-day cycles. It's very likely that the week cycles have run uninterrupted at least since the days of Moses (c. 1400 B.C.), possibly even longer.

It's time for a change!

I have a dream job at *Runner's World* magazine; the only tough part of my job is dealing with injured runners. I hate to see someone train six months for a race and then get injured in the training phase. The most common injuries runners encounter are from overuse. I always hear runners say they got injured on one of their tempo workouts, speed sessions, or long runs, but more often it is really the accumulation of stress, not some specific activity. If you can master the Perfect 10 technique, you will avoid injuries by resting more and going easier on the easy days to recover fully for the quality days. One of the many lessons I learned from several trips to East Africa is that the Kenyans go very easy on their easy days and very fast on their quality days. Make sure you go easy on the easy days, and you will notice the strength you have on the quality days. The easy days can be anywhere from five to eight miles depending on how you feel. The pace on your easy days should be at a conversation pace or approximately two minutes per mile slower than your 10 K race pace.

Rest days and easy days can be interchangeable to be more flexible with the program that follows. However, the quality days should stay where they are.

CROSS-TRAINING: Cross-training will strengthen the heart and the muscles you don't use in running. It will enhance your fitness level, build muscle, reduce body fat, and aid in flexibility. Flexibility is something we need as masters runners. Cross-training should involve sustained aerobic activity like cycling, or an elliptical trainer; rest day cross-training should be no-impact activity like stretching, yoga, pool running, weight training, or swimming.

HILL REPEATS: Find a hill that will take you at least two minutes to climb, and mark off a "short" repeat (about halfway from the bottom) and a "long" repeat (all the way to the top). Do a set of "short" hills: three or four sprints up the short repeat, then a jog back down. Then do a set of "long" hills: three or four loops of a hard run to the top, a jog back to the top of the "short" segment and a sprint to the bottom; then another three or four "short" hills. Adjust the repeats depending on the miles you need. You should be doing two miles of warm-up and cool-down before and after the hills, so the workout should involve three or four miles of work.

The downhill sprints in the long sets are nearly as important as the uphill parts. Try to run smoothly, without slapping your feet.

MPW: The marathon-pace workout, or MPW as I call it, should be a 15-minute warm-up at easy pace, then 30 to 60 minutes at marathon pace. Followed by a 15-minute cool-down. Make sure you pick a course that can best simulate the course you will be racing.

HMPW: Half-marathon-pace workout is the same as the marathon-pace workout only done at half-marathon pace.

LONG RUNS: LSD with a twist: that's "long slow distance". LSD runs are purely for the purpose of endurance. LSD is the cornerstone of endurance. It increases your aerobic fitness, teaches your body to run efficiently, and helps you build mental discipline. It will give you the endurance to tackle the tempo and speed workouts, and also to recover from them quickly. Long-run pace should be a minute to a minute and a half slower than marathon pace. Try long runs with this twist: running the last three to four miles of your long run at either marathon or half-marathon pace. The horse smells the barn type of ending to your long run. This will enable you to develop a "negative split" mentality, running the second half of your race slightly faster than the first half.

SPEEDWORK: Speedwork will condition your body to run fast on demand. You can do the speed workout on the track or on a road; just make sure the course is accurately measured. Make sure you warm-up two miles and cool-down two miles very easy. Always jog half the interval distance for recovery.

Classic workouts are mile repeats. It's pretty simple: Run a mile at your 10 K pace, jog a half mile for recovery, and repeat three times.

Yasso 800s are the rage for marathon runners. (Amby Burfoot, the winner of the 1968 Boston Marathon, named the workout after me.) If you want to run a 3:30 marathon, then train to run a bunch of 800 meters in 3:30 each. Between the 800s, jog 400 meters. Training doesn't get any simpler than this, not on this planet or anywhere else in the solar system. Begin running Yasso 800s a couple of months before your goal marathon. The first week, start with four or five. On each subsequent week, add one more until you reach 10. The last workout of Yasso 800s should be completed at least 17 days before your marathon.

Use 400 meter repeats to keep up some of that leg speed. Twelve times 400 with a 200 recovery is always a great workout.

TEMPO RUNS: For 5 K and 10 K races, warmup 15 minutes, run 20 to 30 minutes at half-marathon pace, then cooldown 15 minutes. The tempo runs can be done on trails or a grass surface.

AND SOME OTHER THINGS: Run as many miles as you can on soft surfaces. I recommend that 70 percent of your running is done on a cinder, hard-packed, or trail surface.

To run comfortably, remember one word: breathable. Wearing breathable fabrics allows perspiration to evaporate from your skin. This cools you off in the heat and keeps you dry. Cotton, as natural and desirable as it may be, is just about the worst fabric you can wear. In the warmer weather, it soaks up sweat and sticks to your skin, and its rough fibers may chafe you. So as you train, wear a lightweight, breathable shirt and shorts made from high-tech fabrics. They're available at running stores everywhere. Microfibers cost more than cotton, but you get a big payoff every time you go for a run. Also, select breathable socks that work well with your shoes, and check to make sure there are no seams in the toe area that might cause you trouble. If, for some reason, a piece of apparel chafes your skin, apply a lubricating product before you run, such as petroleum jelly, Runner's Lube, or BodyGlide. You may need to carry a small tube with you on longer runs.

And last but not least, don't forget sunscreen. The effects of sunlight on the skin have to be taken seriously. Overexposure to the sun causes wrinkles, precancerous growths, and malignant melanoma.

If you run marathons, don't always train as a marathoner. Don't be afraid to mix things up a little. For instance, you can do lower mileage and faster pace on timed and tempo runs.

THE PERFECT 10 (5-K and 10-K)

Day	Cycle One
One	Tempo, HMPW, 15-minute warm-up, 20 minutes at half marathon pace, 15-minute cool-down
Two	Rest or Cross-train
Three	4 miles easy
Four	Track workout – 6 Yasso 800s
Five	Cross-train
Six	3 miles easy
Seven	5 miles easy
Eight	Long run - 5-7 miles LSD
Nine	Rest day
Ten	5 miles easy

Day	Cycle Two
One	Tempo - 15-minute warm-up, 25 minutes half-marathon pace
Two	Rest or Cross-train
Three	3 miles easy
Four	Track work – 12 x 400
Five	Cross-train
Six	4 miles easy
Seven	5 miles easy
Eight	Long Run - 6-8 miles
Nine	Rest day
Ten	4 miles easy

Day	Cycle Three
One	Tempo – 30 at half-marathon pace
Two	Cross-train
Three	5 miles easy
Four	Track 3 – 1 mile repeats
Five	Cross-train
Six	5 miles easy
Seven	3 miles easy
Eight	Long Run - 8-10 miles
Nine	Rest day
Ten	4 miles easy

Start back at cycle one

THE PERFECT 10 HALF-MARATHON

Day	Cycle One
One	Tempo, HMPW, 15-minute warm-up, 20 minutes at half-marathon pace 15-minute cool-down
Two	Rest or Cross-train
Three	5 miles easy
Four	Track workout – 6 Yasso 800s
Five	Cross-train
Six	5 miles easy
Seven	5 miles easy
Eight	Long Run - 8-10 miles LSD with a twist
Nine	Rest day
Ten	5 miles easy

Day	Cycle Two
One	Tempo - 15-minute warm up, 25 minutes half-marathon pace, 15-minute cool-down
Two	Rest or Cross-train
Three	5 miles easy
Four	Track work – 12 x 400
Five	Cross-train
Six	5 miles easy
Seven	5 miles easy
Eight	Long run - 10 – 12 LSD with a twist
Nine	Rest day
Ten	5 miles easy

Day	Cycle Three
One	Tempo – 15-minute warm up, 35 minutes half-marathon pace
Two	Cross-train
Three	5 miles easy
Four	Track 3 – 1 mile repeats
Five	Cross-train
Six	5 miles easy
Seven	5 miles easy
Eight	Long - 12-15 miles LSD with a twist
Nine	Rest day
Ten	5 miles easy

Start back at cycle one

THE PERFECT 10 MARATHON

Day	Cycle One
One	Tempo, MPW, 15-minute warm-up, 40 minutes at marathon pace, 15-minute cool-down – 8-10 miles
Two	Rest day or Cross-train
Three	6 miles easy
Four	Track - 6 to 10 Yasso 800's
Five	Cross-train
Six	5 miles easy
Seven	8 miles easy
Eight	Long run - 12-15 miles LSD with a twist
Nine	Rest day
Ten	6 miles easy

Day	Cycle Two
One	Tempo, MPW, 15-minute warm up, 50 minutes at marathon pace, 15-minute cool-down 10-12 miles
Two	Rest or Cross-train
Three	6 miles easy
Four	Track - 12 x 400 - 8 miles
Five	Cross-train
Six	6 miles easy
Seven	8 miles easy
Eight	Long run - 15-18 miles LSD with a twist
Nine	Rest day
Ten	8 miles easy

Day	Cycle Three
One	Tempo, MPW, 15-minute warm-up, 30 minutes at marathon pace, 15-minute cool-down, 7- 9 miles
Two	Rest or Cross-train
Three	6 miles easy
Four	Track - 4 x 1 mile — 9 miles
Five	Cross-train
Six	8 miles easy
Seven	6 miles easy
Eight	Long run - 18-20 miles LSD with a twist
Nine	Rest day
Ten	8 miles easy

9 quality workouts and 3 days off

Now that you have adjusted to a 10-day cycle, let's start the 13-month calendar year.

Earl Fee

Earl W. Fee, BASc, MASc, age 76, a coach and world class master runner for 18 years, has 40 world records in track events: 300m hurdles, 400m, 800m, 1500m and mile. After graduation as a mechanical engineer in 1953, he studied nuclear power in England on an Athlone Fellowship for two years. For 34 years he worked as a design engineer supervisor/consultant in the Candu nuclear power industry. After retirement in 1994 he wrote two books on running and fitness: *How to Be a Champion from 9 to 90, Body, Mind, Spirit Training*, self published in 2001, and a colourful 440 page tome titled *The Complete Guide to Running* published by Meyer and Meyer Sports in 2005. He is also a poet and motivational speaker on fitness, longevity, and running.

Aging Slower Than Your Rivals
(Reprinted with Permission)

Earl W. Fee

GENERAL

This chapter applies to *all* masters who desire to keep young and stay injury-free, but particularly to older masters over 65. The material is mainly from one chapter in my books: *How to Be a Champion from 9 to 90*, and *The Complete Guide to Running*[1]. The latter book[1] is available in major book stores, from the publisher (www.meyer-meyer-sports.com). And directly from the author (www.feetnessforlife.com).

For an athlete to succeed as one gets older the biggest secret I can suggest is to age slower than your rivals. Second in importance is to avoid injury through preventative maintenance. Third, is attention to retention of intensity in the training. Fourth, is more recovery and more rest. Fifth, is proper diet, with fewer calories consumed. These and more are discussed below.

IT'S NEVER TOO LATE

There are many examples of master runners who started at a late age and became world champions or showed rapid improvement. I started at age 56 and broke an indoor 400 metres record a year later after a 33-year layoff from running. Scott Tinley and Ken McAlpine[5] reported good examples of improvement in older athletes: e.g., a research study showed a 16% increase in VO_2max (aerobic capacity) among a group of 60 to 79 year olds after only a 13 week training program. Another study reported by Kohrt et al[9], indicated an improvement between 12% to 36% in VO_2max for 53 men and 57 women, previously sedentary for 2 years, and aged 60-71. This was achieved by endurance exercise training over a 9 to 12 month period with no significant difference between men or women. Similarly, Coe and Coe[8] reported a 20% improvement in maximum oxygen uptake in 55 to 70 year old men, previously inactive, after only an eight week period of training. An often reported study done at Tufts University in Boston indicated a 174% improvement in leg strength for a group of 90-96-year-old volunteers after eight weeks of high intensity strength training; gait speed improved by 48% and thigh muscle increased by 15% (Fiatarone et al[4]). Amazing! All this indicates it is never too late in life to start and make big gains in fitness, by gradual progression, and even to become a champion.

Endurance levels and muscle strength peak at between 20 to 30 years of age then slowly decline as we get older. Muscle fibres normally decrease a few percent each decade after age 30. After age 35 the average person loses half a pound of muscle and gains a pound of fat every year (Dr. Ken Sparks[3]). This doesn't have to be. With consistent exercise (particularly intense exercise) one can reduce muscle loss considerably as one ages. For example, I have maintained my weight (150 pounds) and body fat (5%) nearly constant over the last 10 years (from age 65 to 75). Research has shown that VO_2max declines by about 10% per decade in most individuals but with intense exercise only about half as much. This is largely due to the lower decrease in maximum heart rate with regular intense exercise over many years. Every decade the sedentary man's maximum heart rate decreases about 10 beats per minute, but with regular intense training, your maximum heart rate can stay nearly constant or decrease very little for decades, as in my case.

AGING SLOWER THAN YOUR RIVALS

Longevity—this is one of my favorite subjects. Who wouldn't be interested in living longer and at the same time enjoying higher quality living as well. I have given some speeches on this subject and I sometimes say, "I am going to show you how you can easily earn a million dollars or more and it's practically guaranteed." This really keeps them awake. The secret I let out eventually is: by leading a healthy, active life as described below you will live decades longer. Therefore, you will collect your pension for an extra 20 or 30 years; for example 25 years at $40,000 per year is one million dollars. Of course having the right parents helps tremendously but the following will take many years off your biological age and thus add decades to your life.

Your real (biological) age depends on your everyday habits of eating, sleeping, drinking, physical and mental exercising, stress level, or smoking, etc. You can determine your present real age from the internet web site www.realage.com; this is based on thousands of individual studies, so it has some validity.

With proper rest, diet, and exercise, you can prevent chronic disease, increase your life span by decades and at the same time add more life and speed to your years. The following is a short course in longevity, covering all the essentials:

- *Avoid atrophy.* Slowing down is more due to rusting out (atrophy) than aging. Get rid of that "I'm slow because I'm old" thinking.
- *Supplements.* To fight the free radicals that damage body cells take antioxidants: vitamin E, C, A, selenium, and grape seed extract daily. Older women may benefit from estrogen replacement. I highly recommend grape seed extract. It is: a very powerful antioxidant, enhancing the activity of vitamin C and E, helping you to live longer; fighting heart disease, stroke, and high blood pressure; and for athletes, enhancing endurance.
- *Improve immune system.* Take supplements daily (e.g., Echinacea, beta carotene, Zinc, vitamin C with bioflavonoid) and plenty of fruits and vegetables to improve the immune system. Strengthening the immune system is the preventative maintenance way to prevent disease. Wash the

hands frequently. Take one baby aspirin (usually 80mg) each day to thin the blood and reduce the possibility of stroke and heart attack.

- **Get adequate sleep** and keep a regular sleep routine. Also if possible take a 15-30 minute nap every day; a nap too long or too late in the day will interfere with sleep at night. Eat dinner about five hours before bedtime. A late dinner or alcohol or coffee late at night robs you of deep sleep and contributes to aging. Also poor sleep results in less release of growth hormone with consequent lowering of the immune system.

- **Memory** deteriorates with age in the normal individual at an increasing rate along with other bodily functions. Memory is a skill requiring constant practice. Your mind needs exercise similar to the body. To reduce memory loss keep the mind active; for example, with chess, reading, taking courses, writing, memory games, memorizing poetry and intelligent conversation. Also physical exercising makes for a more alert mind due to more oxygen to the brain. Finally, remember this: Bortz[10] described a study where three groups in a nursing home were given memory training. The group which was rewarded for correct answers had better memory and alertness; and two and one half years later only 7% of this group had died compared with about 30% in the other two groups. My interpretation of this is that a person with active mind habits survives longer.

- **Balance** deteriorates with age and causes falls, but can be improved by exercise. Exercise makes for stronger bones, so that a fall can be more easily survived. One good balance exercise is: stand on one foot for 30 to 60 seconds in bare feet, then the other foot.

- **VO₂max** declines by about 1% per year in healthy untrained men but intense exercise can reduce this decline considerably or even increase oxygen capacity. See "It's Never Too Late" in a section above.

- **Proper diet.** Eat plenty of fruits and vegetables for the vitamins and minerals and fibre that they contain. Have a high carbohydrate, low protein, high fibre, low fat diet with minimum sugar and salt. Eat fish at least twice a week for the Omega 3 fatty acid to minimize stroke, heart disease and heart arrhythmias (irregular heartbeat).

- **Drink distilled water**, and preferably at least eight glasses per day. Tap water and spring water contain inorganic minerals which are indigestible and clog the arteries resulting in premature aging. But drinking distilled water results in more efficient functioning of body organs, removal of wastes and toxins, and absorption of nutrients in the body cells. Distilled water is also important in the treatment of arthritis. See Water by Dr.P.C. Bragg and Dr. Pat. Bragg[11] for more details.

- **A high alkaline, low acid diet** will assist to combat heart disease, cancer and other maladies. It also combats lactic acid which accumulates more rapidly in older athletes for any given speed during anaerobic exercise. Alkaline foods are, for example most fruits and vegetables whereas acid foods are, for example, flesh foods, baked goods, grains, eggs, cheese and sugar.

- **Minimize coffee, and also alcohol** (it prevents glucose production in the liver and robs energy). Definitely rule out smoking.

- Research indicates that **under-eating** improves longevity. Smaller meals result in less energy expended in digestion. Allow enough time between meals for digestion; the digestive system should not be constantly at work.

- Take good care of your **dental health**, e.g., dental checkups and daily flossing to prevent plaque formation that leads to periodontal disease. With gum disease bacteria travels through the body causing or worsening health problems; and it has been linked to heart disease, stroke, diabetes, pneumonia and other respiratory diseases. Daily flossing adds several years to your life.

- **Activity creates energy**. It is strange but true that "activity begets energy"; the more you exercise the more energy you will have.

- **Continue regular exercise**, preferably with some intensity. Exercise is probably the most important of all anti-aging habits. Studies have shown that longevity is affected more by exercise than by your genes. "Use it or lose it." It is the intensity, more so than the volume that keeps you young.

  However, master runners and especially master competitors above 60 need to be cleared for exercise activity by a physician. Then after the body adapts to the activity, "A trained 60 year old can outperform 95% of untrained 20 year olds" (Dr. Richard Mangi[2]). I have a better quote of my very own: "A very fit 70 year old can have a better sex life than a not so fit 50 year old." That reminds me of my barber who one day told me he got up at about 6am to run for 20 to 30 minutes three days a week. I said, "That's got to be good for your sex life." He laughed, but shortly after, he increased his length of run and now runs five times per week.

- **Stretch** (t'ai chi, yoga, Pilates exercises, etc.) regularly. Static stretching should be done every day and weight training at least twice per week to compensate for loss of flexibility and strength with age. As we age we lose fast twitch fibres and associated motor neurons, and hence muscle power. Therefore, it is very important to compensate by regularly doing reasonably intense weight training, and rapid intensive movements.

- **Massage** on a regular basis will increase joint mobility and flexibility, and strengthen and maintain normal elasticity in muscles.

- **Hanging from a bar** for a minute or less, or chin-ups on a regular basis will help to compensate for the compression of the spongy discs in your spine, which occurs with age. This exercise will maintain your posture and prevent shrinkage in height. I call this the "Poor Man's Stretcher." For the more affluent there is the inversion or tilt table, where you can hang upside down.

- **Avoid stress** as much as possible. This has to do with proper attitude and controlled emotions in daily life situations (such as in driving a car, etc.) Practise transcendental meditation. Avoid the hectic, driving, uptight (Type A) behavior. Pace yourself, keep calm. Don't over-react or over-dramatize a situation.

- *Maintain a positive outlook*, and a sense of humour. Laughter has many health benefits.
- *Be optimistic*. We control the quality of our days within us. Positive thinking makes good things happen.
- *Maintain a good posture* at all times. A good posture when sitting or walking results in a good attitude automatically.
- *Active positive associates.* Associate and train with young people and other active, positive people as much as possible.
- Have a *yearly check-up* with your doctor.
- *Have goals and challenges* in your life. Age should be no barrier to new knowledge and experience.
- Work on your *emotional and spiritual health* just as you work on your physical health. This involves keeping the mind active, for example, with chess and other games, bridge, reading, studying, and relaxing with music or painting. A healthy, contented mind contributes to a healthy body.

Avoid Injury

As we age, we lose suppleness and strength in the muscles. The joints, ligaments and tendons are less well lubricated and more rigid. Also, there is wear and tear due to repetitive training. A chronic injury, particularly to the knees, can finish your running career. Aim for the long term. Therefore, preventative maintenance is recommended to compensate for the above.

Injuries are more prevalent as we get older and recovery could take 25% to 50% longer. During my running days at high school and university I was never injured but at age 70: four times. Injuries can slow you down drastically. For example, at age 71 (year 2000) my injuries (to plantar tendon, hip and broken toe) resulted in training mileage reduced to about 60%, indoor track workouts reduced to about 40% and only three outdoor track workouts. This caused a 4% slower time (+2.5s) in the 400 metres, and 7% (+10s) slower time in the 800 metres compared to the previous year. At this age a fit world class middle distance runner should experience only about 1.5% decline/year.

Therefore, the older athlete has to be extra cautious. The following will assist in preventing injuries:

Stretch at least once a day and do weight training three times a week. Be careful how you stretch. The wrong stretch or position, or too intense can cause injury.

- *Plyometrics* are recommended to strengthen tendons and ligaments. Start easy with skipping and progress from two-legged to one-legged exercises. (In 1999 I had four injuries requiring physiotherapy. These were all for ligaments and tendons and could have been prevented with prior plyometric training).

- **Massage**. Get into the habit of regular massage particularly after a hard training session. Regular massage will also prevent loss of elasticity from intense training over several months. Self massage is beneficial too.

- **Practise preventative maintenance.** For example massage, the plantar tendon daily and do toe raises on a flat surface every other day to prevent plantar fasciitis. If you are a hurdler, do the trail leg exercise daily (as I often do) to strengthen the groin/adductor. Do exercises with surgical tubing to strengthen the quadriceps, hamstring, adductor and abductor muscles.

- If a muscle has been previously injured, make sure to do **strength training** for this muscle to keep it strong to prevent reoccurrence of the injury.

- **Visit the chiropractor** once a month to ensure your body is in alignment. This will assist to prevent future injuries. **"Rolphing" massage** will realign the fascia. The fascia (covering muscles, tendons, ligaments and practically all body parts) is as important as the bones for body support.

- **Cross-training.** Pay immediate attention to a small injury. Back off, do cross-training, and get massage or physiotherapy.

- **Training shoes.** Wear proper training shoes and replace frequently when worn. Rotate your running shoes frequently.

- **Run on soft surfaces**. (trails and grass) as much as possible; avoid running on the roads and sidewalks. The trails are also more relaxing and with more oxygen and less smog.

- **Increase the cross-training** and reduce the running training. Cross-training will assist in keeping keep your body in balance by working different muscles.

- **Adapt gradually.** Be wary of anything new and different in your training. Your muscles take time to fully adapt—usually six weeks.

- **Prevent dehydration.** In exercising during hot weather, ensure adequate fluid intake as this could be more of a problem in the older athlete, especially the unfit older athlete. Drink 16 ounces two hours before exercise and about six ounces 15 minutes before. Replace the weight lost in sweating with water; for example drink 16 ounces of water to compensate for the loss of each pound in body weight due to exercise.

- **Take longer to recover**. This means more time between repetitions in interval training and more rest days.

- Slow down with any sign of **abnormal fatigue** or breathlessness.

- Above all: **avoid "too much, too soon, too fast."** Think of this before each session. Be gradual in all training. See chapters on Recovery, and Injury Prevention and Causes in *The Complete Guide to Running*[1].

AFFECT OF AGE ON RACE RESULTS

It is of interest to examine the decline in performance with age from the Age-Graded Tables[6] as this information gives some idea of what to expect as you age.

The results in the table below are based on my examination and plotting of approximate world record race times for 100 metres, 800 metres, mile, and marathon vs. age from these Age-Graded Tables. These race times, if achieved, would produce 100% age grading.

Average Decline in Performance, Percent Per Year, vs. Age

Event	Between 35 to 65	Between 65 to 80	Between 85 to 90
100m	0.73	1.1	1.7
800m	0.88	1.5	2.8
Mile	0.94	1.5	2.7
Marathon	1.1	1.5	2.7

The following is seen from the table:

- There is more drop-off in speed with age as the race distance becomes longer. I.e., sprinters decline least with age and marathoners the most.
- From plots of race times vs. age it is seen that the there is a more rapid decline after about age 65 +/- 2 years and then an even greater decline after about age 85 +/- 2 years. The more rapid decline with age is to be expected. However, it appears there is something biological happening after about age 65, and then again after about age 85.

Some highly fit world class individuals decline at a much slower rate up to age 65 and even delay the more rapid decline until several years past 65. For example my 800 metres indoor time stayed nearly constant from 2:16 at age 60 to 2:17.05 at age 69; the latter indoor race in Boston 1998 was age-rated at 102%. For most less fit, less motivated individuals, the decline in performance up to about age 65 would be much greater (perhaps 1.5 or 2% per year) rather than 0.7 to 1% per year since these latter numbers are based on world record performers.

Why do sprinters decline in speed or performance at a significantly slower rate than middle distance or marathon runners? The reason for this is strength, flexibility and intensity of exercise. Strength is speed. As we age we lose strength and flexibility. Sprinters are working more on maintaining their strength and flexibility than middle and long distance runners so they decline in speed at a slower rate. In addition, it is well known that to stay young, intensity of exercise is more important than volume. Sprinters have it all since they also have a higher percentage of quality training; i.e., higher intensity than middle distance and marathoner runners, with regular weight training, plyometrics and lots of drills for flexibility. These activities help to retain the fast twitch fibres and associated motor neurons which decay with age unless frequently activated.

It is important to age slower than your rivals. All this indicates the importance to stay younger and live longer by regular weight training, frequent stretching and maintenance of intensity and fast movements in training.

Also, don't focus on race times from past years but focus on your particular age-graded percentage from the Age Graded Tables[6]. If you improve in age-graded percentage as you age, you know you are getting better—like an old wine.

TRAINING OLDER COMPETITORS

The American College of Sports Medicine (ACSM) makes the following general recommendations or guidelines for developing cardio-respiratory and muscle fitness for healthy adults of all ages. Scott Tinley and Ken McAlpine summarize these basic guidelines in their book[5] and state that these can be applied with minor variations to an exercise program whether you're 45 or 85. These sound guidelines serve as a basis and can be modified (increased or decreased) according to the individual's fitness, experience, and age. But as expected, the frequency, volume and intensity is normally reduced with age: see discussion below these guidelines.

Strength Training:

2-3 days per week, a minimum of one set of 8 to 12 repetitions for those less than 50 years and 10 to 15 for those more than 50, for 8 to 10 major muscle groups, in a 20-30 minute session.

Two or three sets per session provide only relatively small gains compared to one set. The weight should be heavy enough to cause some muscle burning sensation (fatigue) on the final repetitions. Allow 48 hours between strength training sessions. Strength training preferably should be done for many weeks before aerobic training is started. If possible standing exercises with free weights should be included to improve balance and coordination.

Aerobic Exercise:

3-5 days per week, 55 or 65% to 90% of maximum heart rate (MHR), for 20-60 minutes continuous (or two to six 10-minute sessions of activity). The 55% MHR applies to unfit sedentary types [or the extremely elderly]. [Approach these times gradually over many weeks, normally at 60% of maximum heart rate, and at 90% heart rate only when highly fit and doctor's clearance is obtained.]

[In aerobic training the 90% upper limit above could be achieved by an athlete running long intervals (800m to a mile) at 10K race pace; called aerobic capacity training or VO_2max training. The shorter intervals and lower volumes would be applicable to older runners. Normally for endurance training, the heart rate is above 70% MHR for at least 30 minutes.]

Stretching:

2-3 days per week, 4 or more repetitions per major muscle group, holding each stretch 10-30 seconds.

Balanced Training:

There are 26 training principles applicable to cyclists, swimmers, and especially runners listed in The Complete Guide to Running[1]. But I believe the most important is the "Principle of Balanced Training."

There are three energy systems and five training systems; most athletes and even some experienced ones are not fully aware of these training systems. It is essential to know of these and to emphasize those in training which are more specific to their event.

The training systems for distance runners are described briefly below. The recommended maximum mileage per session, listed below, is as recommended in Jack Daniels' Running Formula[7] book. The five training systems consist of four quality, more intensive sessions, and the aerobic conditioning system.

Alactic System:

Short sprints (<20 seconds) to develop pure speed at 100% MHR. Mainly for sprinters or to develop a rapid finishing kick in a distance race. Usually <600 metres in a session.

Anaerobic Lactic System (S):

Short intervals (30 to 90 seconds) at mile race pace or faster to develop speed and speed endurance. Recommended maximum weekly mileage /session = 5%[7].

Aerobic Capacity System (VO₂max):

Long intervals (2 to 6 minutes) at 10K or 5K race pace (85–95% MHR respectively) to develop aerobic endurance and mental toughness. Recommended max. weekly mileage/session = 8%[7].

Anaerobic Threshold System (AT): (also called **Lactic** and **Ventilatory Threshold**): Intervals (1.5 to 6 minutes or continuous, usually 20 minutes at conversation pace or 15 seconds per mile slower than 10 K race pace). Recommended max. weekly mileage/session = 10%[7].

Aerobic Conditioning System:

Long continuous runs usually at least 30 minutes at 60 - 70% of MHR to build endurance, tolerate stress and also for recovery at the easier pace.

The quality sessions for distance runners are the **S, VO₂max, AT** systems. It is essential to know which training system should be emphasized in training. The order of importance is listed below for middle to long distance events.

800m, mile	S, VO₂max, AT
3K, 5K, 10K	VO₂max, AT, S
Half-Marathon, Marathon	AT, VO₂max, S

The quality sessions as a percentage of weekly miles varies from 15 to 20% for elite master 50 year olds to 5 to 8% for 80 to 90-year-old experienced runners. See The Complete Guide To Running[1] for more details and typical workouts.

REDUCED TRAINING WITH AGE

Quantity And Intensity Of Training Has To Be Reduced As One Ages

For older runners less (intensity and quantity) is often more (meaning improved times or improved age-graded percentage). However, it is important to maintain the intensity (quality) although it is reduced. This is what keeps you young and maintains race times as you age. As a rough idea of how much to reduce the quantity and intensity in particular, consider that up to age 65 race times are declining between 1 to 2%/year depending on how hard you are training and your level of expertise. So as a rough guide: a 60-year-old compared to a 40-year-old of the same caliber (same age-graded percentage) would do about 20 x 1% less intervals. This fits in roughly with my experience in running with younger runners. Also, an 80-year-old compared to a 60-year-old of the same caliber would do about 20 x 2% fewer intervals if they were national class (above about 80% age graded) but about 20 x 3% fewer intervals if they were average club runners. Since everyone is different, your body, and particularly the recovery of the heart, will normally dictate how many repetitions are practical. See also the "Recovery" section below. When form drops or speed deteriorates, it's quitting time. Your workout should be such that the cool-down is not a big chore and you are not overly tired the next day. Also, as you get older, it becomes even more important always to under-train rather than over-train. Payton Jordan, with many world records in master's sprints and head coach of the USA 1968 Olympic track and field team, recommends under-training also for sprinters of any age.

Reduce Intervals At Near Maximum Heart Rate

Dr. Jack Daniels[7] recommends "a program for older distance runners that minimizes VO₂max training [called 'intervals' in his book] and that minimizes anaerobic/speed intervals [called 'repetitions' in his book] and focuses more on anaerobic threshold training [lactate threshold] as the main quality emphasis. This statement is more applicable to *long* distance runners. There is no doubt that "tempo" training at anaerobic threshold is less strenuous than VO₂max or anaerobic speed training due to the lower heart rate, for example about 75 % MHR compared to near 100% MHR. But for middle distance runners and sprinters in particular the anaerobic/speed type of training is essential. "To stay fast you have to train fast" (Sparkes[3]). To slow down the fast twitch muscle deterioration - speed training intervals, hill training, weight training, fast arms drill, fast feet drill, fast step-ups and fast strides are required on a regular basis. Also, regular weight training on a weekly basis should be retained for all seniors to reduce loss of muscle mass with age.

Adapt Gradually

Adapt slowly over a longer period of time than when you were younger. Remember it takes about six weeks for a training effect to set into the body. For instance, leaving most of your speed training to the last two or three weeks is a big mistake. All training: stretching, running, and weight training has to progress gradually over the sharpening period leading up to your main race. Sudden changes lead to possible injury.

There is the "Principle of Diminishing Returns" (one of the 26 training principles in my book The Complete Guide to Running[1] that you should be aware of. Initially, progress is rapid and as the weeks go by progress is slower and slower. I estimate the last six weeks in the 12 week sharpening schedule will be required to improve by only two or three percent.

Warm-ups and cool-downs need to be gradual too. Start your warm-up with a walk. In doing fast strides or accelerations and speed intervals, the first and last repetition should preferably be slower. Finish your cool-down with a walk. It is very important not to stop suddenly after some hard intervals or a race. Keep moving as the heart is working harder for about a minute without the benefit of quick body movement to assist blood flow; also some movement prevents blood pooling in the legs.

The "Principle of Anti-Shock" in The Complete Guide To Running[1] deals with avoiding sudden changes in body temperature and sudden changes in heartbeat during and after intense exercise for safety sake. Also, it is wise in doing intense intervals always to train with one or two others, especially during extreme weather conditions; this is particularly pertinent to older runners.

Recovery

As you age, recovery becomes more important. More rest is required to prevent injury and burnout.
- Start the next interval when you feel ready to restart. (For younger athletes with a maximum heart rate near 200 beats per minute it is customary to restart the next repetition when the heart returns to 120 beats per minute. If it takes longer than 90 seconds to return to 120 the

speed is too fast or the run too long. This practice is not recommended for older runners.)

- Older athletes should take longer to cool–down gradually.
- Instead of one rest day per week, you may have to take two or three. Your body will normally tell you how much, as everyone is different.
- Instead of the old routine of hard (one day)/easy (the next day), you may have to go to hard/easy/easy days as you get older.
- Taking one easy week per month (periodization) becomes more important as one gets older.
- After the summer track season, rest two or three weeks before cross-country or base-training. Another one or two weeks rest is required after the indoor season and the start of the outdoor season. During these rest periods, do cross-training mainly but retain speed with fast strides. Note complete inactive rest of a month could take three months or more to come back to where you left off; so this is not recommended. Also, a year off could require two years or more to come back to near the previous fitness (or to your previous age-graded percentage).

THE SPRIGHTLY 80 TO 90 YEAR OLD

> When you approach the end of the line
> Slowly creeping up to eighty nine,
> You run the hundred or mile if you dare.
> And your effort may not be speedy,
> But win or lose it's a victory,
> You must agree, just to be there.

When I think of a sprightly 90-year-old I think of the late Paul Spangler of the USA. In 1993 at the World Masters Championships in Miyazaki Japan, at age 94 (I believe), he won seven gold medals: the 10K cross-country, 10K, 5K, 1500 metres, 800 metres, 400 metres, and 200 metres. Even though there was no competition in his races, this was an amazing feat of endurance for this age. In the cross-country he finished in 2 hours 41 min. 11sec; at one particularly steep hill they had to push him up the hill. I asked some of my American friends, "Is this legal?" They said, "It is if you are 94." In the 200 metres I saw him fall at least twice and struggle on again to finish in 1:38.5; no one dared to touch him or he would have been disqualified.

A friend of mine, Judith Kazdan, age 85 (in year 2005), is a good example of what an older athlete can do. She broke many world records in distance running and ran 39 marathons. She says, "I finished them all." I recall her saying, "In the beginning [in her early 60's] I had difficulty in running half-a-mile." During her competitive years until age 80, six days a week she swam over a half-mile in the morning and then ran six miles or more at night. Her dedication and determination paid off.

Older distance master competitors should follow the minimum guidelines of the American College of Sports Medicine if possible. See the section above on Training Older Competitors. Add also at least one quality session per week, i.e., anaerobic threshold, Fartlek, hills, or speed training. A typical quality session would normally involve repeats at a pace near (or building up to) the competitors' race pace. At age 80 to 90—easy days or cross training between running days are recommended and preferably with two days of rest per week.

Of course, at age 80 or older most competitors have been at it for many years and they know, or should know, what their body can and cannot do. With experience and trial and error one must find his or her own best way to achieve success and avoid the dreaded injury. In any case, it is always best to proceed gradually and under-train rather than over-train.

Here's hoping your healthy/active life-style and the Ultimate Race Director allows you to collect your million dollars (in pension) but more importantly allows you to run on and on and on with a smile on your face. Also, if you slow down a lot, look on the bright side. You are still able to run and besides, you get to train with (or coach) your grandchildren.

GOTTA RUN, GOTTA RUN

Gotta run, gotta run—
I feel the voice within.
It will not let me be.
Gotta run, gotta run—
though sleet, hail or rain.
Flying low o'er the ground.
Feeling high as an eagle.
Gotta move, gotta move—
Defeating indolent ease.

Then near the end of the trail
in the yawning years
when each sunrise and sunset
appears more dear,
The Ultimate Race Director
calls out our number.
Then with life collapsing—
hopefully we recall
when we did fail or fall:
How we rose up again—-
hardened for the fray—
unvanquished;
How we played the Game,
slaying the beasts of Fear and Pain—
giving all;

Befriending Confidence and Courage;
And making the world a better place
in passing by.

REFERENCES

1. Fee, E.W., **The Complete Guide To Running**, Meyer and Meyer Sports, Aachen   Germany, 2005. www.meyer-meyer-sports.com

2. Mangi, R., Jokl, P., and Dayton, W., **Sports Fitness and Training**, Pantheon Books, New York, NY, 1987.

3. Sparks, K., and Kuehls, D., **The Runners Book of Training Secrets**, Rodale Press, Emmaus, PA, 1996.

4. Fiatarone, M., Marks, E., Ryan, N., et al, **High intensity strength training in nonagenarians. Effects on skeletal muscle.** JAMA 263: 3029-3034, 1990.

5. Tinley, S., and McAlpine, K., **Sports Endurance,** Rodale Press, Emmaus, PA, 1994.

6. Compiled and edited by World Assoc. of Veteran Athletes (WAVA), **Age Graded Tables,** National Masters News, Van Nuys, CA, 1994.

7. Daniels, J., **Daniels' Running Formula,** Champaign, IL, 1998.

8. Coe, S., and Coe, P., **Running For Fitness,** Pavilion Books, London, England, 1983.

9. Kohrt, W. M. et al, **Effects of gender, age, and fitness level on response of VO$_2$max to training in 60-71 yr olds,** J. Appl. Physiol. 71(5): 2004-2011, 1991.

10. Bortz, W.,M., **We Live Too Short And Die Too Long**, Bantam Books, New York, NY, 1991.

11. Bragg, P.C. and Bragg Pat., **Water, The Shocking Truth**, Health Science, Santa Barbara, CA, 29th printing.

THE MOTIVATION ZONE

"There are as many reasons for running as there are days in the year, years in my life. But mostly I run because I am an animal and a child, an artist and a saint. So, too, are you. Find your own play, your own self-renewing compulsion, and you will become the person you are meant to be."
[George Sheehan]

Steve King

Steve King is an avid runner, race-walker and triathlete who holds national age group running records, has raced at Ironman and Ultraman triathlon distances and has been a member of Canada's national 100 km team as well as being a British Centurion (having race-walked 100 miles within 24 hours). In 2001 he became only the second Canadian to complete the arduous 135 miles Badwater Death Valley run.

He was the publisher of *Tri-Fit Quarterly*, a national triathlon magazine, author of *Rapid Recovery* a book on energy healing techniques, and a triathlon training log, as well as having been CBC's colour commentator for the sport of triathlon. Steve is also the race announcer for numerous sports events, including Ironman Canada.

His work history includes stockbroking, private investigation, well-drilling, child care, hospitality management and being a Justice of the Peace. He is a Registered Clinical Counsellor and, since 1989, has been an outpatient addictions counsellor at Pathways Addictions Resource Centre.

He has an avid interest in healthy balance and wholism and lives with his wife Jean in the City of Penticton in beautiful British Columbia.

You can visit Steve's websites at **www2.vip.net/~stking/** and **www.triathlon-tips.com**

Attitude And Energy

Steve King

I have no doubt that since taking up running you will have noticed that you have developed some positive attitudinal shifts, not just chemically induced by the exercise, but also through the social, environmental, relationship and racing experiences that have transpired.

I have been fortunate enough to have been involved in the sport of running for over 50 years and know that it has afforded me opportunities for personal experience, insight, growth and ultimately wisdom, that can be put to very good use if I choose to focus on what works and let go of what doesn't.

Whether through watching great sportsmen and women or through analysing my own successes and failures, it is obvious, with the exception of fast-twitch activities, that relaxation is a big part of the key to being successful; i.e., letting one's natural ability and body wisdom be in a FLOW state.

Attitude is everything. It will determine how you do and what you take from any experience, as well as what you give to any experience/performance. Having an Attitude of Gratitude allows for one to be in a natural FLOW state and to both give and receive positive energy in the forms of fun, joy and satisfaction.

When we are young or first getting into any sport, we are usually involved simply for fun, fitness and friendships. With time, we may choose to move into a more competitive mode or reach a certain level of comfort or competence, whether by comparing ourselves to others or hopefully, by comparing with our "former" selves and our previously perceived limitations. It is interesting to note that, as we get older, we tend to return to those same initial fun, fitness and friendship motivations.

Performance is usually presented as the pooling of three things; 1) Ability: the potentialities that are developed and refined by knowledge and experience. 2) Focus: taking notice of just one thing by narrowing one's attention to other input, including the modulation of energy levels; i.e. being able to calm down or energize oneself at will. 3) Motivation: the reason one does something - which incorporates perspective, the ability to generate short and long term goals, and the flexibility to move from one to another.

I believe that to achieve absolutely the best possible personal performance, we need to also include one's Attitude/Mindset and Energy State.

Firstly, let it be understood that "Winning is independent of the outcome". It is about achieving the best result in less than ideal circumstances, or doing the best one can under the given circumstances at that time.

It is by focusing on the process rather than on the outcome, such as winning the event, that will allow you to achieve the best possible result. The key is concentrating only on the execution (such as when driving a car) thus - being in a flow state.

To achieve our personal best, we must be prepared in the physical and nutritional realms, as well as having worked on the necessary technical/tactical issues, but most coaches would agree that the most important ingredient is in the mental arena.

Chiropractors and other health practitioners refer to the Triad of Health, meaning the structural, chemical and emotional/mental elements of our makeup. If any one of these is out of balance, then the other two areas get negatively impacted.

Hans Selye, an authority on the issue of stress, gave the name `Eustress` to identify and differentiate a healthy level of stress; i.e., a motivating and rewarding level, from unhealthy stress. Unhealthy stress can cause panic, anxiety, hyperventilation, uptightness, anger and performance anxiety. The underlying feelings that stress provides are fear, pain, and fear of more pain. Suffering does indeed suck!

One item that gets little attention is the importance of sleep. Deprivation of it often lends itself to some form of mood disorder; therefore some discipline is needed and it should be viewed as training – a time when the batteries get re-charged.

If we seek a balance of performance and personal excellence, then we firstly need to ask ourselves whose needs are being satisfied by our performance? We need to honour our personal choice and desire, and not that of another. Trying to provide vicarious satisfaction for someone else or to attain another's approval is not being true to oneself.

At some levels you may note that you have been your own worst enemy and that you find yourself constantly self-sabotaging when the palace of possibilities stands before you.

If we have that awareness, then it behooves us to stop living with the problem and start living with the answer; to recover or we'll continue to repeat the sabotaging cycle.

By virtue of our past experiences, our energy levels and our attitude, we can find ourselves feeling spirited/motivated/enthused/passionate. By the same mechanism, we can also find ourselves feeling dispirited and lacking the wherewithal to perform anywhere close to our true potential.

It is important for us to figure out by whom or by what are we inspired or motivated. Nowadays, many runners are motivated to run for the pursuit of fitness, camaraderie, challenge or charity; whereas, prior to the running booms, performance was the main motivator. By virtue of the "everyman" involvement in the sport, there are many who provide the inspiration that drives others to participate.

I have always found that my performances were `stronger` when, without his/her awareness, I dedicated a race to somebody of significance to me. The other times that I noted I always put in a full effort were in road relays. By dedicating a race to a person or a cause (inspiration/motivation), I believe we draw upon the inner passion, enthusiasm and spirit that manifests in those team road relay events.

Having and harnessing the necessary mental components used to equate to being mature in an age-related sense, but it doesn't need to be seen that way any longer. It is really about application of the knowledge. It is about letting go of what doesn't work and focusing on what does. We are the experts on ourselves and there is enough external expertise such as personal coaches and written material that we do not need to keep re-inventing the wheel. There will always be new information and training methods that are worthy of our attention; i.e., the Pose method, but we do not need years and years of trial and error to figure out a good personal goal-oriented training program for ourselves.

If we have stuck to a routine that has never paid the dividends we have sought, we need to be willing to risk and work at change, as performance and experience alone do not lead to confidence. Confidence and belief are the biggest determinants of excellence and we have to make a personal commitment to excellence to reach the highest levels.

This commitment is purposeful, planned and is based around fidelity to oneself. One should not rely totally upon outside support to provide opportunity, encouragement and motivation. All of this is essentially within the individual who has the internal fortitude, combined with confidence, belief, experience and wisdom to focus on what works and let it flow, while embracing and enjoying the process.

Our biggest fear is usually the fear of failure. But failure need only be negative if we look at it that way. The most used acronym for Failure is **F**ound **A**nother **I**mportant **L**esson **U**pon **R**eviewing **E**xperience. Another way to reframe the concept is to view a perceived failure as being feedback or fuel for future reference. Regardless of success or perceived failure, there is always a result - it is what you do with the result that counts. Are there any lessons from it that you can take away with you?

If you start putting yourself down with negative internal dialogue or "roof brain clutter" then you have created and are already competing against one extra opponent! Worse, it will be an opponent whose goal will not just be to beat you to the finish line, but rather to stop you from getting there by discouraging you at every step along the way. We therefore need to modify our self-talk. We can focus by using a written personal script list, which we can verbalise internally and can share with others, such as coaches or supporters, to use during an event. These scripts would be personal commands - positive, technical, mood phrases that can be used to counter pain and fatigue. They could be a reminder of a dedication/charity or simply to push/pull etc.

It does not mean that we need to analyse every little thing to the point of "paralysis by analysis", but gaining confidence minimizes the worries. Remember that "Worrying is praying for what you don't want". After some racing experience, and possibly with the help of a coach, we should be able to identify our own key to consistency. The only difference regarding pre-competition and competition conditions is having versus not having control - the predictable versus the unpredictable. We can have routines and rituals in our training but, given all the possible challenges a race or event can present, we need to be very flexible in order to achieve flow and high performance.

Emotion can be thought of and felt as either negative or positive, but it's how one chooses to use it that determines whether or not it will be productive and work for you or be destructive and self-sabotaging. Emotion is energy in motion and "energy flows where attention goes" (see below). Attention and intensity equals focused emotion. Over-arousal can be an issue - the antidote for which is relaxation.

Lance Armstrong, the six-time Tour de France winner, uses the acronym CANCER to represent those things that helped him survive the disease and fully grow as an athlete and humane being. The acronym stands for **C**ourage, **A**ttitude, **N**ever give up, **C**urability, **E**nlightenment and **R**emembrance (of fellow patients). Millions of his yellow wristbands have sold as a result of people being inspired by the man and his cause. As a result, 'Livestrong' has become a motivational personal script or mantra for many people.

Dr. Martin Collis of Vancouver coined the acronym MELLOW to encompass those areas which I believe allow for a balanced triad of health. They are **M**ind, **E**xercise, **L**aughter, **L**ove, **O**ptimal nutrition and **W**onder. These are indeed ingredients for a `spirited` existence. The one thing we know for sure is that none of us will get out of this existence alive, so we might as well make our life something that we truly want it to be.

We know that what the mind dwells on, the body reveals. Therefore, our primary goals should incorporate becoming a friend to the self and not, at times, being our own worst enemy. We will inhabit our body 24 hours a day for the rest of our lives, so we might as well make peace with the vehicle we drive in and provide it with the best possible fuel!

There are some important questions that we can ask ourselves in order to assist us in determining and developing our other life and athletic goals:

- How do you want to be, and how will you know when you are there?
- What dreams did you have as a child that you have given up on?
- Who do you wish you could be like?
- What would you like to do that you haven't been able to do yet?
- What would you do/attempt/be, if your success was guaranteed?
- What legacy of self would you like to leave behind?

I am not a religious person but I do subscribe to the Huna philosophy, which consists of seven basic principles:
1) The world is what you think it is.
2) There are no limits.
3) Energy flows where attention goes.
4) Now is the moment of power.
5) To love is to be happy with - love is the only ethic needed in Huna.
6) All power comes from within.
7) Effectiveness is the measure of truth.

As Frank Outlaw wrote, "Thoughts become words, words become actions, actions become habits, habits become character, character becomes your destiny".

Being the world's leading experts on ourselves, I suggest we need to utilise our own `inner coach` wisdom. We can do this by being aware of what I call the `Independent All-Knowing Expert Observer` part of oneself. By stepping `outside` of ourselves we can avoid athletic and other forms of self-sabotage by asking questions such as, "What advice would I give right now if I really cared for this person and I were watching him/her training/racing, or if I were coaching a runner in this predicament." When we hear our own loving advice, then we need to heed it by applying it to ourself, even when a part of us doesn't believe that we deserve it. It is so easy for us to see what another person is doing, yet we are generally stone-blind to our own actions and thoughts. We would all know what to do if we could just see. As Robbie Burns said in *To a Louse*: "O wad some Power the giftie gie us, To see oursels as ithers see us!"

When, at some future point, you reflect on this particular stage in your sporting life, ask yourself how you want to think of your performance and attitude or your own part in the team's performance. Do you want it to be one of enjoyment and satisfaction or disappointment and frustration? Define the attitude you wish to adopt and observe the difference it brings to your overall experience.

The way you train or practice will define your performance. For high performance you should incorporate deliberate practice, which is designed to take you out of your comfort zone, and pressure practice; i.e., tactical. Do not avoid focus on weaknesses. In fact, the purpose of a drill is to expose and correct weaknesses. We are forever involved in self-dialogue and if we find ourselves in a state of inner turmoil some healthy reframes that we can use could include, "I am cordially invited to change my mind," "I can choose peace instead of this," "I can elect to change all thoughts that hurt." If you have not yet achieved a goal and find yourself internally using put-downs, it is more productive to use a reframe such as, "To this point I haven't hit the stride that I want to".

Sports psychologists now play a big part in elite athletes' training arsenals and regimens. Mental rehearsal is of vital importance to all goal-oriented athletes, regardless of comparative performance level. If our visualisation is of watching or observing a third party, then it is passive and external; i.e. modeling. However, if it is in the first person; i.e., seeing and feeling oneself doing it, then it is internal, active and kinesthetic, which creates the desired simulation. It is therefore possible to use mental rehearsal as one's basic warm-up and it re-defines dry-land training. Dr. George Goodheart developed a means (Applied Kinesiology) by which, I believe, we can test the effects of beliefs, thoughts, statements, images, etc. on our physical well-being and ability.

Applied Kinesiology has demonstrated that an athlete's motivation has a major impact on the mind/body/spirit energy level. This could, in part, be a reason for someone who has little pressure on them to set a new personal record in the heats, but who then falls apart in the final due to the added pressure and mindset motivation shift it could facilitate! Fuller details are also available in my book *Rapid Recovery* or via my website (see below).

The reason for many doctor's visits is hypoadrenalism, though it will often be given other names such as fatigue or depression. Nutrition is a big factor for all, but especially so if you are engaged in athletic activity. It is easy for our system to become depleted of essential nutrients, vitamins, minerals, amino acids etc. Water and electrolytes such as potassium and sodium are vital. Dehydration is a major issue that was only really appreciated as such with the running boom of the 70's when aid stations became more readily available in road races. The body is made up of around 70% water. Through Dr. Masaru Emoto's fabulous book *Messages from Water*, which beautifully illustrates the impact of thoughts and images on water, (see the film *What the Bleep Do We Know*) we are only now becoming fully cognisant of the statement 'what the mind dwells on the body reveals'. Dr. William Tiller, a Stanford professor who is working on the genome project, has spoken about the major role of 'loving intentionality' in healing and his work and opinions are also featured in the same film. Dr. Wayne Dyer has been the host of a popular TV program called the 'Power of Intentionality'. These issues have been somewhat minimized in the past, but clearly they have a major impact in our overall athletic, fitness and wellness goals and successes.

Most people carry with them some form of miasm or predisposition to a certain ailment, such as the chicken pox virus, which, if it gets 'expressed', can manifest as a painful case of shingles. However, we do have the ability to create much healthier forms of cellular memory by means of visualisation, training and racing experience that we can specifically gear towards expression at the peak time in order to experience the desired athletic goal. Visualisation is now an accepted and validated tool of sports psychology (remember that the body does not know the difference between what is real and what is imagined) and the whole system will start to respond well as it gains a comfort level 'knowing' that it has been in the imagined scenario many times before.

Success will be more likely if one has an expectation of success. Therefore, by changing one's goals to that of performance process rather than only the outcome, the event will be a fully present one with constant access to one's 'inner coach', and the body/mind/spirit will have shifted from an anticipatory anxiety-based to an excitement-based experience.

It has been said that you cannot have a strong emotion while you are physically relaxed. Therefore, if you find yourself having strong emotions that stiffen the body and stifle the possibilities, you might need to consciously remind yourself of that and choose to do the simple `Wet Noodle` exercise. Just allow yourself to relax as much as is possible in a given situation and give an internal command for every part of you to relax, release and totally flop, just like a wet noodle. The progressive muscle relaxation combats any pressure or perturbation. Notice whether or not you have the ability to observe thoughts in your head without any reaction to them (sympathetic nervous system or otherwise). If you are able to, then you are in a *Tapas* state, which allows for total psyche and physical relaxation. (Rapid Recovery p.105)

The simple Serenity Prayer contains a magnificently powerful message that has been a guide for millions. It states, "Grant me the Serenity to accept the things I cannot change, the courage to change the things I can and the wisdom to know the difference."

Dr. David Hawkins, author of *Power vs. Force* (which fully endorses the use of Applied Kinesiology), stated that, "All stress is internally generated by one's attitudes."

Gerald Puls, a 75+ yr-old Ironman competitor from Pueblo, Colorado sent me a card that stated, "Exercise is the chain that links us to the Chariot of well-being. Well-being means happiness, but happiness is also an attitude, and the best attitude is one of gratitude." How lucky we are to be able to choose to run for fun, fitness, adventure, competition or to complement and honour our existence. Our attitude of gratitude needs to extend to those who help make it possible, whether they be our loved ones, race directors, volunteers or those who assist in our healthy overall maintenance. Putting out positive words, thoughts and vibrations - and being willing to receive them, allows for the quantum possibilities to impact personally and globally.

We have to recognise that life is indeed, at times, a struggle and that winning or losing is in the hands of the gods. We must therefore learn to celebrate the struggle!

From the viewpoint of coincidence, providence or serendipity, you might find it interesting to note that, the word ATTITUDE and the number that corresponds with the letters of the alphabet, A(1) T(20) T(20) I(9) T(20) U(21) D(4) E(5) for a grand total of 100! The attitude you choose to carry with you directly determines your experience of everything!

Albert Schweitzer stated that, "The greatest discovery of any generation is that human beings can alter their lives by altering their attitudes of mind".

RECOMMENDED BOOKS

Armstrong, Lance. with Sally Jenkins. *It`s Not About the Bike.* New York: Berkley Books. 2000.

Diamond, John. *Your Body Doesn`t Lie.* New York: Warner Books, 1979.

Emoto, Masaru. *Messages From Water.* Tokyo, Japan: Hado Kyoikusha. 2001.

Hawkins, David. *Power vs. Force: the Hidden Determinants of Human Behavior.* Carlsbad, CA: Hay House, Inc. 2002.

King, Serge. (not related – honestly!) *Mastering Your Hidden Self: A Guide to the Huna Way.* Wheaton, Ill: Quest Books. 1985.

King, Stephen P. *Rapid Recovery: Accelerated Information Processing & Healing.* Victoria, B.C.: Trafford Publishing. 2004.

Lepore, Donald. *The Ultimate Healing System.* Provo, Utah: Woodland Books. 1988.

Nickel David J. *Acupressure for Athletes.* New York: Henry Holt & Co., Inc. 1984.

Lynn (Williams) Kanuka

Lynn is an Olympic Medalist, Canadian record holder and elite athlete who has gone on to carve out an entirely different role for herself in life and in the world of running. Top among her accomplishments, she lists being mother of four children, two boys and two girls.

Her running credentials are impeccable including a Bronze medal in the LA Olympics (1984 – 3000 m), Commonwealth Games Gold (1986 – 3000 m) and Bronze (1986 – 1500 m). Lynn also held Canadian records at 1,500 m, 3,000 m, 5,000 m and 10,000 m and has been inducted into the Canadian Olympic, BC and Saskatchewan Sport Halls of Fame. She was selected to receive the YWCA Woman of Distinction Award.

After her active running career, which spanned 10 years from 1979 to 1989, Lynn took on the challenge of being a TV host and color commentator covering events including the Barcelona Olympics (CTV), Roadrace of the Month (ESPN), and the Commonwealth Games from Victoria, BC (CBC).

From 1996 until mid-2004 she was co-owner of Peninsula Runners (White Rock and Langley) and North Shore Athletics: walking, running and fitness stores.

At present Lynn is working with Sportmed BC as "Intraining" program coordinator. She is responsible for program development, communications, leadership and promotion for InTraining for SunRun - Annual 10K event which attracts 45-50,000 participants to the streets of Vancouver. She is responsible for over 60 clinics throughout the Lower Mainland and Interior regions of British Columbia, which assist people to prepare for the SunRun, able to walk, jog, run the distance safely and enjoy the experience. She also continues to coach and coordinate Track and Field and Cross Country programs for local elementary and secondary schools.

Today, Lynn still runs, but for her own pleasure and health rather than competitive goals. She brings an interesting and important perspective regarding attitudes and approaches to life-long running. She even admits that these days, long hikes through the mountains attract her as much as running does.

Motivation: You're In Charge!

Lynn Kanuka

MY STORY...

I grew up in Regina, Saskatchewan: 5 foot nothing and 105 pounds soaking wet...Sure I was a good little athlete, but nobody looked at me when I was a kid and said, "THAT GIRL is going to be an Olympic athlete one day!"

Did I really stand on an Olympic podium, and see that beautiful Canadian flag rise up as I received an Olympic medal? You bet I did! It's still sometimes a wonder to me how I got there...such a combination of so many good things, and not without some very good luck.

I was part of an amazing and supportive family; including parents willing to move the earth for their kids, wonderful coaches, and a life path that evolved with all kinds of forks in the road, requiring choices to be made along the way.

Some 20-plus years later, my four children are my Olympic Gold Medals, and these days I draw huge inspiration from the people with whom I work. I coordinate Walk-Jog-Run clinics for all kinds of people, most of whom are new to the sport of running and walking. They are from all walks of life, champions and experts in their own fields, all shapes and sizes, with a majority between the ages of 40 and 50 years old, but some as young as 20, and perhaps as old as 75. It's wonderful to see people learn to walk or run, to be united in their pursuit of this sport, and to be part of the amazing difference an exercise program can make in the quality of their lives.

PHILOSOPHY...

I'm learning all the time. Life is wonderful in all its stages. Me? I'm not old (I'll never be old). It's a relative term. When I was 20, a 30-year-old was old. When I was 30, a 40-year-old was old. Now that I'm well into my 40's, I'm proud of it, proud of my wrinkles and blonde (grey?) hair, and I realize that for me, 50 won't be old, nor will 60 or 70 or 80. Common sense tells me I'll just have to keep up what I enjoy doing, modify it according to what my limits evolve to be and I'll still be me, and for me, that means doing my best to stay healthy and active.

BE INSPIRED...

As an Olympic Medalist I've been somewhat humbled over the years in that people have given me the privilege of sharing my stories as an athlete, and in so doing I'm told I provide inspiration for them in their varied walks of life. I say privileged because, in fact, it's I who draw inspiration from those I tell my stories to...people who have embarked on a commitment to make their lifestyles healthier and more active. You see, for me, the notion of a healthy lifestyle was never my motivation. I was gifted as an athlete, and it was the impending competition that motivated me to train and stay fit. Now in my mid-forties, I find myself in their position, redesigning my goals for exercise to simply stay fit and healthy, without the competitive goal in the background. I've discovered it is, in fact, more difficult, because I was never really a fitness person. The training and fitness components were necessary to achieve the goal. Life is very busy, and it's hard to fit fitness into one's life, so I seek inspiration both from those around me, and in quotes from others who have walked in my shoes, or have wisdom beyond my years. Here are a few words of wisdom I have come to appreciate:

"Whether you come in first or not, performing at your highest level makes you a winner. At age eighty-three, I've had to adjust to the fact that I'm not as fast as I was at seventy-three or even sixty-three. Even if I don't win the medals, I get up and do my best, and I'm satisfied with my performance.

You have to do the best you can under the circumstances and realize there's no point in getting upset. You'll run into difficulties, and if you can change or improve the situation, change it. If you can't, don't fret about it."

-Bob Boal
Masters Gold Medalist, Track and Field

"I'm now over sixty years old and enjoy competing in the Masters Program. But Mother Nature is trying to take charge of my life. I can live with Mother Nature, but if she thinks her struggle with me is going to be an easy one, she's got another think coming. (After all, I'm the one who used to jump over barbed-wire fences.)"

-Phil Mulkey
Olympian, Decathlon
(the great decathlete Bob Matthias was his inspiration when as a young boy on a farm, he trained for decathlon using pitchforks minus the forks for javelin, a round plow shear for a discus, and jumping barbed wire fences for hurdles...)

"We're never too old to learn new skills and polish the ones we have. To grow in strength and to increase our speed and endurance is satisfying at any age.
My words of wisdom go like this: If you're going to work at something, no matter if it's cleaning out a trash can or running a race, do a good job. I can't imagine doing anything and not doing my best."

-Betty Vosburgh
Most Outstanding Female Athlete in USA 1991

(64 years old. Began running strictly for health...did it for 5 years as a jogger until she heard about the Masters Track and Field champs. She went on to set a world record for her age group in the heptathlon at the Masters World Champs.)

THE TWO RULES OF PERSEVERANCE

RULE #1: Take one more step.
RULE #2: When you don't think you can take one more step, refer to Rule #1.

-H. Jackson Brown, Jr.

"The important thing to remember is that the essence of our humanity is the spirit that lies within our container. We all have this spirit, and it is a reservoir of tremendous potential. When you tap into this potential, you can move mountains. And if you can't do that, you can still drill right through them."

-Rich Ruffalo
Paralympic Gold Medalist, Discus
Outstanding Coach and Teacher of the Year in 1998

TO EXERCISE?...

We're dealt the set of cards that we've got, and we're here on this planet only for a short time, so the way I figure it, we've got to keep on dancing, in our minds, our bodies, and our hearts.

A sound body goes hand-in-hand with a sound mind.

If you don't have your health, your quality of life will suffer. As I grow older I appreciate every day. I understand how quickly time passes, and how quickly it could all be gone.

Find an activity that you like. If it's running or walking, that's great.
Learn about it; take a class; find a group or a friend for support.

Assess yourself realistically: If you've never climbed a mountain and you'd like to, that's great, but don't arrange your trip to the Himalayas just yet... do things in stages.

If you have a terrible fear of heights, don't skydive right off the bat. Try something like the Capilano Canyon suspension bridge near Vancouver. If you're me, you try ziptrekking at Whistler...

Shakespeare said, "To climb steep hills requires a slow pace at first".

TAKE THE PLUNGE!...

If you like the water, then swim! Or learn to swim! When I'm with my family on vacation, I'm always inspired by the mature person-athlete who enters the water at the lake and proceeds to swim back and forth from dock to dock, consistently and effortlessly. Clearly they've been doing it a long time. Then a random person near me on the beach says something like, "Oh that's so-and-so, and she swims that route every single day".

Seek inspiration in those around you.

If you love to be outside, then walk, run, hike, cross-country ski, or snowshoe. But, moderation has to be the key. Do it first and foremost for the joy. Maybe more will come later, maybe it won't. Balance in one's life is so important.

COMMITMENT?...

Don't be too busy to fit exercise into your week. It isn't a luxury. Make an appointment with yourself. Write it down and stick to it. Keep a log on your kitchen calendar, or in a special diary, so you can be proud and motivate yourself.

HOW OFTEN?...

Depends on you, and your lifestyle. Three times per week for half an hour to an hour is a nice easy, manageable schedule. Every day? Not necessary, but if it's who you are, then go with it, as long as you are not obsessive.

If you become "depressed" because you miss a day, then you're not healthy and your program isn't helping as it should. Moderation and balance in one's life are the keys, with a few spontaneous moments tossed in to keep things spicy! We are creatures of habit by nature, but I think it's good to remember that change and variety can be good things.

BELIEVE IN YOURSELF...

If there's one thing sport has taught me, it's to never give up, never be a quitter. You can always be proud if you've given your best effort.

Set a goal, and simple is best. Mine is to simply go for a 30 minute jog three times per week: an escape from chaos... that's all it is for me. If I have more time, a day or more, and perhaps some company, my favourite activity and escape? A hike in the mountains. It is so much a favorite that my long-term goal is to stay healthy and to live in a country community where nature is at my doorstep and I'll be able to walk and hike every day in my mature years.

"I think to feel peaceful in one's life there has to be balance. My running gives me that. Among all the chaos with my kids, household, and business, a 30-minute jog in the woods allows me to really breathe and keep the demands of the day in perspective. I always finish a run feeling that my life is pretty good." -Lynn Kanuka   August 2000 Runners World

WALKING AND RUNNING: WHY DO IT? ...

Most anyone can do it. One only has to attend a local fun-run event to see people of all shapes, sizes, age groups and walks of life out there walking and running. In my home town of Vancouver, the major footrace event of the year happens to be the Vancouver SunRun 10 K, and we saw nearly 45,000 people take to the streets and cross that finish line this year (2005). In fact I remember standing on the starting line of the inaugural SunRun as an elite athlete, poised to win the event, never for a second imagining some 21 years later it would be my responsibility to provide the actual walk-jog-run programs to help prepare people to safely complete the distance! At that time I had very little awareness of those folks lined up behind me, focused as I was on performance.   I most definitely had no inclination of the great satisfaction and inspiration I would one day receive from helping people discover the joy of walking and running!

For the last 15 years my passion has been with the people who have never tried the sport I love: people embarking on a beginning walk or run program, unsure of themselves, but with proper guidance, discovering how simple it is, and how it can make such a difference in their lives. I'm grateful I now understand their huge sense of pride in their accomplishment, and moreover that it is not at all unlike the pride I have in my own accomplishments as an athlete.

The beauty of walking and running is its simplicity: all you need is a good pair of shoes and you can do it anywhere, anytime.

SOME THOUGHTS ON "RUNNING ON THE SHADY SIDE OF 50"...

As I've discovered, whether you bring loads of experience to the table as a goal-oriented high performance athlete like myself, or whether you've got the spirit of adventure and have decided it's never too late to begin something new (good for you!), I believe the ultimate motivation has to be to stay healthy and enjoy yourself.   With that in mind, and patience to listen to your body, I've come up with a few points that will apply to any program, elite or otherwise.

1. Make sure you develop a good relationship with your doctor, and follow through with a regular thorough medical check-up, at least once a year. It's important to ensure you are fully aware of all that is happening with your body at this stage in your life. It will be preventative in that it will create an important sense of body awareness as it responds to exercise.

2. Remember, the only piece of equipment you truly need as a runner is a good pair of running shoes that fit your type of foot properly and support you where you need to be supported. Generally speaking, a pair of shoes is good for about 500 miles. If you train a lot, you'll understand the "dead leg syndrome", and that it probably has to do with your shoes being worn down to where they are no longer supportive enough. If you're only just beginning, and exercising about 3 times per week, you'll probably need to visit your local running store about once a year for a new pair of shoes. Always make sure you bring in your old shoes so the staff can analyze your wear patterns and gait, ask you questions, and advise you properly on the shoes you need. Be prepared to take some time and try on a few pairs. It'll be the best investment you make. The clothes and accessories are functional and fun, but it's the shoes you can't do without.

3. Elite athlete or newbie, make sure you are following a well thought out program for the kind of walking or running you are doing. There are books, classes and clinics out there for help. That goes for walking AND running. It needs to be proven to be successful, and that means it will be a gradual program that guides you to progress easily and slowly. There needs to be a macro-cycle, in which the program progresses from week to week and month to month, and there also needs to be a micro-cycle in which the program progresses within the week.

4. The bulk of any walking or running program is general endurance, and that has to be at a comfortable talking pace, whether you are training for the World Masters Championships, or not! Unless you are doing a workout that involves special intervals for good reason, most of your work should be slow and comfortable. If you are unable to carry on a conversation, you are going too fast. In my experience, the beginners I work with are successful if they go SLOW. You have to respect the forces imparted everywhere on your body because of the impact. When you walk, you place 1-2 times your body weight against all the bones, muscles and tendons in your body, from your feet to your ankles, knees, hips, back, neck and everywhere in between. When you take it up to a slow, easy shuffle-jog, in which you are airborne for just a split second, you are suddenly imparting 2-3 times your body weight with each step. When you jog faster, the forces go up and become more and more significant. The same principles apply to the Masters Runner, and all elite athletes at any age for that matter. The old adage applies here: If I'd known back when I was seriously training what I know now, I wouldn't have been afraid to slow down on my easy days, and even take a few days off for proper recovery once in a while. As a mature athlete you need to be wiser. Work hard when the program tells you to, but easy recovery runs and all warm-ups and warm-downs need to be at an easy talking pace.

5. Vary the terrain, routes and distances. Soft surfaces are best, like grass or trails, and even asphalt is softer than concrete, although neither is a good idea all the time. Personally, my legs can't take any asphalt at all, so I drive to a park or field or set of trails every time I run. The variety is fun, but is also practical because it helps to prevent over-use injuries by varying the angles at which your feet hit the ground. The same route day in and day out will eventually become boring anyway.

6. Make sure you give great importance to a good stretching and flexibility program, and that you warm up and down properly. You'll feel better and will reduce your chances of injury.

7. Our bodies don't heal as quickly when we are mature. I had a tendon problem not too long ago that I know would have lasted only a week or so when I was 25. At my present age it took a month before I was able to resume activity. Listen to your body. When you have an unusual ache or pain, take a day or two or three off, and please don't let it worry you. It's a lifestyle activity and a few days, early on, are much better than a lot of time later because you are truly injured. I like my personal "Discomfort Awareness Scale". When I was a serious athlete, my coach and doctor, Dr. Doug Clement had me analyze what I was feeling, and the scale still holds true today. On a scale of 1-10, where "1" is very little awareness, and "10" is very painful, it's a good idea to give your discomfort level a rating. A "1-2" is fine, even "2-3-4" can be fine if you're careful, but consistently getting up to a "5-6" means you better give your body a break from walking and running until it's back down to a "2-3" again and on its way down. I found cross-training to be effective. Take some days or weeks off the road, and get into the pool or on a bike for a change.

8. Include cross-training in your schedule of activity. Try activities other than walking or running: swimming, cycling, cross-country skiing or snowshoeing do wonders as a transfer to your walking or running fitness, but you could choose to try anything. Work on your core strength through yoga, Pilates, aerobics, water aerobics or dancing. Variety is always good. It will help prevent injury and improve your overall fitness. I now wish I'd discovered yoga long before my forties. It most definitely would have improved my core strength and prevented injury, not to mention the strength in my mind and heart.

9. In my experience, everybody, and I mean everybody, tends to do too much. Trust me, more is not better. Be smart, patient, and listen to your body. Once again, a good program or coach will be able to help you. I also find most people in group situations tend to be very competitive. You have reached a stage in your life where you should be able to stop and smell the roses! Slow down, enjoy yourself, and be honest with yourself and what you are feeling. Your inner instincts will always tell you if you

are doing too much for your conditioning or capability. It's irrelevant for you personally, what the guy beside you is doing.

10. If you truly are into high performance in your age group, that's fantastic. If competition is what motivates you, then go for it, but at the risk of being repetitive, let me reiterate that it is no different than a beginning running program in that being cautious with a well thought out program has to be paramount. "Rest days" are as important as "hard work-out days". I wish I'd had a stronger sense of that when I was training seriously in my mid-twenties! I know for certain I'd have spent less time injured. I would suggest that, as a very serious mature middle distance runner, one moderate-hard effort session, one easy effort session, and one longer run per week is all that would be necessary. Most definitely my advice would also be to build in at least one full rest day every week, without any physical activity whatsoever. In the old days I did back-to-back hard sessions, and most certainly did 2-3 hard sessions per week plus a good long run, with of course, easy runs every day in between, often twice per day. Those days are over! (Thankfully!)

11. Enjoy yourself! Listen to your body and do stop to smell those roses! Running and walking are both great and equally as good for you. When you need to walk, WALK! If you have no desire to run, then don't run, stick to walking. Be flexible according to how you feel every day.

FINAL THOUGHTS...

> *"You have to stay in shape. My grandmother, she started walking 5 miles a day when she was 60. (Impressive eh? 5 miles a DAY!) She's 97 years old today and we don't know where the hell she is!"* -Ellen Degeneres

I don't think who we are at 20 years of age is any different from who we are at 40-plus. Our principles remain the same. We just have to modify a few things to fit our natural limitations. Remember, good healthy eating and snack habits, taking care to have adequate sleep each night, and reducing day-to-day stresses in your life will help you maintain your health. You'll definitely feel better for it whenever you run. It's lifestyle we're talking about, with balance, and good common sense. I'd run more than my usual 30 minutes-3 times per week if I could, but I'm listening to my body, a body that served me so well in my 20's when I was an elite athlete and I know if I do more, I'll wind up unable to do any running at all. It's a no-brainer for me. I can accept where I'm at because I don't ever want to jeopardize that peaceful jog in the forest I look forward to every other day.

Seize the day! Take charge of who you are. If your health is important to you, then take the steps necessary to do what you want to do, be who you want to be, and live your best life. Happy Running!

Don Kardong

Don Kardong grew up in the Seattle area. He graduated from Stanford University in 1971 and received a second bachelor's degree and a teaching certificate from the University of Washington in 1974. He moved to Spokane that year to take a job as an elementary school teacher.

In 1976, Don finished fourth in the Olympic marathon in Montreal, and the next spring he founded the Lilac Bloomsday Run.

In 1977 he left teaching to open a retail sporting goods store in downtown Spokane (1977-1986), and after selling the business in 1986 he pursued a career as a writer, primarily for Runner's World magazine, for the next 16 years.

From 2002-2004 Don served as executive director of the Children's Museum of Spokane. In August of 2004, after many years as a member of Bloomsday's Board of Directors, he took over as Race Director. He is married (wife Bridgid), and has two college-age daughters.

Back On The Wagon

Don Kardong

After 40 years and over 100,000 miles of running, I finally developed an injury worthy of surgery. Running may be blamed for a myriad of aches and pains—I've had my share of those—but I've almost always managed to bounce back quickly from whatever was ailing me. A few days on the bench, a few strategically placed bags of ice, a few days at reduced pace and distance, and I'm back at it.

Call it persistence, benevolent genetics, or dumb luck. Whatever the reason, in all my years as a runner, recovery has generally been a cakewalk. A week off erodes conditioning very little, so recovery is straightforward. Go easy until the body rebounds.

This time, though, was different. I had developed what was described as a complex tear of the meniscus in the right knee. The meniscus is a crescent-shaped piece of cartilage in the knee joint, and it can tear during weight-bearing, twisting activities—soccer, tennis, basketball. It's not typically a running injury, and the doctor puzzled over how I had gotten it.

So did I. But the meniscus wouldn't heal on its own, so while I was puzzling over how I tore it my doctor performed arthroscopic surgery to fix it. Remove the offending area, reshape the meniscus, and send Don on his way. Let the patient, more or less, chart his own path to recovery.

As I charted, in the back of my mind was the mother of all running recoveries. In 1984 Joan Benoit had arthroscopic surgery to repair a faulty knee. Seventeen days after surgery she won the U.S. Olympic Marathon Trials. It was an incredibly quick turnaround, one that stunned anyone familiar with the challenges of running a marathon, and it put her in position to win the first Olympic marathon a few weeks afterward. Arthroscopic surgery? No worries.

Wrong. Or at least wrong in my case. So here's rule #1 for anyone beginning running after a long layoff. No two recoveries, no two new beginnings, are alike. Seventeen days after my own surgery, the thought of running a marathon was ludicrous. Walking around the block was a challenge. Joan Benoit's recovery, I decided, was a freak of nature. My own moved slower than a frozen snake.

Worse, when I finally started doing some easy jogging again, I had another surprise. The other knee went south. The pain wasn't as acute, and the doctor said I could tough it out for a while if I wanted, but the diagnosis was identical. I had my second surgery in December, just as winter hit with both barrels.

This may have been my first surgery and thus my first real attempt to begin running again, but for most runners the need to restart is as familiar as the rationale for stopping in the first place. Why does a perfectly good running routine die?—let me count the ways. There are the mundane—new job, bad weather, ebbing attitude (It just wasn't fun any more). There are the distracting—new infant, second divorce, third marriage—times when life careers away from the pursuit of personal fitness. And there are the physical—shinsplints, torn meniscus, myocardial infarction. Sometimes the mind is willing, but the flesh just can't hack it.

No matter the reason for stopping, some runners never begin again, and that's a shame. Running is the fastest, cheapest, most accessible way to maintain fitness, and its ability to reduce stress and moderate temperament is the stuff of legend.

Fortunately, there are a variety of prods to restart: five (or more) extra pounds around the middle, an unwelcome wheezing after climbing a couple of flights of stairs, a certain indefinable emptiness on a weekend morning, and the sharp recollection that in better days those same hours were spent with friends, padding down a trail somewhere near the river, watched, on occasion, by a bald eagle or two.

All of these, I think, were on my mind as I finally faced the prospect of trying to restart what had once been an admirable running program. Admirable, even if increasingly unremarkable over the years. I may not have been cranking out double workouts and hundred mile weeks when that first meniscus tear reared its frayed head—those days were long gone—but I was still out there most mornings for 40 minutes at 8-minute-per-mile pace or better, 12 months a year, no matter the weather. People still told me my looks belied my chronology, an admission of running's benevolent trump of the aging process. Diminished perhaps, but my commitment to running was solid, and I was proud of having kept at it for 40 years.

When all was said and done, though, as two arthroscopic surgeries were finally receding in the rearview mirror, I felt totally disconnected from my former fit self. The first surgery had been on September 22nd, the second on December 8th. It wasn't until mid-February that I did any jogging again. It had been nearly seven months since I had done what used to come so naturally. Run.

By then my weight, which had been "trending upward" (my doctor's words) by a pound or two a year, had skyrocketed nearly 20 pounds. Friends squeezed the spare tire around my waist and commented on the fullness of my face. The elevator started seeming like a better option than the stairs. Worst of all, I struggled with a certain pervasive sadness, something that was most likely due to the absence of those wonderful chemicals produced by vigorous exercise—endorphins, seratonin, whatever. I wasn't exactly depressed, but I wasn't radiant with life either. I especially missed my weekend runs with friends. We males don't share our burdens easily. Hell, we don't even talk much. Except, that is, on a nice long tromp in the woods. Man, did I miss that.

I had gotten to this point because of two injuries and two resulting surgeries. But unfortunately, there are many paths to the same sorry spot, plenty of ways to get disconnected from fitness, a multitude of methods of falling off the wagon.

The question is, how do you get back on?

Here I turn to the ancient Chinese philosopher. The journey of a thousand miles, saith the sage, begins...with one step.

The man may not have been a runner, but he knew his stuff. And so, on a Monday in February, I took my first step of recovery. My first jogging step, that is. I had been walking for some time after surgery on the treadmill, three or four times a week, but jogging was different, a related but fundamentally different activity. Now, after a few minutes of fast walking, I jogged for one minute at 5.5 miles per hour, which a punch of a button tells me is a sluggardly 10:54 per mile pace. That's one of the beauties of using the treadmill, and also one of the negatives. You know your pace, your overall time, your caloric expenditure—all the gory details. I jogged at a paltry 5.5 miles per hour for a minute, then geared it back down to 4.0, a fast walking pace. I did this five times.

Five minutes of jogging. And it felt horrible.

Still, I had restarted. I knew my conditioning was terribly lacking, but at least I had begun the process of recovery. There was no light yet in the distance, but at least I had entered the tunnel.

Nor did I have a real plan, but rather just a general sense of how to build a running program. Start slow, build gradually, be patient. At the end of the first week I increased to 9 minutes of jogging during 30 minutes on the treadmill. By the end of the second week I was up to 13 minutes, and my speed upticked to 5.7 miles per hour. By the third week, 16 minutes at 5.9 mph. The amount of walking time decreased as the jogging increased. By the fourth week, it was 20 minutes of jogging (6.1 mph) and 10 of walking.

There's no magic to retraining, no hard-and-fast rules, but if you need guidance, follow the rule I was using: start slow, build gradually, be patient. That's actually my second rule (#1 was that no two recoveries are the same), and it's really three rules in one package. But you get the idea.

Of course if the event that precipitates a layoff is as serious as a heart attack, rule #2 is going to get a lot more detailed than "start slow, build gradually, be patient". Cardiac rehabilitation has become a sophisticated process in the past three decades, not to mention a lifesaver. If you need real advice, the cardiac pros have got it.

But faulty heart plumbing wasn't my problem. For my measly meniscus surgeries, "don't overdo it" was the gist of the advice I got from my doctor. That's certainly right on the money, but you've got to admit that it's somewhat lacking in specifics. My physical therapist's prescription was more detailed in terms of how much to do, how often to do it, and which machines to do it on, so if you'll allow me to inject another rule (#3) into this narrative, it's this: Do your exercises. Whether your layoff has been the result of injury or indolence, the rule is the same. Do your exercises.

I proffer this advice as someone who is historically antithetical to stretching, strengthening, cross-training and all those other non-running activities that running magazines spend so much time prattling about. I don't doubt them, I just don't do them.

After an injury or an extended layoff, though, those things seem especially relevant to rebuilding. The sedentary body loses structural support, primarily in musculature, and it's prudent to rebuild systematically. Hamstring curls, leg presses, leg extensions, abductor exercises...I did them all, just as my therapist recommended, three days a week.

I also started doing 45 minutes of biking twice a week. Stationary cycling had bothered my knee more than running in the weeks immediately following my second surgery, but I really needed something besides running to burn calories. I also knew that cycling was typically a great way to strengthen muscles that support the knee. Over time the knee reacted better and better to pedaling, and cycling became a key component of my ability to return to running.

As spring beckoned things really seemed to fall into place. By the middle of March I was jogging 30 minutes on the treadmill at 6.5 miles per hour, Monday-Wednesday-Friday, and one weekend I did the first run I had done outdoors in eight months. It was only three miles, ponderously slow, and my left knee fired a couple of sharp warning shots midway. But I was back at it, for real, outside.

But here's the next rule, #4 if my count is right. Restarting a running program will never be the steady progression it ought to be, even if you follow rule #2 (Start slow, build gradually, be patient). The body is way too mysterious and mischievous to allow logic to prevail.

My steady, gradual, patient building of speed and distance on the treadmill progressed nicely all the way to the end of March. Increasing speed at the rate of two-tenths each week, I reached 6.9 miles per hour in the first week of April. I was outside running on Sunday mornings, building my distance incrementally each week. Then, suddenly, my left knee stopped cooperating. The pain was sharp and constant, and on a Monday treadmill ride I was barely able to finish 30 minutes.

Here's rule #4, restated: There will be setbacks: aches, pains, fatigue, a recalcitrant body. Or maybe the setback will be a distraction that upsets the training apple cart: a crisis at work, sickness, trouble on the home front.

For me, it was my blasted left knee. It simply wouldn't behave. I cut my speed, reduced my time on the treadmill, hoped for the best. That helped, but I was still limping quite a bit. I added two degrees of incline to the treadmill and kept the speed low. That worked better. The knee seemed to stabilize, and after a few days I was able to increase my treadmill time to 30 minutes again.

And then, on a miraculous Sunday morning in mid-April, two running buddies and I met at our traditional starting spot for a six-mile run. We were all slower than Klondike sludge that morning, but it was a major uplift to be rekindling our tradition. I hadn't run trails with friends in over 10 months.

So here's rule #5 for restarting a running program: Recruit some teammates. Running is often characterized as the obsession of self-absorbed loners, but that's not even close to the truth. Yes, plenty of runs are monastic sojourns. But there's nothing like social support, a reliable running buddy or two, to keep you connected to your program.

In fact, my "teammates" had been a help long before that morning when we finally ran together. A week or so after the first surgery they came over, bearing gifts of fermented grain, and grainy videos of classic races of the past. We passed an evening watching Jim Ryun, Marty Liquori, Lasse Viren and Seb Coe during their wonder years.

And they emailed. "How's your recovery coming?" "Ready to try running trails again?" "Need more beer?"

And they called. "Want to put together a team for the next Masters championships?" "What about running the Boston Marathon next year or the year after?"

They noticed. They empathized. They checked in now and then. And that made a world of difference. It buoyed my spirits, calmed my irritability, rejuvenated my optimism.

At those times when running five miles felt like a distant dream and the possibility of running a marathon seemed as remote as Pluto, their support was vital. If you follow no other rule when you're restarting a running program, follow #5. Recruit some teammates. Find friends.

And that carried me all the way to the first Sunday in May, the weekend of the Lilac Bloomsday Run. Bloomsday is a 12-kilometer run that I started in my home town of Spokane, Washington in 1977. Between 40,000 and 50,000 runners, joggers and walkers participate. I've run it every year since its inception, but this year would be my biggest challenge. My knee was still bothering me, I was at least 20 pounds overweight, and even with my recent buildup I was in the worst shape of my life.

No matter, I was focused on rule #6: Have a goal. Mine was to complete Bloomsday, and I relied heavily on rule #5 to do it. I recruited a buddy. Both of us were ailing, both trying to regain our running legs, both unsure about our chances for success. So we leaned on each other, ran conservatively, and hung on till the finish. It was my worst time ever for the distance, but I was well pleased.

In fact, reaching that goal, still with my knee far short of 100 percent, seemed to give me a much-needed confidence boost. I had miles to go before I could realistically claim to be back in shape, but I had completed the longest run I had done since the previous July. That had to mean something.

And perhaps it did. As I marched through May, my knee seemed to rally on a gradual but clearly favorable incline of improvement. I increased my treadmill speed to 6.6, 6.8, and 7.0 miles per hour. My weight was on an equally gradual, but clearly downward trend. I began to believe I might reclaim my pre-injury weight some day.

This is not to say that it was all clear sailing from there. In fact, I'm convinced that this was only the first of many rebuildings in my running future. Some will be major, some minor, but the process will be ongoing. I'm going to need to have all my rules handy to stay aboard the wagon and keep rolling.

In the meantime, my buddies and I are back at it on Sunday mornings. Not 15 or 20 miles like in the good old days, but a solid six. Limping and wheezing a bit, perhaps, but still chugging along our favorite trails once a week, telling stories and enjoying the wildflowers.

And if all goes well, maybe one of these weeks we'll try 8 miles. And if 8 miles is possible, can a marathon be far behind?

Diane Palmason.

Diane Palmason's first running career, as a sprinter, ended in 1955. Twenty years and four children later she started running again - this time in the marathon. She's been running ever since, and has held Canadian and World records in 40+ to 65+, and from 100 meters to the marathon - plus one 80K.

Her Canadian records include the 45+, 55+, 60+ and 65+ marks for the marathon. When a chronic-fatigue-like illness kept her from racing in her early 50s, she obtained coaching certification in Canada in 1988-89, and in the U.S. in 1991. She now coaches full-time from her home in Blaine, WA, and races both in her native Canada and in the northwestern U.S.

Being the Best Runner You Can Be
At Your Present Age

Diane Palmason

"Maybe I'll run my best performances ever when I'm 70 years old." With this cheery remark I ended my part of a workshop presented in October, 2004 for the entrants in the next day's Royal Victoria Marathon. The other four presenters and I, all 60+ runners, had been asked to talk for a few minutes on what motivates us to keep running, training, and competing long after we had last set a personal best or record (PR). At the end of the workshop, the moderator, Steve King, asked each of us to write an article summarizing what we had said that day. My plan was to write about how I used age-grading to help me set goals and stay motivated despite my ever slower performances.

At the time of the workshop and my bold prediction, I had not run a "fastest ever" race in 20 years. But I explained to the group that, thanks to using calculations in World Association of Veteran Athletes (WAVA) publication "Age-Graded Tables", I had been able to rate my more recent performances, on a percentage basis, against standards set for my age. WAVA, which has since changed its name to World Masters Athletics (WMA), has been publishing and updating these standards since 1989. (See the Resource Zone - page 220). Using these percentages I could compare performances from one distance to another, thus learning in which event I had been strongest at any given age. I could also compare the percentages I had earned at my present age with the percentages for that same distance in the past. I told our audience that the times I had run to break World Records (WR) for 65+ women in the 400 and 800 metres on the track in 2003 had been two of my best performances ever – age-graded. I also told them that the other two WRs I had broken that summer - for the 1500 metres and the mile - did not rate such high percentages. Thus it had been no surprise to me to learn that the 1500 metre mark had been surpassed the following June.

The Age-Graded Tables had given me a realistic assessment, telling me which were my strongest performances. They told me that the 2:41.51 I had run for 800 metres at the age of 65 had been much better than my 2:20.9 for 800 metres at age 41 – age-graded, of course. They also allowed me to put my 2:46:21 marathon PR, set when I was 46, in perspective. I was able to calculate that although I had Canadian Records (CR) for the W45+, W55+, W60+ and W65+ age categories, my W45+ performance ranked the highest. But, I could change that by earning a higher percentage for a marathon I might run this year, at age 67. What a good goal! Over the years, the highest percentages I have earned have been for the 800 metres on the track. If I could run a really strong 800 metre race when I'm 70 I would, indeed, have my best performance ever - again, age-graded. In October 2004, this seemed like a possibility worth striving for.

Now? Maybe not. From November 2004 to February 2005, I experienced a series of symptoms while training and racing that had me wondering if my running career might soon be over. Fine! How was I going to write an article about staying motivated, and training to be the best runner I could be, when I was not sure I would ever be able to race again? The problems seemed to be cardiovascular in nature, and I was reminded of an article I had read recently in the January-February 2005 issue of Marathon & Beyond. In "Coping With the Inevitable", Paul Reese, an extraordinarily accomplished masters road-racer and ultra-runner, describes how he was sidelined, at age 86, by a heart problem diagnosed as aortic valve stenosis. How could this happen to someone who, at 73 years of age, had run 3,192 miles across the USA, crossing 12 states and averaging 26 miles a day; and then gone on, between the ages of 75 and 80, to run across the other 38 states? Thinking of him brought tears to my eyes, just as it had when I first read the article. By that time I knew that Paul had died the previous November, from complications following the surgery to correct his aortic valve problems.

At about the same time that I was reading about Paul's cardiovascular disorders, I received a message informing the members of the Canadian Masters Athletic Association (CMAA) that my long-time running friend, Dr. Danny Daniels, had just undergone quadruple bypass surgery in a Victoria, BC hospital. What? I remembered running beside Danny in the National Capital Marathon back in the late '70s. More recently, Danny had moved his competitive activities from the road to the track, competing nationally and internationally in 70+ masters pentathlons. I knew him to be fit and active, putting his energies in his retirement years into coaching young track athletes and volunteering for administrative roles in Masters athletics. News of his heart failure was a shock.

The heart function troubles of these two men were certainly in the back of my mind as I underwent a series of tests to assess the condition of my own cardiovascular system. When the results of the first tests failed to reveal any major disorders, I started doing some easy training - while always wearing my heart rate monitor (HRM). Maybe I wouldn't be able to race any more, but at least I could run. Paul Reese's article came back to me again. Its subtitle is "Aging and Diminished Physical Capacity Are Part of Life. We Need to Work Around Them". Paul had done exactly that. In fact, looking at his life from a different perspective, I dried my tears. Here was a man who had lived an active, adventurous, full life well into his 80s. I was amused to reread his statement that, "I am not yet at the point where I think and act like an old man. (I'm talking about the motions of life, not exercise here.) Translation: Elaine and I still live very active lives." I knew, from reading previous articles and books by, or about Paul, that he always credited his wife Elaine as the person who made all his transcontinental runs and walks possible by devoted service as the driver of their van. I gathered that they had shared a wonderful life together.

Describing how he felt when he learned his racing days were behind him, Paul wrote, "Reflecting on 40 years of running and racing, I've come to the realization that the most important consideration ...is not how fast you can run, not how far you can run, but rather, the degree and manner in which running and racing enhance your life". Thank you, Paul, for this reminder to be thankful for the myriad ways in which running has enriched my life. Paul concluded his article by contacting several of his friends, men in their sixties to eighties, who could still run, but whose PR days were far behind them. These men came up with several interesting lists of the philosophies and strategies they had devised to keep up their motivation to train and race even though, as 82-year-old George Billingsley recounted, "in my prime I could run 50 miles at sub-8:00 pace. Currently I can't run one mile in 10 minutes". George's advice? "Be slow - to give up." "You can do more than you think you can." Paul's friend Abe Underwood advised, "Set – or reset - some realistic goals", and "Keep, rekindle, or make new running buddy connections". These and other thoughts sounded like good material for my article on "Being The Best Runner I Could Be". But all of Paul's respondents were men. What would older women runners have to say about their continued participation in running and racing?

If the older man who is still an athlete is unusual in current society, how much further from the norm is the older woman athlete; and how is she coping with the effects of aging? During my 30 years of competitive running, I have met some amazing older women runners; women who have been both my role models and my inspiration. Maybe they would be willing to help me with my article by providing input on what keeps them still setting goals, still training, still racing as their paces gradually slow.

Thus it was that in late February I sent out a short set of simple questions to thirteen women I knew had been running for many years, and who were at least in their sixties. This was not a scientifically designed survey, but rather a gathering of information from some of my contemporary running friends. All 13 responded immediately. By adding my own responses, I had input from 14 women. What a remarkable cohort we are, even if I do say so myself. The following data describe this group in more detail.

*Ages ranged from 61 to 83 years, with 70 being the average.

*With one exception, the respondents had not been runners in their school or college years. This was no surprise, since middle and long-distance running opportunities for girls did not even exist until the mid '70s.

*All have been participating in races for from 21 to 30 years, with some having had even longer histories as fitness runners before the racing bug hit.

*While three participants recorded their best times within five years of starting, the rest took from seven to eleven years to hit their peak, with one posting some best times 14 years after she started (the oldest informant).

However, it had been at least 11 years, and up to 21 years in my case, since any of us had last run a PR. The average was 16 years. Yet, it was obvious that the fact that our fastest days were behind us had not discouraged anyone. In response to the question, "Do you plan to enter races in the current season?", respondents wrote summaries that included such goals as running in the WMA World Championships; competing in the US Masters Championships; running a local 10K before leaving for a cycle tour in Europe; going to Ethiopia to run with Haile Gebrselassie (!); competing in the World Masters Games in Edmonton (two respondents, both in the 70 to 74 age group); running a 12-hour race in the spring and a 50K in the fall; aiming to set single-age 64 records at distances from 5K to the Half; running a marathon to qualify for the 2006 event in Boston (a 77-year-old); and completing a Grand Prix schedule of races at distances from one mile to the marathon (and probably setting some 65+ American Records (AR) in many of these events).

An ambitious group! I did not ask them how they trained, but I did inquire about their sources of support as they train and compete.

Do they have coaches?

Do they train with a group or club?

Do they have partners or spouses, and if so are they supportive?

Here the answers were as varied as I am sure their accounts of their training would have been. Of the 14 respondents, only five had coaches at present, though seven mentioned that they had had coaches in the past, and two described having had an advisor in the past. One still has an advisor. Of the 13 who replied to the question about company as they trained, while all ran with groups or training partners at one time or another, eight reported that more than 80% of their running was done alone, or with a dog. Another three ran with partners or friends more than 80% of the time. Two estimated that their running time was evenly split between running alone and with company. Five did not have a spouse or partner. Of the other nine, two had partners who trained with them, five others described their partners as supportive, while two stated that their partners were not involved.

From this mixed response it seems that, regardless of the support they may or may not receive from coaches, team-mates, running friends or partners, this is a very self-motivated group. Their comments in reply to the last question: "What motivates you to train and race when you know you are unlikely to run as fast as you have in the past?" confirms this. To quote some of their comments:

Louise Adams, Colorado (83)

I just enjoy running. All my best friends are runners, as well as one of my sons. I have always liked competition. I have met many new friends at races, and enjoy visiting foreign countries for meets. I must admit I enjoy the praises I receive from younger runners.

Grace Butcher, Massachusetts (71)

My own self-image is that I am a runner. Age-group competition allows us to feel competitive forever, whatever our "forever" might be. The joy of running is so strong that I can't imagine not doing it. As long as I'm capable of being vertical, I'll be a runner.

Vicki Griffiths, Washington State (61)

I enjoy training with my running partner. I enjoy different types of races, from 800 meters on the track to ultras on the trails. I love the camaraderie at races, the feeling of accomplishment after running a race. I love running.

Mary Harada, Massachusetts (69)

If the name of the game is to always run faster than in the past I would have packed it in years ago. I will be 70 in June, and age will work as it always works. The question is how much longer can I hang on to such speed as I have, and how much faster than I do will my age-group competitors slow down than I do. None of us will get our pictures on a Wheaties box, but it's a sport. It's about having a good time, and a healthy lifestyle, and it surely beats the noon lunch and bingo at the senior center. It brings a richness to life, an excuse to travel, and a chance to play like a child.

Carol Judd, British Columbia (63)

I still do well in my age group. I enjoy pitting myself against myself. (Carol cycled across Canada in the summer of 2003.) Just last week I ran 10 seconds faster than last year in an 8 K race. I find this very encouraging. I fell back 6 to 8 minutes in the 10 K within a couple of years in my mid-50s. That big loss was hard to take, but I have adjusted now. I have accepted that this happens to most women.

Helen Klein, California (82)

I have never been about "fast". (Helen holds the 80+ WR for the marathon.) My goal is to finish strong, to inspire others to a healthy lifestyle. I will go anywhere I am invited as long as I can run. I have seen much of the world by these invitations.

Barb Macklow, Washington State (70)

Hey, almost everyone gets slower with age. Older runners can still compete in their age groups and see how they place with their peers. The basic reasons for running (health, enjoyment) are still there even if one's pace is slower.

Shirley Matson, California (64)
To not give in to the aging decline, and to run my best regardless of my age. (Shirley holds many 55+ and 60+ ARs for various distances.) The age-graded percentages help a lot, and keep me motivated. I'm still running in the 90% age-grading which is equivalent to my faster times at a younger age. It's all relative, and I have to keep that in mind. I'm also motivated by the veteran runners who are still out there. They haven't given up!

Betty Jean McHugh (BJ), British Columbia (77)
I enjoy running and the feeling of wellness it generates. (BJ holds the 75+ WR for the marathon.) Also, I have a lab dog who loves running and needs daily runs, rain or shine. I also run with a group of younger women. They are always there for me. A word of advice as you age - develop young friends! I also enjoy racing as I age. It's an opportunity to rejoin with all my friends I have competed with over the years.

Suzi McLeod, Oregon (71)
I feel like I am a forerunner, blazing a path for older women runners. See! You can do it! 70 is not old. ARs are nice, too - and age-graded results are very gratifying.

Barbara Miller, California (65)
Even though I'm not as fast, I can always measure my times by my peers (Barbara holds the 65+ WR for the marathon.) I really like to run and train. It is a great feeling to be part of the running community. I like the way running makes me feel strong and fit. I enjoy being out in the fog and the rain. I guess I enjoy almost everything about running.

Lenore Montgomery, British Columbia (74)
Running keeps me fit and healthy. (Lenore holds many 70+ CRs at various distances on both the track and the road.)

Those comments gave me some major insights into what motivates these women to continue to strive to be the best runners they can be. To read of their enthusiasm, commitment and love for their running, you would think that they had never experienced the injuries, illness and traumas in other aspects of their lives that the rest of the world has to deal with. And, you would be wrong. All kinds of injuries were cited, including lower back problems, plantar fasciitis, torn hamstrings, stress fractures, patella and Achilles tendonitis, plus bouts with asthma, high blood pressure, and other disorders. And yet I detected an unwillingness to dwell on these setbacks. They would say "I can't remember what year that was", or "I did have Achilles tendonitis, probably about age 50". Obviously they recovered and carried on. As for Danny Daniels, he later explained to me that he had long been aware that his genetic history was not favourable. His father had suffered from angina for years, before dying at an early age. How fortunate that Danny's active lifestyle had given him so many more years, and that his basic good health helped him to recover quickly. He is looking forward to competing in the BC Seniors Games for years to come.

And me? What will motivate me to train and race, particularly if my current challenges make it unlikely that I will run my best age-graded performance, at any distance, at the age of 70? I'm in the process of finding that out. What I have learned, so far, is that I'm still able to get out there and do what I so enjoy - running down to the dock, or up into the hills. I have a rather hilly nine-mile circuit that takes me out into the country, past alpaca farms and beside bubbling creeks. I love visiting with the alpacas! They're so responsive. When I'm out running like this, I don't care what my pace is.

And then there are the people I coach - men and women at all levels of running ability and experience, whose ages range from 28 to 74 years. I never give them a track workout that I have not tried myself. That will continue to keep me heading over to the track; trying new combinations of distance and recovery; experimenting with new drills to improve their strength and coordination. Standing on the sidelines holding a stopwatch is not my way of coaching. So I will still be out there, training to do what I ask of them: to do the best they can, given their background, abilities, time available for training, and all the other variables that affect their participation in an activity they so enjoy that they are willing to put out a little extra on the track and hills once or twice a week.

But racing? I have already tried a couple of races, though not in my usual style of going as hard as I can. I am like the runner whose injury is healing, gingerly trying a few steps or a few miles to see how I am doing. The difference is that I do not have any injuries - no sore hamstrings, no tight calves, no aching Achilles even though I ran 26 miles (carefully) a few days ago. How lucky is that? As for the motivation to enter races on the track and road; is it still there? Apparently it is. As in years past, I have noted on my calendar the dates of my favourite track meets, and of some road races that I really want to run.

So I will do just as the title of this article suggests. I will be the best runner I can be, given my present age and my present state of health. As I write, the signs and symptoms that led me to undergo all those tests remain to be explained and resolved. The next step will be an appointment with a cardiologist specializing in electrophysiology. Will that session lead to answers that will let me go back to my old style of racing? I don't know. I do know that I am learning a lot from this experience. Included in this learning is all that I have gained in reading the responses of my extraordinary 60+ women runner friends. I hope that others will be inspired by their words and deeds, and by my experiences as well. And whether my racing days are over or not, I know I will never forget Paul Reese's admonition to be grateful for the innumerable ways in which running has enriched my life.

Mae Palm (Wilson)

Born in Johannesburg, South Africa in 1939, Mae emigrated to England in 1956 and moved to Canada in 1966. Although she is also known by her married name, Wilson, Mae uses Palm for all her races in memory of her parents. Because of the apartheid problems in South Africa her father would often say "You are a Palm and you are Number One!" She is of mixed origin.

Mae started running in 1978 and started racing in 1980, at the age of 40. She only took up swimming at the age of 58 so she could compete in triathlons and has never looked back. She has not only completed over 100 marathons, but also regularly racks up a 1st place finish in her category! Known as "Marathon Mae", Ms. Palm is a Canadian and North American record-holder and an inspiring individual to meet.

Mae is the mother of a son, Brendan and a daughter, Breanna and now a grandmother and even though she now resides in a seniors residence, she surely qualifies as the fastest senior in town!

One of Mae's running highlights has been competing in the "Diamond Head Duet" a pre-marathon fun-run team event which is part of the Honolulu Marathon. For several years her partner was 1972 Olympic Marathon champion, Frank Shorter, shown with Mae in the photo, above.

Unfortunately, Mae finds the cost of entry fees, especially for international competitions, prohibitive and in the past has had to pass up competing in events for which she has qualified, including the Boston Marathon and the Hawaiian Ironman due to the expense. She relies on sponsors to help offset the athletic costs involved in competing in triathlons and other events. Supported by Triathlon Canada, Mae was recently recognized with a grant from the Canadian Athletic Achievements of Women in Sport (CAAWS) and will use the WISE Fund for registration fees for upcoming competitions, including the World Ironman Championships in Hawaii. In 2005 Mae received the Community Sports Hero Award (Sea to Sky Community Area) in recognition not only of her volunteering but also as a motivator and promoter of sport.

You can learn more about Mae Palm at the website: **www.marathonmae.ca**

They Call Me Marathon Mae!!

Mae Palm

I was born in Johannesburg, South Africa on December 26, 1939. At that time my family lived as 'coloured' in an area that became known later as Soweto, but then it was known as Alexandra Township. It was for Blacks and Coloureds only. My father had the pride and inner courage to open a business in a town for Whites called Ferndale, so we hid our true identity to be accepted as White. My Dad had the audacity to claim our darker coloured skin was due to Portuguese heritage! I credit this upbringing and my experience from that time with empowering me to be the best at whatever I do, whether it is working as a maid (something I did for a time) or competing as an ultra runner.

When it came time for me to find work, my birth certificate had to be shown and it told the real story. In those days my options and opportunities were severely limited due to apartheid. In 1956 I emigrated to England, where I lived until 1966. I was able to do this thanks to my Mum, who saved any money she could in her special little "brown bag". Mum and Dad ran two stores side by side called – you guessed it - Palm Stores. My Dad was a very proud man, and did not want to 'yes sir'/'no sir' anyone. He went into business for himself and became his own boss. When you go through hard times, I believe it makes a better person out of you. Dad would often tell us: "You are a Palm and you are Number One".

For me running started when I was in my late 30's. It was about the time when I started driving a car, walking less and noticed that I was gaining weight. Being just 4'11" in height, I didn't want to wind up as wide as I was high! As a 'stay at home Mum' of two children, it didn't take too long to realize that if I was going to do it, I needed to walk or run at 6:00 a.m. to have my then-husband at home with the sleeping children. For me, this was simply the best timing. I think most people will quit running if they do not choose the right time of day. When I began working in Whistler in 1982, I found that this early morning exercise schedule could be continued with good effect. It is when I became a "5-9" person. That is right: five to nine. It included my 9-5 p.m. work schedule, something with which most people are more familiar. I would be up at 5:00 a.m. to go for a run and hit my bed at about 9:00 p.m., soon after the kids. That has been my routine for over 25 years now. For me, it's now just part of life. I guess I run for the health of it!

My first race was in 1980 in Squamish, BC - an 8 km run. Maybe more to my own surprise than anyone else's, I placed first in my age category – the rest is history! This first race hooked me on racing. As most of my running and training has been achieved by self coaching, I really have nobody to blame but myself when I don't do well. Still, I strongly believe that I have managed to stay uninjured by listening to my body and backing off when I need to do so. That is to say, I have never missed a race that I have entered due to injury. I live by a personal rule to never bite off more than I can chew and that has been a key component of any success I have achieved. I run because I love it and if I manage to place first in any competition, well that is just 'icing on the cake'.

I truly thrive on other people's achievements, especially if they are older or are physically challenged. It is seeing and hearing success stories in the sport world that inspires me. Knowing what others can do, especially those with some kind of extra challenge to meet or overcome, helps me to grow stronger. I have a great appreciation for the volunteers at races and always try to let them know that in real terms. I once had a running friend comment, "If you would only stop thanking all the volunteers you would improve on your time!" To me that is neither important nor possible. It just isn't my way. I love the healthy friendly enjoyment of the run itself, the longer the better. It's like being at a big party where you dance for three or four or five hours.

There was a time (age 13-26) when I used to smoke and drink but that was the limit of my use of any kind of drugs, and I have always stayed away even from pain killers. I want to know what my body is feeling and how it is doing. I stopped smoking when I was three months pregnant with my son Brendan, more than 36 years ago. And, while on the subject of family, I also have a daughter, Breanna, who is seven years younger than her brother.

Quitting willy-nilly is not in my nature, so I always try to make sure I can finish whatever I start. Experimenting in a new sport is a real 'high' for me. That attitude has taken me to marathons, ultra running and triathlon. But, let's start at the beginning. After running for a bit I found out that I had the mental strength to endure long distance running, so over time I went from running two miles every day in the first couple of years of my regular running, to the slightly further distance of 100 miles. That transition took until 1994 at the Western States 100 Miler. I did that run in a time of 29 hours 54 minutes and some seconds, only 6 minutes to spare before the cut off of 30 hours! But, I did it!

I had the pleasure of meeting Helen Klein. She actually passed me in the dark of the night – what an amazing woman – she was in her early 70's at the time. Even though she only started running in her mid-50's, she is a superb senior athlete and has held many age category records. She is a great inspiration and gives me hopes for my own endeavours in the 65-69 age category.

One of the happiest, most pleasurable, and OK – luckiest, parts of my running career came when I partnered with Olympian Frank Shorter (1972 and 1976 gold and silver medalist for the marathon) in "the Diamond Head Duet" a pre-marathon fun run which is part of the Honolulu Marathon. The "Duet" is a 4.6 mile marathon primer and with our combined ages we were placed in the 100-119 age category. In the four or five years we competed together, we always placed first because Frank was so fast. Frank, through the inspiration he gave, drove me to compete at my highest level and to work very hard for him. He was always so gracious. He came, this Olympic hero and fantastic runner, to pick up

Breanna and me and to take us to all the events he had to attend. We met his wife and their baby girl. We went to the beach with them and were treated like old friends.

I found myself amused and amazed to be standing side by side with Frank (after the main event - the marathon) while waiting for the results to see how we did and discussing the race. It seemed so strange to be there alongside an Olympian who just treated me like a buddy (in between signing autographs, of course!).

I love running. It is really that simple. It has brought me through troubled times and is a great stress releaser. It just always makes me feel like I am beaming and smiling not only on the outside but from within. What keeps me going is really quite simple. I want to continue setting the best example I can for anyone who might be interested. But most of all, now that I have a grandson, my dream is to be able to do a run with him one day.

Dag Aabye, a Squamish forestry worker, and locally well-known skier and runner, encouraged me to believe in myself and believe that I could become a long distance runner. He used to see me on my early morning two-mile runs as I would pass his house and one day he just came dashing out of his house, stopped me and said: "You are a runner and you should do a marathon!" It was his encouragement that sparked a personal and ongoing passion for marathons even though I barely knew what a marathon was at the time. It was also what inspired me to compete in the grueling Whistler Marathon in 1982 and again in 1983.

During my ultra running days, I was so pleased to meet Ann Trason, female winner of the 1994 Western States 100 Miler. This was a real highlight for me. Ann is an amazing woman and, I think, very shy. Two weeks after the 100 Miler race, I completed the North Shore Knee Knacker 30-mile ultra marathon (North Vancouver, BC) and won my division. As I crossed the finish line, race organizer Enzo Federico announced that I had run the Western States 100 Miler as a "training run" for the Knee Knacker. I hadn't actually thought of it that way, but......

In 1995, I raced again in the North Shore Knee Knacker wearing a pair of Nike racing flats and I elected to not carry any water. The bottom of my racing flats had slight ridges but no tread. I am pleased to say that I bettered my time of the previous year by over one hour and finished in 7:20:26, breaking my own race record of 8:21:33 which I set in 1993. In 1996, I was thrilled to be one of 10 trail-runners highlighted in the Discovery Channel show "Go For It!" The show followed the runners through the terrain of the 30 Mile Knee Knacker course and filmed the trail running experience.

Medals and ribbons and trophies are good, but my personal reward for running a marathon is Häagen-Dazs ice cream! Well, that is if I have done really well; actually any ice cream is good and originally my favorite treat was waffles with oodles of cream and blueberry sauce. Treats are rewards and not for all the time. I have to earn them. Of course, I am the only one keeping track, but that is the way it is.

As the clock and calendar tick away, I take nothing for granted. Even though I enjoy good health and do marathons and other such endurance races, I am grateful to be able to walk to the bathroom and just be able to be self sufficient. I feel very fortunate to be in good health, when I know that others are not and that there is no guarantee for any of us. I like to challenge myself, but not to the point of being ridiculous. I know my limits and run against my own times.

I think it was quite fitting and made a bit of personal history to plan my 100th marathon for Vancouver. Although I go by Mae Wilson for most things, I use my maiden name, Palm, for running. I do this as a memorial to my late mother who passed away in 1990 on the very date of the Vancouver International Marathon. When my good friend Steve King announced this at the race, it was very special and heart-warming. Steve always has a way of making one feel so good through his encouraging and kind words.

In September 2002, I was featured in the article 'The Ages of an Athlete" in an issue of Sports Illustrated Women. The feature was on growing old gracefully and the changes an athlete experiences. I was the only Canadian featured in the article and represented the 60's category. Like everyone, I have had lots of photographs taken by family, race photographers and even a reporter or two, but it was my first 'photo shoot' with a New York professional photographer. To say the least, it was a memorable experience and I felt truly honoured to be chosen. The article featured athletes from a 9-year-old basketball player through the decades to a 93-year-old swimmer.

A local internationally recognized triathlete, Bob McIntosh, was tragically and brutally killed in 1999. In that same year, in recognition of him, the Bob McIntosh Triathlon was organized in Squamish, BC. While I didn't know him well, he had joked with me about becoming a triathlete. Little did he realize that I could not swim with my face in the water or that when I first tried my hand at triathlon in 1989 in Whistler on a dare, I was the last one out of the lake. I did every stroke I knew (including the backstroke) to avoid putting my face or nose in the water. I concluded at that point that I was not triathlon material! So, I thought I would volunteer for the 1999 event. When the local paper called to find out if I would be entering, I laughed at the idea. Apparently, they didn't know much about my swimming abilities either. After I put the phone down from the local reporter, I gave the race another thought. Why not try? Other people swim - I could take swimming lessons. I began to build my courage, telling myself that 'you are never too old to try'. I still feel the swim is the scariest part of triathlons, but my determination and perseverance motivated me to take lessons, practice and force myself to swim more effectively and conquer my lifelong fear of swimming. I participated in the 1st Bob McIntosh Triathlon as a personal memorial to Bob.

In 2001, I won my age category in the very windy and scary World Ironman Championship Triathlon in Kona, Hawaii. As far as I know, I was the only Canadian representing my age category at the World Championships. As someone who has always been content to finish each race, this was an achievement I had never even considered. This win was definitely 'icing on the cake'! Sadly, my family was unable to attend the race and celebrate that special victory. Still, it was a glorious moment to share the win with fellow Ironman athletes while sitting at the awards ceremony at an 'all Canadian' table. I will admit that there is some loneliness in being a long distance athlete, especially when you are self coached. However, the win in 2001 was a very proud moment that makes it all worthwhile. It was like a dream, but it encouraged me and made me feel there was still so much to learn and improve on with triathlons. More than that, it gave me the confidence to know I can achieve both the learning and the improvement.

The goal today is to remain healthy and injury free so I can enjoy having athletic fun with my grandson and the rest of the family. I sometimes dream of 'finishing' what my young hero, Terry Fox, could not do, at least in a physical sense. It is my dream and my ambition to do runs and events for a cause rather than just selfishly doing them for my own achievement and satisfaction. I often dedicate a given run to the memory of someone, but would like to be doing more. I truly believe in being careful and listening to my body. With this attitude and approach, I think I could live up to the example of my young hero and do a marathon a day for as many days as it would take. The inspiration of Terry Fox tells me there is something out there that will one day click with me and then I will know what my cause will be.

Bernd Heinrich

Bernd Heinrich's running passion was ignited in x-country while in high school at the Good Will School in Hinckley, Maine. He went on to the University of Maine in Orono, where he ran year round (track and x-country). During grad school at UCLA and as a professor at UC Berkeley he redirected his passion to science but still ran recreationally. Nearing 40 years of age he decided to cap his running "career" with a marathon, and ended up running about a half dozen in all, including finishing as the 1979 overall winner of the Golden Gate marathon at age 39, and subsequently coming in as first master runner in the Boston marathon, a day after his 40th birthday .

After that he quit the marathon entirely, and at age 41 concentrated to try to cap his career with "an" ultramarathon. He ended up running nearly ten races. In one he set the overall (any age) USA record at 100km (road) in 6:38:20 in October '81, running a 5:10:12 fifty mile split. (Both are still masters world records). Other major USA records include the 24 hour run (156 miles 1388 yards) in 1983, and the 12 hour run (95 mile 1217 yards) and 100 miles (track) in 12:27:01, in 1984. He was twice named "Ultramarathoner of the Year" by Ultrarunning Magazine.

Presently Bernd's daughter Erica, age 35, has taken up running, and he has "retired" from competition in order to devote his full energies to biological science and writing, and to a new family with two kids, Lena 6, and Eliot 8. Five years ago he set the over 60 age-group fifty mile road record.

The Race
(Reprinted with Permission of Harper Collins Publishing)

Bernd Heinrich

*You don't run against a bloody stopwatch, do you hear? A runner runs
against himself, against the best that's in him. . . . Against all the
rottenness in the world. Against God, if you're good enough.*
  - BILL PERSONS, fictional coach in Hugh Atkinson's The Games

"On your marks - get set - "

The sharp report of a starter's gun sounded. I'd heard it hundreds of times in
over two decades past. But this time was different. I was forty-one years old.
There would not be another chance. That's what made this fearsome. My one
comfort was that I'd promised the beast in me that this would be my last effort,
and my best.

Klecker and the others up front took off like antelopes pursued by wolves. Keep
calm, keep calm, I kept telling myself. Don't get sucked out. I've got to run my
race, on my schedule. Trying to hold myself back, yet going fast enough to hit
about a 6:15 per mile pace, took concentration. I had to be like a camel, although
a very fast one. I had to make sure I started slower than the pace of most of my
training runs even while factoring out possible adrenaline effects that would
make me feel light at the start. I would check my pace by listening to timers
along the course who'd holler out the elapsed race time at the mile, 5 miles, 10
miles. . .

We had barely taken off, it seemed, when I heard the first mile split - several
seconds over 6 minutes - just a tiny tad too fast, but right about where I wanted
to be. Ray Krolewicz, the indestructible ultramarathon camel, was alongside and
tried to make small talk. I could neither listen nor talk, and I soon passed him. A
big crowd was ahead, and after only 3-4 miles I had lost visual contact with the
leaders.

Jack came alongside me at the first-aid station to hand me my first drink. I
grabbed, squirted the juice into my mouth, dropped the squeeze bottle, and kept
on, trying to keep the same pace. The key to winning this would be: never speed
up, never slow down, don't stop till the finish. Most important in a race, never get
sucked into someone else's program. And, oh yes, believe.

I'd drink all I could force down. I had to rely on fat metabolism for endurance,
but I'd burn carbohydrate for as long as possible-all of what I had loaded into
muscles and liver and all I could process from the gut along the way-to boost my
speed. Still, I worried that I might drink too much juice, because I had no way of

knowing how fast I was losing liquid from sweat. It all depended on pace and temperature, both of which seemed to be rising quickly.

At the 10-mile mark I anxiously listened as the times were again called out as we rushed by. One-o-three ten, one-o-three fifteen. . ." At sixty-three minutes and 10-15 seconds (at 6:20 per mile) my time was almost a minute slower for 10 miles than what I was aiming for. A little alarm bell sounded in my brain-but the rational centers said, better slow now than later. Like antelopes, Paul and Klecker had already passed through the 10-mile mark a full 8 minutes ahead of me, and I had not been loafing! Such an incredible lead - but then, since last year Klecker had been the best ultrarunner at that distance in the world, ever. What could I expect? Some of the best runners' strategy, which the great late Pre (Steve Prefontaine) was famous for, is to try to control the race and lead from the start, intimidating the competition and then hanging on by sheer guts. Obviously not my style.

I speeded up only a tiny bit to try to get back on an even pace. I did that surprisingly successfully, because I later (eighteen years!) learned that I finished the first four 10-mile loops in 1:03:16, 1:01:31, 1:01:33, and 1:01:03.

At the end of the first 10 miles my mind was still clear, and I could concentrate on the running machine. There is always plenty of time for taking inventory of one's otherwise automatic responses on an ultramarathon. I still had 52 miles left to go.

Keep those thumbs up, I told myself, to avoid floppy wrists. Motion must be forward and back, minimizing up and down. Keep the knee lift to a minimum. I'd lock my mind on the movements, checking them out to make sure I was feeling smooth. Now-loose, loose-keep it loose. For a half mile I continue my mental tour of the running body, visualizing loose thighs, calves, arms. . . Then a focus on my legs. Creeping tiredness can cause inefficient motions.

Relax. Swing each leg far forward while at the same time loosening all the muscles; that way only the relevant ones do the work, and none work against each other like a bumblebee's shivering response, which burns energy to produce heat but accomplishes no work. I visualize matching the stride of my right leg in synchrony with the swing of the left arm. For a quarter mile or so, I feel the rhythm and switch my conscious editing to concentrate on the opposite limbs. Once in a while, I vary the length of my stride, to contract my leg muscles for slightly different durations, like frogs varying the length of their calls. The rhythm of my footsteps is steady, unvarying, and like my heartbeat, it is unconsciously timed with my breathing. As long as I'm at rest, I can normally feel the beat when I switch on my conscious awareness. There are either one or two beats with each inspiration, and the same number with each expiration. During running I feel my breathing. Like my heartbeat, the breathing rhythm is usually also unconscious. It is timed to the same unconscious metronome that times the footsteps. I like the feeling of the strong, steady rhythm with everything in sync. At times I listen to it-in just one instant I can bring it up on my screen of consciousness. Three steps with one long inspiration, a fourth step and a quick expiration. Over and over and over again. My mantra. My mind goes blank. Sometimes I vary the beat, with only two steps during the inspiration. I can do this switch-over consciously, but it normally occurs unconsciously as I increase my effort. The harder the effort, the deeper the breaths, until there is the sudden switch in number of breaths. The rhythm preserves synchronicity, synchronicity translates to smoothness, and smoothness means energy efficiency. The body's metronome has been fine-tuned by more tens of thousands of miles than I can begin to comprehend, which have long been deleted from my working consciousness, just like the breathing rhythm itself. Only the feeling of it remains. And it feels good.

Meanwhile, Klecker's lead is continuing to grow ever wider. I'm almost to the marathon mark and about to grab my juice bottle when I hear Jack yell: "He is heading for a new world record." That would be in the 100-kilometer, I presume; he has already set his astounding world record in the 50-mile, last year. "You couldn't reach him now with an airmail postage stamp," Jack continues-just as I drop the juice squeeze bottle-perhaps to forestall later disappointment or to prevent me from overreaching.

I will remember his comments for as long as I live. It took some wind out of my sails. Klecker was indeed intimidating. I knew then that if I couldn't beat him, even in this one race, then I obviously couldn't have a U.S. record, either. To try to succeed, I needed to start off with fantastic dreams, but ultimately I'd have to be realistic. I tried to console myself with the thought that I must simply do the best with what I have. Giving it my all, that's all I can do. That's all I can care about, and therefore that's what really counts. Nevertheless, things can happen. Any weakness or flaw-no matter how slight-will be magnified in the next 10,20,30 miles, and after that it will be hell for all of us. That still gives plenty of room for the unseen, the unplanned, the unanticipated, in any of us. I recall Bert Hawkins, twenty-two years ago at Hinckley, Maine. . .

My time at the marathon mark was 2:42. I'm on pace again, although Klecker, of course, is far out of reach. I'll not be trying to outsprint an antelope. If I tried to be too brave, I'd overreach. I'd blow up. I'd end up a casualty alongside the path. Once you speed up to the point that you're breathing hard, you dip too deeply into the carbohydrate stores, and possibly pass the anaerobic threshold, when lactic acid is produced faster than your metabolic and cardiovascular systems can get rid of it. Lactic acid is like sand accumulating in the gears of a car that soon bring all to a grinding halt.

Don't speed up, don't slow down, and above all, never stop. . .

Soon enough it gets harder. Much harder. But I'm not sure anymore whether I'm slowing down or overcompensating and possibly speeding up. I just keep working harder and harder, and steadily going by one runner after another, using them to cinch myself along. A runner up ahead - move up on him – pass - the next one.

Coming by Jack again. He yells: "Paul has dropped out-Klecker is still going strong."

The cranberry juice is becoming increasingly hard to 'stomach. I lose both my thirst and my appetite and have to force myself to swallow. Fatigue to the point of pain is overwhelming other sensations. My body is screaming at me to stop, and it would always win if it did not have a mind to play tricks with it, boss it around, and delude it.

To psych one-self up takes self-delusion. That's where the use of logic comes in. Logic is less an instrument for finding truth than a tool that we use to help us justify what our lower emotional centers direct or demand. Lacking this self-delusionary logic, we would be less able to rationalize, and so be unable to succumb to such mad, senseless, crazy things as trying to see how fast one can run 62.2 miles without stopping. Ultimately, our logic may get wacky enough that we see through our rationalizations, and then they don't make sense anymore. This almost invariably occurs sometime around halfway through the race, and you ask yourself, Why am I doing this? Why am I here? Why? There is no answer.

At that point, one needs faith-a combination of ignorance, deliberate blindness, hope, and optimism. It defies logic yet makes us able to strive and to survive. Maybe it also distinguishes the mind from a computational machine. It's what made our ancestors chase the antelope on and on till it tired.

"To run a good ultra-marathon," the world's best ultramarathoner, Don Ritchie, has said, "you need a good training background and a suitable mental attitude-i.e., you must be a little crazy." I had the first. But the second? I ask myself: Is there anyone else in America who might be an even greater lunatic than I, who might push himself even harder? A small voice says, Probably. So I push again, a little harder. Am I crazy? Perhaps. But I must judge both my and others' ability accurately, maintain absolute integrity to my vision, and be guided strictly by cause and effect, by empirical reality. As Yogi Berra said about baseball, "It's ninety percent mental. The other half is physical."

After about 4 hours, the sun is blazing hot and the wind has picked up. Jack still holds out the welcoming squeeze bottle full of cranberry juice every few miles. I grab, squirt, swallow, drop the bottle, and am glad to have both hands swinging free again. . . "Klecker is fading," I thought he said as I went by. What? Really? Fading? Did I hear correctly? I'm still passing people. Another 5-mile lap, another cranberry juice. "You're in second place. . ." So what? I think-he is still miles ahead.

Every handoff is now a welcome event. Every handoff ticks off another 5 miles completed.

I don't really feel thirsty, but I drink anyway, because on my training runs I had often had a lot of fluid weight loss without feeling thirst. Thirst arrives too late.

"He's dying!" Jack says at another handoff. I did hear it right. I think of Billy Mills as he, a complete unknown, is coming out of the last turn charging into the lead of the Olympic 10,000-meter, saying over and over to himself, I can win, I can win, I can win. I feel a shiver all over my body. Jack's two words have an electrifying effect. Although my body is weakening, I'm carried along now by what amounts to spirit. I don't really know what spirit is, but I feel different. I know I've got a chance! The impossible. Nobody knows me. And I'm charging out of nowhere, and I'm going to catch him! I know what he is experiencing. I know exactly what it feels like to die on the run. Last week was my most recent reminder. There is no way he'll go beyond the 50, and there is no way I won't.

It is time to get excited. It is time to squeeze out the adrenaline. I think of Mike, Bruce, Fred on our cross-country team, mock-growling, laughing, and saying on the run: "Gotta be tough-be an animal." I also know that being ahead means nothing-not till the finish line. Two years earlier, while I was laboring about a mile from the finish line of the San Francisco marathon, I heard snatches of chatter from radios held by spectators along the course. I recall hearing: "Here comes the winner now... it is Peter Demaris." Demaris was just barely visible, far ahead of me. But I wasn't ready to cede defeat, despite the premature announcement of his victory. I speeded up, and just kept going-I don't know how or from where it came, but something made me fly. My finishing time was nothing to brag about, but the San Francisco Examiner the next day (October 29, 1979) headlined, "Tricky ending to Golden Gate Marathon-complete unknown wins." I was that unknown runner. And I know there are many. They can be any of us. I might get the lead now-today-but I, too, could be caught. . . just as Demaris was caught then, right before the line.

During exercise, the mobilization of fuel for use by the muscles is controlled largely by the circulation not only of adrenaline but also of noradrenaline, adrenocorticotropic hormone, glucagon, and thyroxine-all these hormones are controlled by feedback loops through the brain. I obviously don't think of hormones or their feedback loops now, but abnormal performance demands abnormal physiology. How do I change from being normal? I involuntarily draw inspiration and strength from the example of brain power exhibited by others I admire.

Lefty had it. Lefty Gould, who had talked to me for hours when I was mail boy and when I had jogged back and forth twice a day carrying the leather mail pouch. He had looked unblinkingly at me with his pale gray eyes and told me of the "Krauts" who crawled over the lines and held him up at gunpoint, to demand his cigarettes, then let him go. In my mind's eye, I see him next in the hospital as a group of interns wheels him along. Feebly and laboriously he hoists himself up on one elbow and declares with a grin on his face, "I can lick all of you f#@$*rs'" to show them not to pity him, the once great prizefighter. His brave but feeble gesture was a declaration of his generosity-how much he had in him, even when his body was helpless. Not to give an inch is to give everything. The stories he told me, a little kid. . . He'd lean out the teller's window to tell me how he'd thrown his shot-out thighbone at the enemy. . . as he continued shooting even as he sunk into unconsciousness. I draw deep now, on memories-on life, really. The mountain of life. Let there be enough of it to draw from. . . till the finish line. . . Lefty-now I see him-as he lay so still with his hands neatly folded across his U.S. Army uniform, in the casket in Moody Chapel, where I'd been hundreds of times as a kid before running off into the woods on Sunday afternoons. Tears well up. Lefty had been a personal bodyguard of General George S. Patton, a 1912 Olympian. Patton had said, "Now if you are going to win the battle, you have to do one thing. You have to make the mind run the body. Never let the body tell the mind what to do. The body will always give up." The body can handle only little steps. The mind can take great leaps. To that tree. . .

My entire life is compressed into this little life of several hours. The past, present, and future fuse into a searing knot where the body shrinks and the mind is of ever-greater significance. Horizons shrink. I'm dipping into pain, gradually, inexorably. I look up and focus on a tree up ahead. Keep the pace-to that tree. I'd make it and reward myself with a congratulation: I made it! There-now to that tree. And so it goes, one little section of the distance at a time, distance I'd never in my life have to run again. . . ever. . . never again. Now is all that matters. Now-now. This moment.

It's as if I've been in the woods a hundred years, trailing a big whitetail buck forever-I've finally come close physically. I can do it! Don't mess up now. This is the end of the longest hunt, and the biggest buck of all is up ahead. He's that white line across the pavement. My mind locks on, drawing me forward.

Finally, as I'm nearing the end of the 50, Jack hollers excitedly: "Klecker is finished! You are first now, and far ahead of the next runner." Only 12 more miles to go. I grab the cranberry juice and speed on, all the more possessed. If I can finish first, that's all the more reason to run ever harder, because now I have a chance to set a record-if I can only hang on. But anything can happen-a muscle pull, the dreaded wall, dehydration, an ankle sprain. . . a complete unknown. . . .

The end of this hunt is drawing close. The quarry I'm trying to catch will be defined by a number, my finishing time: hours, minutes, and seconds separated by colons. And that number once made will be with me for the rest of my life. Maybe it should go on my tombstone. After all, two sets of numbers designating birth and death dates say little about a person. It is the in-between that matters. The number I am making now is pure. It will define the limits of my animal nature-it will be the measure of my imagination, achieved by gut and spirit. It can't be bought, traded, or achieved through leverage. All other honors are paltry in comparison. It is valuable, because it's a product free of others' judgments, prejudices, jealousies, and ignorance. This is life not as it is, but as we idealize it.

Don't forget the precious past. I'm forty-one. I'm nearing the end of the cat's proverbial nine lives as a runner. The back, the two knee operations, the orthopedic surgeon saying, "If you don't stop running, I'm going to have to take that kneecap off and throw it in the garbage can."

"How many miles do I have left if I stop running?" I wanted to know.

"I can't tell you that. It could go tomorrow, or it could last you twenty years."

"What if I *don't* stop running?"

"I can't tell you."

"In that case," I had told him, 'I'm going to run like hell and get into the best shape of my life, and use those miles to their Utmost." And I did, and won first master in the Boston Marathon. (Inactivity never helped me: this was only one of four very similar scenarios that I encountered in over forty years of running.)

A picture pops up in my mind of the tall man I saw walking across the campus at Berkeley. His face was missing. Burned off by napalm? All of those brave soldiers-many of my running mates. Someone else went, because I didn't. . . . Their heroism-and I'm complaining that I'm tired?

I inhale deeply. I suck in the fresh, clean air off the lake.
I run past strollers on the racecourse sidewalk who see us runners in deep concentration. We look neither right nor left. We stink of sweat. Our glazed eyes stare ahead. . . Runners don't have to smile. We don't have to look pretty. We don't allow ourselves to be judged, and we cringe every time we see a superb athlete such as an Olympic diver, gymnast, or skater having to stand to be judged, waiting for cards with numbers to be held up.

One little distance at a time. One step. Every one is precious. Every step is aliveness, because aliveness is to resist inertia. I draw on all the emotional wells I can think of, trying to kill the demons of indifference that say, Why? Why? It doesn't really matter-why should I care whether I win or if somebody else does? And who cares whether I finish in 6:30 or 6:31 or even 8:30, if I'm first? Nobody will know the vast differences. Except me.

I'm still passing people on successive loops who are miles behind me in the race. Bystanders can't tell who is up front from who is way back in the pack. Just as in real life.

"Suffering is the sole origin of consciousness," Dostoyevsky wrote. My stream of consciousness alternates between vividness and dreamlike somnolence. Sometimes it retrieves peaceful scenes-the antithesis of what I'm experiencing. I envision myself lying in the grass by the cabin, paddling with my pal Phil down Bog Stream, fishing with him as a teenager at dawn on Brailley Brook in the great north woods of Maine. I try to feel the birds, the forest, the people that are in me. I call upon these riches through images in my mind that "flicker about in dreams or can be called upon to relieve an hour of stress or idleness," as Howard Evans, a biologist friend, once wrote. I call upon those images now. . . I see Phil when I ran the state meet at Bates College. He'd driven thirty miles from Wilton, the little town with the roaring, clanging textile mill where he'd gone early each morning most of his life, carrying his black lunch pail with a thermos and a sandwich. He'd driven all the way to Lewiston just to see me run. Nobody had ever done that before. I'd won it for him, against the best distance runner in the state, and in his excitement at seeing me win, he jumped out onto the track-and threw up! I'm running for you now, Phil. . . I see you in bed. Cancer has melted your frame. You can barely move. "It's a hard row to hoe," you say wearily. I have hoed hundreds of rows of beans and corn, many for you in your garden when I was a kid. "Take me to Bog Stream in the canoe," you feebly begged me. You wanted to go out, on our favorite canoeing stream, where we'd found peace together.

Now during the run I tap into another emotion: shame. Did you want us to tip the canoe in order to drown yourself? I had played dumb. It took you another two weeks of agony, lying staring at the ceiling, before you expired. How precious you'd think this moment is now, if you'd had it, ever. How precious I'll think it is, when I'm where you were. . . .

My heart pounds. When will it be my turn? I try next to distract myself with pleasant images-painted turtles slipping off half-submerged logs on the Kennebec River as we glide quietly around a bend with the rowboat, down past the gardens at Good Will. Bumblebees buzzing on the blue pickerelweed blooming along the banks, where the lily pads float and the pickerel lurk . . . Will my kids see these wonders? Feel them? My daughter Erica-only ten years old has just left with her mother to live back in California. Erica-Erica-I love you-I love you. . . And my body shudders. Winning is not enough, I tell myself again and again. I had for months forgotten what the record was, after I knew I'd try for it, because ultimately it didn't matter. My best did.

The miles roll on. My first place finish feels assured, but so little in life really is.

My pace now has to be maintained by a different body. The very landscape has changed. The distance between trees has expanded, the ground has hardened, the scenery is fading. There are no more bystanders. Nothing but pavement 10 feet in front of me, 5 feet, and my mind's constant vision of the quarry ahead-that white line across the pavement. The universe is contracting, constricting. The pavement and the line-is all there is. I've run several times around the globe for this opportunity, and I could still miss it by a second. If I don't run those 100 yards to that next turn as fast as possible, I will later experience a pain greater and more long-lasting than what I feel now. . . To that tree. . . .

I remember only short phrases of songs. I had rehearsed a Cat Stevens song in hopes of distracting myself on the run: "Summers come and gone / Drifting under the dream clouds / Past the broken sun / I've been running a long time, on this traveling ground." I needed stronger and stronger medicine. Images of. . . the cabin in the woods, the tranquillity of the trees and the songs of the birds at dawn, the thoughts of their epic migrations, the feel of wet dew on the grass early in the morning, the humming of the insects on the rhododendron in the bog-the flight of the ducks last spring and their excited quacking in the swamp. . . Memories, distractions, remembrances, and the longing for "the peace beyond understanding" rush me onward.

As I'm rounding the bend with only 2 or 3 more miles to go, I'm elated by one thing, there is one overpowering, delicious thought: This will end soon. I speed up slightly, catching a second wind for the anticipation of release-in minutes-seconds. That foretaste of relief drives me as hard as any other motives. However, even when I finally see the finish up ahead-that group of people-I continue to fear that possibly another runner might be creeping up behind, having saved it to the end, to rush by to take me by surprise. Or if I'm close to a record, any number of them could be invisibly beside me, separated only by a date.

Soon I see it, up ahead-the prize, the white line across the pavement. A hundred feet-50-10 . . . Finally. . . It's over. . . I've done it! I've come through-into a heaven where merely being there is the sweetest ambrosia.

One would think I'd have raised my hands in triumph and pranced about like a mad banshee. However, I was much too exhausted to raise even a finger; instead, feeling a deep, quiet, warm glow, I collapsed onto the soft, cool grass in the shade of a tree. I felt unimaginable contentment as my heart pounded a long time from the hard finishing sprint.

The tall, solid metal winner's cup is inscribed at the base with the words "Winner-100k" and beneath them, "1981 National Champion." The cup is full. It contains what I had put into it. Like catching an antelope, the best things in life that we can experience are served on the challenge to endure and to overcome in the long run.

Editor's Note: "The Race" took place in Chicago on October 4, 1981. The official time was 6:38:21, breaking the previous 100 km road race record by 13 minutes. Bernd Heinrich was recognized by ***Ultrarunning*** magazine as the outstanding male performer of 1981.

THE RESOURCE ZONE

"No doubt a brain and some shoes are essential for marathon success, although if it comes down to a choice, pick the shoes. More people finish marathons with no brains than with no shoes." [Don Kardong]

AGE-GRADED PERFORMANCE

Summary prepared by Diane Palmason

AGE-GRADED TABLES

The following notes, including the uses for age-grading, were taken from the 1994 edition of "Age-Graded Tables", compiled by the World Association of Veteran Athletes (WAVA), and published by National Masters News.

Age-graded tables are a series of "age factors" and "age standards" that can be used to compare performances at different ages in the disciplines of track and field, long distance running, and racewalking events. The tables show how much a person's athletic performance improves during youth and declines during aging. The performance factors vary by event. Standards are published for both sexes for each age from 8 to 100 for the common events in the three disciplines.

The purpose of age-graded tables is twofold:

1) To correct a person's performance, no matter what his/her age, to what it would have been (or will be) in their prime years. By so doing, all kinds of interesting comparisons can be made. You can compare back to your best performances; and you can compare your performances to those of other people of any age, such as open-class athletes.

2) To provide individuals with a percentage value which enables them to judge their performance in any event without bias to age or sex. No matter how old one gets, this performance percentage will always be judged against the standard for one's age. As your performances decline with age, so do the world standards that the tables use to calculate your percentage, giving a true measure of your performance.

Age-graded tables can be used to:

1. Keep track of your progress over the years.
2. Compare your own performances in a given event.
3. Compare your own performances in different events.
4. Compare your progress in the current year.
5. Set goals for the current year and future years.
6. Compare back to your best-ever performance.
7. Compare your performance to people of any age.
8. Estimate your performance in new events.
9. Compare performance of older and younger individuals in the same or different events.

10. Select the best performance in an event among all age groups.
11. Select the best overall performance in a meet or race.
12. Select outstanding athletes.
13. Give recognition to good performances in the younger and older age groups.
14. Enable athletes at the upper end of their age group to compete on an equal level with those at the lower end of their age group.

WAVA (now World Masters Athletics - WMA), is the world governing body for masters track and field, long distance running and racewalking. The first set of tables was compiled in 1989. These were updated in 1994.

Online Calculator.

In the interim, a lecturer in applied statistics at the University of Reading in Britain created an online form that allows athletes to enter their age, event and performance and have the calculations completed for them at the click of a mouse. This form can be found on the web at

http://www.howardgrubb.co.uk/athletics/wavalookup.html

Projected Update of Tables.

A third update of the tables was due to be published in 2004, but thieves stole the computers containing all the data in May of 2003. Huge Excel files containing the single-age world records for all track and field events plotted on a curve had to be recreated, causing a delay in publication. The latest version of the tables will be published by National Masters News, with an expected publication date in 2005. The National Masters News offices are now located in Eugene: PO Box 50098, Eugene, OR 97405. Details on this and other publications can be found on their website: www.nationalmastersnews.com.

EXAMPLE OF AGE-GRADED PERFORMANCES

Running in the Zone is the work of twenty-six individual contributors, including the editors. Both men and women are represented, covering a range of ages from about 46 to almost 80. A number have written about age graded performances and how to use them to put present day achievements into context.

The following two tables are based on the average contributor age of just over 61 years, to set out some benchmark performances for several distances from the mile to the marathon. They were built using the calculator, graded against the age standard for a 61-year-old man and woman respectively. The tables are just an example as the 100% standard changes with advancement of the best recognized performance for the distance. If you want to determine your own performance percentage for a given distance, you can go to the calculator and enter your age and time in the appropriate boxes. The tables below are calculated for our fictional "average" contributor to *Running in the Zone* at the time of publication.

In addition to finding your personal percentage performance for any given clocking at any given distance, you will also get an age graded time, adjusted to the standard age used for the system. For instance, if our man ran a 10K at 41:20 or 80%, the calculator would give him an adjusted time of 33:42.

Table 1. Male: Age 61

%	Mile	5K	10K	Half Marathon	Full Marathon
100	4:41	15:59	33:04	1:12:32	2:32:50
90	5:13	17:45	36:45	1:20:39	2:49:50
80	5:50	19:59	41:20	1:30:35	3:11:05
70	6:42	22:50	47:17	1:43:40	3:38:20
60	7:48	26:38	55:09	2:00:55	4:14:40
50	9:21	31:58	66:10	2:25:00	5:05:36

Table 2. Female: Age 61

%	Mile	5K	10K	Half Marathon	Full Marathon
100	5:24	18:26	38:02	1:22:57	2:53:08
90	6:00	20:29	42:16	1:32:10	3:12:22
80	6:45	23:03	47:33	1:43:40	3:36:30
70	7:43	26:20	54:20	1:58:30	4:07:20
60	9:00	30:44	1:03:25	2:18:17	4:48:30
50	10:48	36:52	1:16:05	2:45:54	5:46:20

INTERNET RESOURCES

NOTE TO READERS: As a service to readers, the Editors requested contributors to provide a listing of their favourite running related web sites for inclusion in the Resource Zone. The editors are providing these sites for the convenience of readers, but can take no responsibility for the content of the sites, nor can we endorse any site listed. While we have made every effort to confirm the listed sites were active at the time of publication, we can make no guarantee of their continuing availability over time. Some of the sites are free, others may require a subscription or other user fee for full access.

CONTRIBUTOR SITES.

Some of our contributors have their own web sites and we are pleased to list them here.

Steve King: **www2.vip.net/~stking/** and **www.triathlon-tips.com**

Joe Henderson: **www.joehenderson.com**

Moe "the Eagle" Beaulieu: **www.eagleruns.com**

Don Kardong: **www.donkardong.com**

Richard Benyo: **www.marathonandbeyond.com**

Mae Palm: **www.marathonmae.ca**

ASSOCIATIONS, CLUBS AND ORGANIZATIONS.

Masters Track Association (formerly WAVA) **www.masterstrack.com**

Prairie Inn Harriers Running Club: **www.pih.ca**

Pacific Road Runners: **www.pacificroadrunners.com**

BC Athletics Association: **www.bcathletics.org**

Age graded Calculator:
www.howardgrubb.co.uk/athletics/wavalookup.html

Road Running Club of America: **www.rrca.org**

GENERAL INFORMATION AND NEWS.

www.keepingtrack.com

www.trackandfieldnews.com

www.Active.com

www.marathonguide.com

www.marathonmaniacs.com

www.ontherunevents.com and www.ontherunevents.com/yrcm

www.runtheplanet.com

www.coolrunning.com.au

www.clubfatass.com/cdn_ultras.com

www.ukathletics.net

www.race-results.co.uk

www.canadianmarathoning.bc.ca

www.halhigdon.com

www.georgesheehan.com

www.JeffGalloway.com

www.runnersofcompassion.com

www.terryfoxrun.org

FAVORITE BOOKS

NOTE TO READERS: As with the other resource listings, the editors have requested contributors to provide a short list of their favourite reading material on the subject of running. And, as with all this material, the editors provide this information for the convenience of readers but cannot endorse nor be responsible for the content of any book listed here.

Personal Best. George Sheehan, MD – Rodale Press (1989)

Galloway's Book on Running. Jeff Galloway – Shelter Publications Inc. (1984)

Running Past 50. Richard Benyo – Human Kinetics (1998)

Why We Run – A Natural History. Bernd Heinrich – Harper Collins Publishing (2001)

Running Start to Finish. John Stanton – Lone Pine Publishing (1999)

The Complete Book of Running. James Fixx – Random House (1977)

The Complete Marathoner. Joe Henderson (Ed) – World Publications (1978)

Running and Being, The Total Experience. George Sheehan, MD – Simon and Shuster (1978)

It`s Not About the Bike. Lance Armstrong with Sally Jenkins. Berkley Books. 2000.

Your Body Doesn`t Lie. John Diamond - Warner Books, 1979.

Messages From Water. Masaru Emoto - Hado Kyoikusha. 2001.

Power vs. Force: the Hidden Determinants of Human Behavior. David Hawkins -   Hay House, Inc. 2002.

Mastering Your Hidden Self: A Guide to the Huna Way. Serge King - Quest Books. 1985.

Rapid Recovery: Accelerated Information Processing & Healing. Stephen P. King -   Trafford Publishing. 2004.

The Ultimate Healing System. Donald Lepore - Woodland Books. 1988.

Acupressure for Athletes. David J. Nickel - Henry Holt & Co., Inc. 1984.

A Step Beyond: A Definitive Guide to Ultrarunning. Don Allison. (Editor) - UltraRunning Publishers, Weymouth, Mass. 2002.

The Runner's Literary Companion. Garth Battista - Penguin Books. NY. 1994.

The Death Valley 300. Near-Death and Resurrection on the World's Toughest Endurance Course. Richard Benyo - Specific Publications Inc.Forestville, CA. 1991.

Running Encyclopedia: The Ultimate Source for Toady's Runner. Richard Benyo & Joe Henderson - Human Kinetics. Champaign. IL. 2002.

More Than A Game. Sport in Our Time. Sebastian Coe, David Teasdale and David Wickham - BBC Books. London, England. 1992.

Runners & Walkers: A Nineteenth Century Sports Chronicle. John Cumming - Regnery Gateway. Chicago, Illinois. 1981.

Boston Marathon: The History of the World's Premier Running Event. Tom Derderian - Human Kinetics Publishers. Champaign, Illinois. 1994.

How to be a Champion From 9 to 90. Earl W Fee - Feetness Inc., Mississauga, ON. 2001.

The Dunlop Book of the Olympics. David Guiney - Eastland Press. Lavenham, Suffolk, England 1972.

To the Edge: A Man, Death Valley and the Mystery of Endurance. Kirk Johnson - Warner Books. New York. 2001

The Ultimate Athlete. George Leonard - Avon Books. NY,NY. 1974.

Mental Discipline: The Pursuit of Peak Performance. Michael K. Livingston - Human Kinetics Books. Champaign, ILL 1989.

Running the Lydiard Way. Arthur Lydiard and Garth Gilmour - World Publications Inc. Mountain View, CA. 1978.

Running to the Top. Arthur Lydiard and Garth Gilmour - Jenkins Publishing. 1962

How They Train. Fred Wilt - Tafnews Press, 1959

Flanagan's Run. Tom McNab - William Morrow & Co. NY, NY. 1982.

Lore of Running: Discover the Science and Spirit of Running. Tim Noakes - Leisure Press. Champaign, Illinois. 1991.

In Pursuit of Excellence: How to Win in Sport and Life Through Mental Training. Terry Orlick - Leisure Press. Champaign, Illinois. 1990.

Running Fast & Injury Free. Gordon Pirie. Edited by John S. Gilbody - Available FREE on the Internet

The Ghost Runner. John Tarrant - Athletics Weekly. Rochester, Kent, England. 1979.

The World of Marathons. Sandy Treadwell - Stewart, Tabori & Chang. NY, NY. 1987

Beyond Winning: The Timeless Wisdom of Great Philosopher Coaches. Gary M. Walton - Leisure Press. Champaign, Illinois. 1992.

The Complete Athlete: Integrating Fitness, Nutrition and Natural Health. John Winterdyk with Karen Jensen - Alive Books. Burnaby, B.C. 1997.

To Run With Longboat; Twelve Stories of Indian Athletes in Canada. Brenda Zeman - GMS Ventures Inc. Edmonton, Alberta. 1988.

Lillian Board. David Emery - Hodder and Stroughton. 1971

My Olympic 10 Days. Kelly Holmes and Richard Lewis - Virgin Publications 2004

The Perfect Mile. Neal Bascomb – Houghton Miflin. Boston. 2004

ISBN 141206857-6